WHAT YOUR COLLEAGUES ARE SAYING . . .

This book places a premium on mathematical thinking. The authors make the compelling case using myriad examples that fluency requires reasoning and relies on conceptual understanding. If you want your students to confidently choose and flexibly use a range of strategies when working with rational numbers and algebraic equations, dig into the treasure trove of engaging activities in this book!

Grace Kelemanik
Author of *Routines for Reasoning and Teaching for Thinking*
Natick, MA

Sixth grade is a challenging time for fluency development—some students are still working on basic fact fluency, while others are starting to engage in a more sophisticated way of algebraic thinking. This book is an excellent resource for scaffolding middle school students on a personal level wherever they may be on the fluency continuum!

Kiersten Campbell
6th Grade Teacher
Clinton, UT

Figuring Out Fluency is a necessary resource for every middle school mathematics educator seeking to grow their knowledge base, learn effective teaching strategies, and gain access to teaching activities they can immediately implement.

Kristopher J. Childs
Chief Academic, Equity, and Social Justice Officer—Open Up Resources
Winter Garden, FL

This book is exactly what the mathematics world needs. Even as a veteran teacher, I need to be reminded that students *need* explicit strategy instruction. Students need to see that there are efficient ways to solve problems and the standard algorithm isn't always the best. This companion book is overflowing with ideas for the classroom teacher to improve mathematical fluency!

Elizabeth Uden
8th Grade Math Teacher
Olathe, KS

Despite striving for students to develop fluency with number and operations, inconsistent definitions of what it means to be fluent and a lack of understanding to implement effective fluency-building practices can leave you feeling defeated. Enter the action-oriented *Figuring Out Fluency* book that clarifies what it means to be fluent with number and operations while providing content specific examples that can be implemented in your classroom to begin seeing the fruit of your professional learning efforts.

Kyle Pearce
K–12 Mathematics Consultant
Belle River, Ontario, Canada

This is a book you keep on your teacher-desk! It's full of classroom activities for your classroom while at the same time, it teaches you how to build your own activities so you can build mathematical fluency for your students.

Jon Orr
High School Math Teacher, Lambton Kent District School Board
Chatham, Ontario, Canada

This book is like a full-course meal. Each course complements the other, from the *amuse-bouche* to the main course where each module, from operations of whole numbers to solving systems, leaves the reader satisfied with figuring out fluency. Lastly, as sweet as the dessert, developing fluency puts it all together. This is the most practical math book for secondary instruction of this time.

Valentin Sotomayor
Mathematics Specialist, Seminole County Public Schools
Seminole County, FL

When most educators hear "fluency," they immediately think of elementary school. The authors do a masterful job of pushing us to think of fluency at the middle grades as well and provide concrete examples of what it looks like. The activities are ready to implement immediately to bring to life the key ideas around fluency for rational numbers and algebraic equations.

Kevin J. Dykema
8th Grade Math Teacher, Mattawan (MI) Middle School Teacher; President (2022–2024), National Council of Teachers of Mathematics (NCTM)
Mattawan, MI

This book is the instruction tool I have been looking for with essential insights to effective mathematical teaching without unnecessary details. Filled with explicit ideas on how to build fluency, the book merges conceptual and procedural learning goals perfectly. A must-have tool for both educators and students looking for a deeper understanding of mathematics.

Kirk Redford
Teacher
Clearfield, UT

This brilliantly crafted book stresses the importance of teaching mathematical fluency as equipping learners with multiple strategies that are not only efficient and flexible but also lead to accurate solutions and are appropriate for the given situation. The fun and engaging activities, examples, and games all stress that fluency is also a matter of equity and access for all learners.

Kanita K DuCloux
Associate Professor and Chair—Mathematics Department,
Western Kentucky University
Bowling Green, KY

This book is awesome! What stood out to me was the deep understanding I gained about what *fluency* actually means. Too often the message has been to focus on fluency and accuracy, especially at the middle school level. By providing teachers with tools for building fluency with integers, expressions, and algebra, this book shifts that message to also focus on flexibility and strategy selection.

Lindsey Henderson
Secondary Mathematics Specialist, Utah State Board of Education
Salt Lake City, UT

Building fluency certainly does not end in elementary! This book guides teachers seeking to help students make essential connections between first, rational number operations and familiar whole-number strategies, and second, number sense and solving abstract algebraic equations. What a great resource for novice and experienced teachers to explore together!

Tiffany Spralding
K–12 Math Curriculum Coordinator
Sanford, FL

Figuring Out Fluency succeeds in delivering a true understanding of mathematical fluency. It encourages a shift from basic memorization of facts to developing and mastering one's math psyche and revelatory understanding.

Steven Geiger
Curriculum, Volusia County Schools
Palm Coast, FL

Operations With Rational Numbers and Algebraic Equations is an excellent addition to the *Figuring Out Fluency* series. This book brings to light how fluency is carried through to the higher grades—a must for math teachers. Bay-Williams and SanGiovanni highlight how fluency beyond whole numbers is possible and should be promoted in all of our students.

Pam Harris
Texas State University
San Marcos, TX

This book paints a vibrant picture of the life fluency can live beyond the confines of basic math facts and memory exercises starting with early grade areas of fluency, through rational reasoning, and stretching far into the heart of algebraic reasoning.

Rachel Bachman
Associate Professor, Mathematics Education, Weber State University
Ulysses, PA

The resource that every middle school educator needs whether you are new or experienced in teaching operations with rational numbers and algebraic equations! The authors walk you through how procedural fluency is achieved by incorporating research-based strategies. There are routines, games, and activities for supporting instruction in the classroom to empower your students as mathematicians!

Micaela Wang
6–8 Math Coach
Louisville, KY

This latest edition to the *Figuring Out Fluency* series is written specifically to address the needs of middle school learners. Finally, middle school math educators have a playbook of research-aligned strategies to support fluency. The focus on the importance of reasonableness, the three moves to support reasonableness, *and* 100+ classroom-ready activities are a welcome addition to any classroom!

Latrenda Knighten
Mathematics Content Trainer
Baton Rouge, LA

A fantastic resource! For years, I have pulled from multiple sources to help teachers develop a comprehensive view of teaching middle grades mathematics. Now it is all in one place! Not only does *Figuring Out Fluency* elaborate on the trajectory of mathematical content, but it also offers a variety of activities, games, and routines to help students reason, strategize, and develop "real" fluency.

Rodrigo Gutiérrez
University of Arizona CRR Co-Director
Tucson, AZ

Figuring Out Fluency: Operations With Rational Numbers and Algebraic Equations
The Book at a Glance

Building off of *Figuring Out Fluency*, this classroom companion dives into strategies across the operations with rational numbers and procedures with algebraic equations.

FIGURE 12 ● Reasoning Strategies for Rational Numbers and Algebraic Equations

STRATEGIES FOR THE OPERATIONS	STRATEGIES FOR COMPARING RATIOS AND SOLVING PROPORTIONS	STRATEGIES FOR SOLVING EQUATIONS FOR AN UNKNOWN	STRATEGIES FOR SOLVING SYSTEMS OF LINEAR EQUATIONS
1. Count On/Count Back	1. Build Up/Break Down	1. Use Relational Reasoning	1. Identify the Point of Intersection on a Graph
2. Make Tens, Make a Whole, Make a Zero	2. Find a Unit Rate	2. Choose a Basic Transformation: ● Combine like terms	2. Identify Values in a Table
3. Break Apart to Multiply	3. Use Scale Factor	● Add or subtract like terms on both sides of the equation	3. Use Substitution
4. Halve and Double	4. Use $y = kx$	● Multiply or divide on both sides of the equation	4. Use Elimination
5. Compensation	5. Find Cross Product	● Use distributive property	
6. Use Partials			

Strategy overviews communicate how each strategy helps students develop flexibility, efficiency, accuracy, automaticity, and reasonableness.

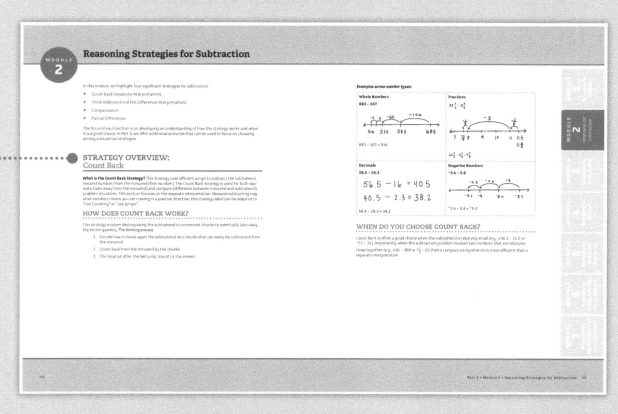

Reasoning Strategies for Subtraction

MODULE 2

In this module, we highlight four significant strategies for subtraction:

● Count Back (Separate Interpretation)
● Think Addition (Find the Difference Interpretation)
● Compensation
● Partial Differences

The focus of each section is on developing an understanding of how the strategy works and when it is a good choice. In Part 3, we offer additional activities that can be used to focus on choosing among subtraction strategies.

STRATEGY OVERVIEW:
Count Back

What is the Count Back Strategy? This strategy uses efficient jumps to subtract the subtrahend (second number) from the minuend (first number). The Count Back strategy is used for both separate (take away from the minuend) and compare (difference between minuend and subtrahend) problem situations. This section focuses on the separate interpretation. Because subtracting negative numbers means you are moving in a positive direction, this strategy label can be adapted to "Use Counting" or "Use Jumps."

HOW DOES COUNT BACK WORK?

This strategy involves decomposing the subtrahend in convenient chunks to eventually take away the entire quantity. *The thinking process:*

1. Decide how to break apart the subtrahend into chunks that can easily be subtracted from the minuend.
2. Count back from the minuend by the chunks.
3. The location after the last jump (count) is the answer.

Examples across number types:

Whole Numbers
683 − 167

516   513   583   683

683 − 167 = 516

Fractions
$11\frac{1}{4} - 3\frac{7}{8}$

$11\frac{1}{4} - 3\frac{7}{8} = 7\frac{3}{8}$

Decimals
56.5 − 18.3

56.5 − 16 = 40.5
40.5 − 2.3 = 38.2

56.5 − 18.3 = 38.2

Negative Numbers
−3.4 − 5.8

−3.4 − 5.8 = 9.2

WHEN DO YOU CHOOSE COUNT BACK?

Count Back is often a good choice when the subtrahend is relatively small (e.g., 436.3 − 14.2 or −72 − 14). Importantly, when the subtraction problem involves two numbers that are relatively close together (e.g., 436 − 388 or $7\frac{1}{2} - 6$), then a compare interpretation is more efficient than a separate interpretation.

Each strategy includes teaching
activities that help you explicitly
teach the strategy.

TEACHING ACTIVITIES FOR COUNT ON

Count On is the first strategy students learn with whole numbers, but it is a useful strategy across number types, and often overlooked as an option. These teaching activities illustrate how the strategy works. The number line is a very useful tool for this strategy. The teaching goal is that students (1) become adept at using Count On efficiently and accurately and (2) know when they will want to use the Count On strategy.

ACTIVITY 1.1
NUMBER LINE COMPARISONS WITH WORKED EXAMPLES

Using jumps works well with negative numbers, though it looks different than counting on with positive numbers. A great way to highlight the differences is by comparing worked examples on number lines. To do this, create a set of related problems, as shown below. Have students work together to compare the examples. Then, bring the class together to share their observations, highlighting points such as how the direction of jumps is connected to the sign of the second addend.

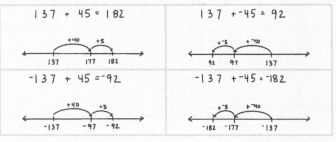

Notice that in these examples students recognize they can count on in chunks, which is more efficient than counting by ones or tens. When negative numbers are introduced, students need to revisit the idea of chunking their jumps. To support such thinking, provide a collection of different ways to count on to solve a given equation.

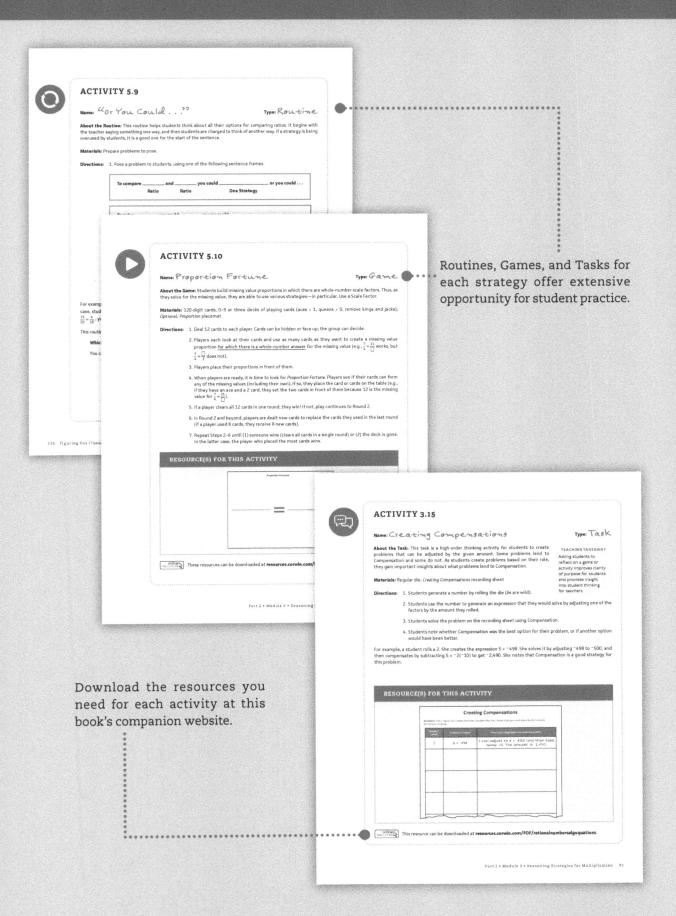

ACTIVITY 5.9

Name: *"Or You Could . . ."*　　　　　Type: *Routine*

About the Routine: This routine helps students think about all their options for comparing ratios. It begins with the teacher saying something one way, and then students are charged to think of another way. If a strategy is being overused by students, it is a good one for the start of the sentence.

Materials: Prepare problems to pose.

Directions:　1. Pose a problem to students, using one of the following sentence frames.

| To compare _____ and _____ you could _____ or you could . . . |
| Ratio　　　　Ratio　　　　　　One Strategy |

ACTIVITY 5.10

Name: *Proportion Fortune*　　　　　Type: *Game*

About the Game: Students build missing value proportions in which there are whole-number scale factors. Thus, as they solve for the missing value, they are able to use various strategies—in particular, Use a Scale Factor.

Materials: 120-digit cards, 0–9 or three decks of playing cards (aces = 1, queens = 0, remove kings and jacks); *Optional: Proportion* placemat

Directions:　1. Deal 12 cards to each player. Cards can be hidden or face up; the group can decide.

　2. Players each look at their cards and use as many cards as they want to create a missing value proportion for which there is a whole-number answer for the missing value (e.g., $\frac{7}{4} = \frac{21}{\square}$ works, but $\frac{7}{4} = \frac{\square}{7}$ does not).

　3. Players place their proportions in front of them.

　4. When players are ready, it is time to look for *Proportion Fortune*. Players see if their cards can form any of the missing values (including their own). If so, they place the card or cards on the table (e.g., if they have an ace and a 2 card, they set the two cards in front of them because 12 is the missing value for $\frac{7}{4} = \frac{21}{\square}$).

　5. If a player clears all 12 cards in one round, they win! If not, play continues to Round 2.

　6. In Round 2 and beyond, players are dealt new cards to replace the cards they used in the last round (if a player used 8 cards, they receive 8 new cards).

　7. Repeat Steps 2–6 until (1) someone wins (clears all cards in a single round) or (2) the deck is gone. In the latter case, the player who placed the most cards wins.

RESOURCE(S) FOR THIS ACTIVITY

These resources can be downloaded at **resources.corwin.com/**

ACTIVITY 3.15

Name: *Creating Compensations*　　　　　Type: *Task*

About the Task: This task is a high-order thinking activity for students to create problems that can be adjusted by the given amount. Some problems lend to Compensation and some do not. As students create problems based on their role, they gain important insights about what problems lend to Compensation.

TEACHING TAKEAWAY
Asking students to reflect on a game or activity improves clarity of purpose for students and provides insight into student thinking for teachers

Materials: Regular die, *Creating Compensations* recording sheet

Directions:　1. Students generate a number by rolling the die (6s are wild).

　2. Students use the number to generate an expression that they would solve by adjusting one of the factors by the amount they rolled.

　3. Students solve the problem on the recording sheet using Compensation.

　4. Students note whether Compensation was the best option for their problem, or if another option would have been better.

For example, a student rolls a 2. She creates the expression $5 \times {}^-498$. She solves it by adjusting $^-498$ to $^-500$, and then compensates by subtracting $5 \times {}^-2({}^-10)$ to get $^-2,490$. She notes that Compensation is a good strategy for this problem.

RESOURCE(S) FOR THIS ACTIVITY

Creating Compensations

This resource can be downloaded at **resources.corwin.com/FOF/rationalnumbersalgequations.**

Routines, Games, and Tasks for each strategy offer extensive opportunity for student practice.

Download the resources you need for each activity at this book's companion website.

FIGURING OUT

Fluency

OPERATIONS
With Rational Numbers
and Algebraic Equations

Grades
5–9

A Classroom Companion

FIGURING OUT
Fluency

OPERATIONS
With Rational Numbers
and Algebraic Equations

Grades
5–9

A Classroom Companion

Jennifer M. Bay-Williams
John J. SanGiovanni
C. David Walters
Sherri Martinie

CORWIN Mathematics

For information:

Corwin
A SAGE Company
2455 Teller Road
Thousand Oaks, California 91320
(800) 233–9936
www.corwin.com

SAGE Publications Ltd.
1 Oliver's Yard
55 City Road
London, EC1Y 1SP
United Kingdom

SAGE Publications India Pvt. Ltd.
B 1/I 1 Mohan Cooperative
Industrial Area
Mathura Road, New Delhi 110 044
India

SAGE Publications Asia-
Pacific Pte. Ltd.
18 Cross Street #10–10/11/12
China Square Central
Singapore 048423

President: Mike Soules
Vice President and Editorial
    Director: Monica Eckman
Publisher: Erin Null
Content Development Editor:
    Jessica Vidal
Editorial Assistant: Nyle De Leon
Production Editor: Tori Mirsadjadi
Copy Editor: Talia Greenberg
Typesetter: Integra
Proofreader: Jennifer Grubba
Indexer: Integra
Cover Designer: Rose Storey
Marketing Manager:
    Margaret O'Connor

Printed in the United Kingdom.

ISBN 9781071825181

This book is printed on acid-free paper.

22 23 24 25 26 10 9 8 7 6 5 4 3 2 1

Contents

Visit the companion website at
**resources.corwin.com/FOF/
rationalnumbersalgequations**
for downloadable resources.

Preface

This book is about figuring out fluency in middle school. Fluency is *not the same* as becoming proficient with a collection of "standard" algorithms and procedures. An algorithmic approach leads students to do such things as solve $x + 7 = 10$ by subtracting 7 from both sides, rather than recognizing that x is 3 (a combination of 10 that they learned in Grade K or 1). Fluency, then, involves sizing up the situation first and then deciding what to do. A fluent person thinks, "What are my options for solving this problem?" and then, "Given my options, which one works best in this situation?" Thus, fluency instruction must make sure that students learn options and learn how to choose from among their options.

Even though our standards focus on fluency (e.g., operations with rational numbers), we haven't even come close to accomplishing this for each and every student. In 2019 only one-third (34%) of our nation's Grade 8 students are at or above proficient and 31% are below basic (National Center for Education Statistics, n.d.). We can and must do better!

BUILDING PROCEDURAL FLUENCY FROM CONCEPTUAL UNDERSTANDING

We are strong advocates for conceptual understanding. In fact, implementing reasoning strategies requires a strong conceptual foundation. However, conceptual understanding alone cannot help students fluently navigate computational situations. Students learn reasoning strategies through *explicit strategy instruction*. According to *Merriam-Webster* dictionary, *explicit* means "fully revealed or expressed without vagueness." In mathematics teaching, being *explicit* means making mathematical relationships visible. A *strategy* is a flexible method to solve a problem. Explicit strategy instruction, then, is engaging students in ways to clearly see how and why a strategy works. Once understood, students need to explore when a strategy is a good option. Learning how to use and how to choose strategies empowers students and thus nurtures a positive mathematics identity and a sense of agency.

USING THIS BOOK

This book is a classroom companion to *Figuring Out Fluency in Mathematics Teaching and Learning, K–8*. In that anchor book, we lay out what fluency is, identify the fallacies that stand in the way of a true focus on fluency, and elaborate on necessary foundations for fluency. We also propose the following:

- Seven Significant Strategies across the operations

- Eight "Automaticities" *beyond* automaticity with basic facts

- Five ways to engage students in meaningful practice

- Four assessment options that can replace (or at least complement) tests and that focus on real fluency

- Many ways to engage families in supporting their child's fluency

In Part 1 of this companion book, we revisit important ideas from the anchor book, focusing specifically on fluency topics in the middle school curriculum: operations with rational numbers, solving proportions, solving equations (one variable and systems of equations). In addition, Part 1 offers a collection of topics and activities for skills and concepts that are "good beginnings"—necessary for using reasoning strategies (e.g., flexibly decomposing a number).

Part 2 modules offer robust collections of ways to teach and practice reasoning strategies. The first four modules focus on each of the four operations and the last three focus on algebra-related fluency. Features of the modules include:

- *Strategy Overviews.* Written for a broad audience—teachers, students, caregivers—these pages explain a strategy, why it works, and when it is useful.

- *Teaching Activities.* These activities help students visualize and make sense of a strategy in engaging ways.

- *Practice Activities.* Routines, games, worked examples, and independent practice provide varied, substantial, and enjoyable practice to ensure students learn to use the focus strategy.

Part 3 extends the focus on fluency with a focus on *choosing among strategies.* The discussion, assessment tools, routines, and games in this section apply to all the topics in Part 2.

Figuring Out Fluency for Rational Numbers and Algebraic Equations, Grades 5–9, is one of five companion books. Each offers over 100 activities to support student reasoning related to different operations and types of numbers:

Figuring Out Fluency for Addition and Subtraction With Whole Numbers

Figuring Out Fluency for Multiplication and Division With Whole Numbers

Figuring Out Fluency for Addition and Subtraction With Fractions and Decimals

Figuring Out Fluency for Multiplication and Division With Fractions and Decimals

WHO IS THIS BOOK FOR?

With over 100 activities and a companion website with resources ready to download, this book is useful for multiple audiences. For classroom teachers, it offers ways to extend and enhance core resources and better support fluency. For special education teachers, it offers explicit strategy instruction and quality practice. For teacher leaders and university mathematics educators, this book can be used to galvanize teachers' understanding of fluency and provides them with a wealth of classroom-ready resources.

Acknowledgments

We would like to begin with you, the reader. As we shared in the preface, we can do better to have more students fluent, and developing positive mathematics identities. We acknowledge your professionalism as you seek to figure out fluency for each of the students in your setting. Having said that, there would be no book to write if it were not for:

- The researchers and advocates who have defined procedural fluency and effective practices that support it. We ground our ideas in your findings.

- Classroom teachers and their students who have taken up "real" fluency practices and shared their experiences with us. We piloted and shaped our ideas in your experiences.

- Our editing team. We re-crafted and polished our ideas with your keen eyes on the message and the audience. Erin Null has gone above and beyond as a partner in the work and the entire editing team has been creative, thorough, and supportive.

- Our families and support systems.

From Jennifer: I am forever grateful to my husband, Mitch, who is supportive in every way; my children, MacKenna and Nicolas, who get a lot of extra math in their lives; and my parents for their decades of support. Deep thanks and appreciation to John—an amazing writing partner across six books figuring out how to write about figuring out fluency, and Sherri and C. David for helping figure out fluency in 5–9. Finally, I am so grateful to so many Kentucky teachers and their students who have helped me figure out fluency—along with a lot of other things.

From John: I want to thank my family—especially my wife—who, as always, endure and support the ups and downs of taking on a new project. Thank you to Jenny for being an exceptional partner in this series. And thank you for dealing with my random thoughts, tangent conversations, and fantastic humor. As always, a heartfelt thank you to certain math friends and mentors for opportunities, faith in me, and support over the years. And thank you to my own math teachers who let me do math "my way," even if it wasn't "the way" back then.

From C. David: To my daughters, Even and Eloise, I am continually amazed at how resilient and patient you are whenever I embark on a writing project—thank you! I am also grateful for my mom, Shellie, who has never wavered in her support and belief in me. Thank you to the teachers in Northern Utah—I learn so much from working with these wonderful humans. I've also learned so much about fluency from my colleague Dr. Rachel Bachman, who is a brilliant educator and incredible mathematician. Finally, thank you to Jenny, John, and Sherri for collaborating with me on this book.

From Sherri: Thank you to my children—Curtis, Peter, and Lucy—who have patiently waited on me while I finish "one more thing" and whose math thoughts and math work have provided me great insight. Thank you to my husband, Brian, who is encouraging and supportive. Thank you to my colleagues and mentors, especially Jenny and John, for including me in this project. Finally, a special thank you to my math students over the years who continue to inspire me to be a better math teacher.

As with fluency, no component is more important than another, and without any component, there is no book, so to the researchers, teachers, family, and editing team, thank you. We are so grateful.

PUBLISHER'S ACKNOWLEDGMENTS

Corwin gratefully acknowledges the contributions of the following reviewers:

Kevin Dykema
Math Teacher, Mattawan Consolidated Schools
President-elect, NCTM
Mattawan, MI

Ruth Harbin Miles
Math Consultant and Instructor, Mary Baldwin University
Madison, VA

Jennifer Novak
Director of Curriculum, Instruction, and Assessment, HCPSS
Elkridge, MD

About the Authors

Jennifer M. Bay-Williams is a professor of mathematics education at the University of Louisville, where she works with preservice and practicing PK–12 teachers. She taught middle school in the United States and Peru. She has authored numerous books, such as *Teaching Student-Centered Mathematics: Grades 6–8* and *On the Money: Math Activities to Build Financial Literacy (Grades 6–8)*, as well as many journal articles, all of which focus on developing aspects of effective mathematics teaching and learning. Jennifer is a frequent presenter at national and state conferences and works with schools and districts around the world. She has served as a member of the National Council of Teachers of Mathematics (NCTM) Board of Directors, the TODOS: Mathematics for All Board of Directors, and as president and secretary of the Association of Mathematics Teacher Educators (AMTE).

John J. SanGiovanni is a mathematics supervisor in Howard County, Maryland. There, he leads mathematics curriculum development, digital learning, assessment, and professional development. John is an adjunct professor and coordinator of the Elementary Mathematics Instructional Leadership graduate program at McDaniel College. He is an author and national mathematics curriculum and professional learning consultant. John is a frequent speaker at national conferences and institutes. He is active in state and national professional organizations, recently serving on the board of directors for NCTM and currently on the board of directors for NCSM.

C. David Walters is an assistant professor at Weber State University. He teaches mathematics content and methods courses for elementary and secondary teaching majors as well as creates professional development opportunities for local K–12 teachers. He is active in several professional organizations and has presented at conferences for the Research Council on Mathematics Learning, the Association of Mathematics Teacher Educators, and NCTM. He has reviewed for the *Journal for Research in Mathematics Education, Mathematics Teacher: Learning and Teaching PK–12*, and for the National Science Foundation DRK–12 grant program. C. David also has experience teaching middle and high school mathematics for the New York City Department of Education.

Sherri Martinie is an associate professor of curriculum and instruction at Kansas State University, where she teaches undergraduate and graduate courses in mathematics education. Prior to taking her position at Kansas State, she taught elementary, middle, and high school mathematics for a combined 20 years. Sherri is an author, professional development leader, grant writer, and conference speaker. She is continually seeking innovative ways to support preservice and inservice teachers in their development and refinement of effective mathematics teaching practices.

PART 1

FIGURING OUT FLUENCY

Key Ideas

WHAT IS FLUENCY WITH RATIONAL NUMBERS AND ALGEBRAIC EQUATIONS?

To set the stage for figuring out fluency for rational numbers and algebraic equations, find the solution to each of these problems using a method other than what you learned as the standard algorithm:

$14.99 + 7.07$	$7\frac{1}{4} - 5\frac{1}{2}$	$1\frac{3}{4} \times 16$	$2.49 \div 0.3$
$^-38 + 57$	$\frac{5}{15} = \frac{x}{9}$	$3(x + 5) = 6x + 9$	$3(x - 1) = 2(x - 1) + 2$

If you had difficulty strategizing beyond using the standard algorithm, you are in good company. It is common for adults to have multiple strategies for adding 48 + 49 or multiplying 12 × 25, but once the problem moves beyond whole numbers, that flexibility and strategy selection diminishes. Here are possible alternatives to the standard method for these examples:

$14.99 + 7.07$	$7\frac{1}{4} - 5\frac{1}{2}$	$1\frac{3}{4} \times 16$	$2.49 \div 0.3$
Move 0.01 from 7.07 to 14.99 to Make a Whole: $15 + 7.06$ 22.06	Find the difference (Think Addition): $5\frac{1}{2}$ to 6 is $\frac{1}{2}$ 6 to 7 is 1 7 to $7\frac{1}{4}$ is $\frac{1}{4}$ Total jumps is $1\frac{3}{4}$	Break apart the mixed number and multiply each part by 16. $1 \times 16 = 16$ $\frac{3}{4} \times 16 = 12$ (think one-fourth of 16 is 4 (i.e., 16 ÷ 4), so three-fourths of 16 is 12). $16 + 12 = 28$	Think of it in fraction form, $\frac{2.49}{0.3}$, and multiply by $\frac{10}{10}$ to divide by a whole number, $\frac{24.9}{3}$. Then use partial quotients: $24 \div 3 = 8$ $0.9 \div 3 = 0.3$ The answer is 8.3.
$^-38 + 57$ Decompose 57 into 38 + 19 to Make a Zero: $^-38 + 38 + 19$ 19	$\frac{5}{15} = \frac{x}{9}$ Notice that $\frac{5}{15}$ can be simplified to $\frac{1}{3}$, and another equivalent of $\frac{1}{3}$ is $\frac{3}{9}$. So, $x = 3$	$3(x + 5) = 6x + 9$ Notice that there is a factor of 3 on both sides. Factor and divide to create a simpler equation and solve: $3(x + 5) = 3(2x + 3)$ $x + 5 = 2x + 3$ $2 = x$	$3(x - 1) = 2(x - 1) + 2$ Notice that there is a common factor of $x - 1$, so combine like terms and solve: $3(x - 1) - 2(x - 1) = 2$ $x - 1 = 2$ $x = 3$

Reflect on how you thought about these problems. How did you decide which strategy to use? Did you start with one strategy and shift to another? Fluency involves selecting strategies that are efficient for the numbers given in the problems. While some problems lend to a single option, other problems have several efficient methods. For example, $3(x + 5) = 6x + 9$ could have been solved about as efficiently by first applying the distributive property on the left side to get $3x + 15 = 6x + 9$. Standard algorithms are not always efficient, either. For example, a fluent person will not use the standard algorithm to solve 14.99 + 7.07. Real fluency in mathematics is the ability to select efficient strategies; to adapt, modify, or change out strategies; and to find solutions with accuracy. Fluency involves decision-making, reasoning, and reflecting on how the process is going, instead of simply replicating steps or procedures for doing mathematics.

Procedural fluency has several subsets. *Basic fact fluency* attends to fluently adding, subtracting, multiplying, and dividing single-digit numbers. *Computational fluency* refers to the four operations. *Procedural fluency* encompasses both basic fact fluency and computational fluency (see Figure 1), along with other procedures like solving proportions for missing values and solving systems of equations.

TEACHING TAKEAWAY

Real fluency is the ability to select efficient strategies; to adapt, modify, or change out strategies; and to find solutions with accuracy.

FIGURE 1 ● The Relationship of Different Fluency Terms in Mathematics

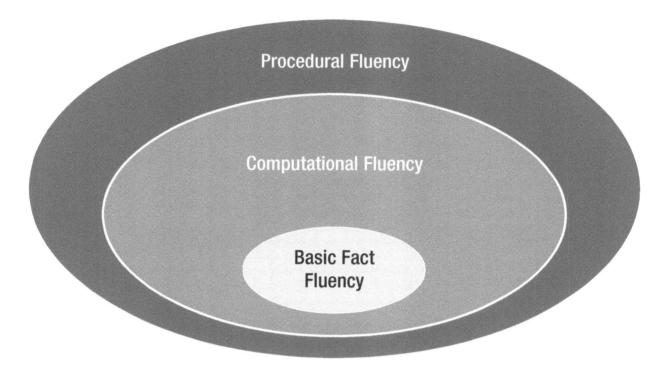

Procedural fluency is defined as solving procedures efficiently, flexibly, and accurately (Kilpatrick et al., 2001; National Council of Teachers of Mathematics [NCTM], 2014). These three components are defined as follows:

1. *Efficiency:* Solving a procedure in a reasonable amount of time by selecting an appropriate strategy and readily implementing that strategy.

2. *Flexibility:* Knowing multiple procedures and applying or adapting strategies to solve procedural problems (Baroody & Dowker, 2003; Star, 2005).

3. *Accuracy:* Correctly solving a procedure.

Strategies are not the same as algorithms. Strategies are general methods that are flexible in design; algorithms are established steps implemented the same way across problems.

To focus on fluency, we need specific, observable actions that we can look for in what students are doing in order to ensure they are developing fluency. We have identified six such actions. The three components and six Fluency Actions, and their relationships, are illustrated in Figure 2.

FIGURE 2 ● Procedural Fluency Components, Actions, and Checks for Reasonableness

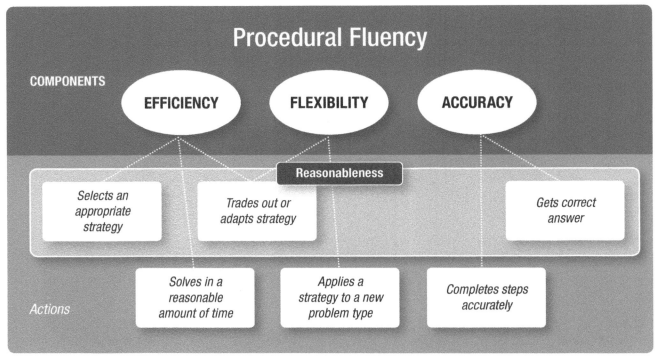

Source: Adapted with permission from D. Spangler & J. Wanko (Eds.), *Enhancing Classroom Practice with Research behind Principles to Actions*, copyright 2017, by the National Council of Teachers of Mathematics. All rights reserved.

Three of the six Fluency Actions attend to reasonableness. Fluency Actions and reasonableness are described later in Part 1, but first, it is important to consider why this "bigger," more comprehensive view of fluency matters.

WHY FOCUS ON FLUENCY FOR RATIONAL NUMBERS AND ALGEBRAIC EQUATIONS?

There are important reasons to focus on real fluency. First, the traditional teach-the-algorithm-only approach has not worked. Memorization approaches result in lower achievement (e.g., Braithwaite et al., 2018; Lortie-Forgues et al., 2015; Newton et al., 2014; OECD, 2010, 2016). The Programme for International Student Assessment (PISA), a study of about 250,000 15-year-olds, analyzed learning strategies across 41 countries and found that students' use of memorization/rehearsal strategies is almost universally negatively associated with learning (OECD, 2010). Conversely, we have strong evidence that a focus on reasoning strategies improves student achievement (c.f., Baroody et al., 2016; Brendefur et al., 2015; Siegler et al., 2010; Torbeyns et al., 2015). Having fluency with fraction operations predicts success in algebra and in mathematics in general through high school (Bailey et al., 2012; Siegler et al., 2012; Torbeyns et al., 2015). In solving algebraic equations, students who learned strategies and compared methods achieved greater gains in conceptual knowledge, procedural knowledge, and flexibility, as compared to control students (Rittle-Johnson & Star, 2007; Rittle-Johnson, Star, & Durkin, 2012). Importantly, a fluency focus is about equity and access. Equipping students with options for working fluently with rational numbers and algebraic equations not only improves their performance, it also develops a positive mathematics identity and sense of agency because students are positioned as capable of deciding how to solve a problem.

WHAT DO FLUENCY ACTIONS LOOK LIKE FOR RATIONAL NUMBERS AND ALGEBRAIC EQUATIONS?

The six Fluency Actions are observable and therefore form a foundation for assessing student progress toward fluency. Let's look at each of these actions in the context of rational numbers and algebraic equations.

FLUENCY ACTION 1: Select an Appropriate Strategy

Selecting *an* appropriate strategy does not mean selecting *the* appropriate strategy. Many problems can be solved efficiently in more than one way. Here is our operational definition: Of the available strategies, the one the student opts to use gets to a solution in about as many steps and/or about as much time as other appropriate options.

Sometimes a standard algorithm is the most efficient option to solve a problem, but sometimes it is not. Teaching students to select appropriate strategies involves helping students notice features of a problem that help to decide which is more efficient: a reasoning strategy or a standard algorithm. For example, when adding integers, noticing that the signs are different is a feature that indicates Make a Zero strategy may be a good option (e.g., $-22 + 39$ can be thought of as $-22 + 22 + 17$). Or, when multiplying decimals, noticing that a number is one-tenth away from a whole suggests compensation may be efficient (e.g., 5.9×8 can be adjusted to 6×8, then subtract 0.1×8, or 0.8). While written out here, these methods can be done mentally. Importantly, students can only select appropriate strategies if they have learned more than one way to solve a problem! With fraction addition, for example, there are more ways than just adding the wholes and parts and then simplifying. Figure 3 shows two other strategies that are useful options that students should understand and be able to use.

FIGURE 3 ● Two Appropriate Strategies for Adding $3\frac{1}{2} + 2\frac{3}{4}$

COUNT ON STRATEGY

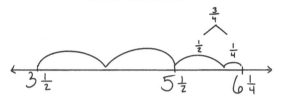

MAKE A WHOLE STRATEGY

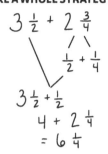

TEACHING TAKEAWAY

Students need to learn different strategies so that they can choose efficiently appropriate strategies.

Students need to learn different strategies so that they can choose efficiently appropriate strategies. Throughout this book, we name strategies so that we can talk about them. But strategies overlap. For example, both strategies illustrated in Figure 3 are also Partial Sums strategies. The focus must be on the ideas (not the naming of the strategy).

FLUENCY ACTION 2: Solve in a Reasonable Amount of Time

The time it takes to solve a problem will vary with the complexity of the numbers or length of an expression. Students should be able to work through a problem without getting stuck or lost. Appropriate strategies can be carried out in inefficient, unreasonable ways. For example, students may add −5.7 + −4.8 by counting on in efficient or inefficient ways, as illustrated in Figure 4. But how efficient a strategy is depends on experience. The first example in Figure 4 is initially a reasonable method that reinforces the meaning of adding negative numbers. With more experiences, jumps can be chunked to solve the problem more quickly.

FIGURE 4 ● Different Ways to Use a Counting Strategy to Add −5.7 + −4.8

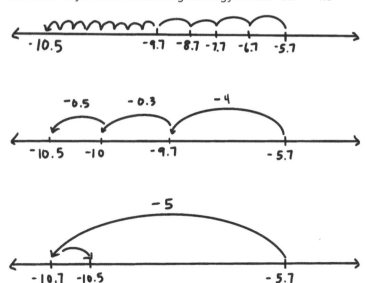

FLUENCY ACTION 3: Trade Out or Adapt a Strategy

As students' number sense and understanding of strategies advance, they are able to adapt and trade out strategies. For example, to solve for the missing value in the proportion $\frac{x}{21} = \frac{15}{35}$, a student might first think cross products, but then notice that $\frac{15}{35}$ can be simplified to $\frac{3}{7}$. At this point, they notice the relationship between the two denominators ($\times 3$) and use that relationship to solve for x.

This Fluency Action is one of three connected to *reasonableness*. If a strategy isn't going well, then the strategy might need to be adapted or traded for another option. This is key to solving equations for an unknown, wherein a common first step, like applying the distributive property, can make a problem messier. A fluent student will stop and trade out the method for another approach:

$$\tfrac{3}{4}(x+3)=9$$

First effort:

$$\frac{3}{4}\left(x+3\right)=9$$

$$\frac{3}{4}x + \frac{9}{4} = 9$$

Second effort:

$$\times \; \frac{3}{4}\left(x+3\right)=9 \; \cdot 4$$

$$3x + 9 = 36$$

$$3x = 27$$

$$x = 9$$

FLUENCY ACTION 4: Apply a Strategy to a New Problem Type

This Fluency Action means that you can take a strategy, like Make Tens, that was originally used with whole numbers, apply it to decimals or fractions (Make a Whole), and then connect it to negative numbers as Make a Zero. The importance of this Fluency Action with rational numbers cannot be overstated. Students benefit from seeing how a strategy learned with fractions also works with decimals (and vice versa).

FLUENCY ACTIONS 5 AND 6: Complete Steps Accurately and Get Correct Answers

These two Fluency Actions are about accuracy, which has been the primary focus of teaching and assessing mathematics, often at the expense of the other actions. But attending to accuracy is important. For example, a wrong answer may be due to an error in how to enact a strategy or an error may be due to a computational mistake. Take a look at the three wrong answers in Figure 5 and decide if the error is related to the strategy or to a computational mistake. In the first error, the student is not understanding integer subtraction and/or how to implement Count Back strategy. In the second example, the student understands how to use Compensation, but makes an error in solving −30.6 + 0.2 (treating the negative side of the number line like the positive side where decimals count up as they go to the right). In the third example, the student makes a counting or adding error.

FIGURE 5 ● Incorrect Solutions for −17.6 − 12.8

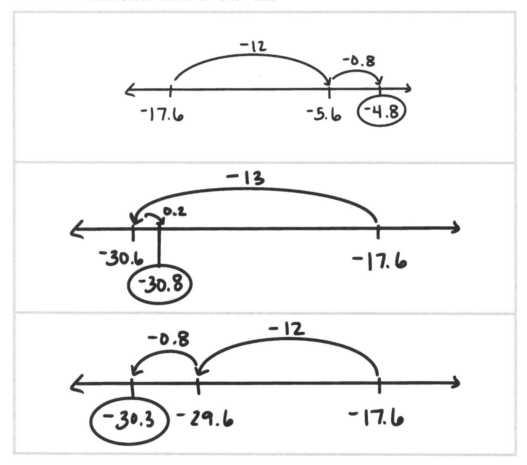

Fluency Action 6 is one of three connected to reasonableness. Within this action is noticing if your answer makes sense. In Figure 5, the answer of −4.8 is not reasonable because taking away a whole number should result in a smaller number, not a larger number. The other two results are both reasonable though incorrect. While reasonableness has been woven into the discussion of Fluency Actions, it is critical to fluency and warrants more discussion.

REASONABLENESS

A fluent student determines if their strategies and results are reasonable. It takes time to develop reasonableness, and it should be practiced and discussed often. Students can develop reasonableness by practicing these three moves (a match to the Fluency Actions 1, 3, and 6 and illustrated in Figure 2).

THREE "CS" OF REASONABLENESS

Choose: Choose a strategy that is efficient based on the numbers in the problem.
Change: Change the strategy if it is proving to be overly complex or unsuccessful.
Check: Check to make sure the result makes sense.

Let's explore how reasonableness plays out for Jessie in solving −65.5 − −49.8.

1. Jessie changes the problem to −65.5 + 49.8 and thinks about using the Make a Zero strategy, but it is too complicated.

2. Jessie decides instead to rethink the problem as −65.5 + 50, and then uses Make a Zero to get −15.5, then compensates by taking away the extra 0.2 to get −15.7.

3. Jessie sees her answer is reasonable, given the negative addend has an absolute value about 15 more than the other addend.

Provide students Choose, Change, Check reflection cards to encourage and support those thinking about reasonableness (see Figure 6). You can adapt these cards into anchor charts for students to use while working on problems and refer to them during discussions.

FIGURE 6 ● Choose, Change, Check Reflection Card for Students

Checks for Reasonableness		
Choose	Change	Check
Is this something I can do in my head? What strategy makes sense for these numbers?	Is my strategy going well, or should I try a different approach? Does my answer so far seem reasonable?	Is my answer close to what I anticipated it might be? How might I check my answer?

Icon sources: Choose by iStock.com/Enis Aksoy; Change by iStock.com/Sigit Mulyo Utomo; Check by iStock.com/Indigo Diamond.

 This resource can be downloaded at **resources.corwin.com/FOF/rationalnumbersalgequations**.

WHAT CONCEPTUAL FOUNDATIONS DO STUDENTS NEED?

TEACHING TAKEAWAY

Developing fluency *begins* with contexts. It is a mistake to "save" story problems for after students have learned to compute, because the stories give students a context from which they can make sense of the quantities and the operation.

Fluency is based on conceptual understanding. As students expand their work to include negative numbers and variables, it continues to be important to start with *contexts* that build meaning and *visuals* to support reasoning. Manipulatives and visuals support conceptual development (Cramer et al., 2002; Monson et al., 2020). For example, number lines are an important representation for numerous reasons. Number lines support:

- locating positive and negative numbers
- the concept of opposites and of zero pairs
- absolute value (distance from zero)
- operations, showing both magnitude and direction
- exploration of both continuous and discrete quantities
- developing relational understanding of variable expressions

Area and set models also support understanding (Van de Walle et al., 2019). For example, fraction circles, fraction strips, Unifix or multilink cubes, base-10 blocks, two-color counters, and algebra tiles help students make meaning of quantity and the action of the operation while also helping them reason about the results. Contexts and visuals also support reasoning strategies and appear through Part 2 of this book. Although the focus of this book is on reasoning strategies—not on developing initial conceptual understandings—here is a short list of what these critical conceptual underpinnings are.

EQUIVALENCIES

Cutting across all rational numbers and algebraic equations is the critical importance of understanding equivalency. Knowing equivalency is both a conceptual foundation and an automaticity. As a conceptual foundation, it means that students "see" that four-tenths means all of these things:

$$0.4 \qquad 0.40 \qquad \frac{4}{10} \qquad \frac{40}{100} \qquad \frac{2}{5} \qquad 40\%$$

There are infinitely many other equivalencies for four-tenths. Students also understand that if they have any fraction and they want to represent it as a decimal, the goal is to find an equivalent fraction with a denominator of 10, 100, and so on. To find the decimal equivalent to $\frac{1}{4}$, for example, students might reason that there is no equivalent fraction in the form $\frac{?}{10}$, so they look for an equivalency in the form $\frac{?}{100}$, which turns out to be $\frac{25}{100}$ or 0.25.

Area models and number lines can help students see the relative size of the numbers: for example, finding multiple names for this value on a number line:

Equivalency is at the heart of proportional reasoning—for example, recognizing that when a recipe is in a ratio of four parts water to one part sugar, then there are infinitely many options, including eight cups of water to two cups of sugar and one cup water and $\frac{1}{4}$ cup sugar. In algebraic equations, students must know which changes they can make that maintain equivalence.

FRACTIONS

Fractions are numbers. This may sound obvious, but many students come to understand fractions as a number over a number or shaded parts over total parts. Researchers include the following significant fraction concepts (Cramer & Whitney, 2010; Empson & Levi, 2011; Lamon, 2020):

- Fractions are equal shares of a whole or a unit.

- Fractions have a location on a number line; unlike shading part of a region, locating fractions on a number line requires recognizing fractions as numbers.

- Fractions may represent part of an area, part of a length, or part of a set.

- Fractions can be decomposed in a variety of ways. For example, $\frac{5}{8}$ can be decomposed into $\frac{3}{8} + \frac{2}{8}$ or $\frac{1}{8} + \frac{1}{8} + \frac{1}{8} + \frac{1}{8} + \frac{1}{8}$.

- Partitioning and iterating fractions helps students understand the meaning of fractions. Partitioning is splitting a whole into equal-size parts and iterating is counting by fractional amounts (e.g., one-eighth, two-eighths, . . .) (McMillan & Sagun, 2020; Van de Walle et al., 2019). For example: $\frac{1}{3}, \frac{2}{3}, \frac{3}{3}, \frac{4}{3}, \ldots$ Or, stacking the counts to show patterns:

$$3\frac{1}{4}, 3\frac{1}{2}, 3\frac{3}{4}, 4$$
$$4\frac{1}{4}, 4\frac{1}{2}, 4\frac{3}{4}, 5$$
$$5\frac{1}{4}, 5\frac{1}{2}, 5\frac{3}{4}, 6$$

- Equivalent fractions describe the same quantity, the difference being in how the same-sized whole is partitioned.

DECIMALS

Decimals are sometimes considered "easier" than fractions, perhaps because the algorithms we use with decimals parallel whole number algorithms. But the conceptual understanding of decimals is at least as challenging as fractions (Hurst & Cordes, 2018; Lortie-Forgues et al., 2015; Martinie, 2014). Number sense with decimals is therefore dependent on an understanding of place value *and* fractions. The following are important conceptual understandings to support student fluency:

- Decimals are a way of writing fractions within the base-10 system.

- The position to the left of the decimal point is the units (ones) place; the position to the right of the decimal point tells how many tenths of the unit.

- The value to the right of the decimal point is a quantity between 0 and 1, regardless of how long the decimal is.

Using appropriate language (tenths and hundredths) throughout the process further supports both the connection between fractions and decimals and the fundamental idea that these numbers are parts of a whole.

NEGATIVE NUMBERS

Negative numbers are introduced with integers—the whole numbers and their negatives or opposites—instead of with fractions or decimals. But students must understand that a number like $^-5.25$ is to the left of $^-5$ (the opposite of where it is located with positive numbers). The following are important conceptual understandings to support student fluency:

- The minus sign has three meanings: (1) to indicate subtraction; (2) symbolic representation of a negative number; (3) to indicate the opposite of (Lamb et al., 2018).

- The minus sign can change meanings as a problem is solved. For example:

  $8 - a = 20$

  $^-a = 12$

  $a = ^-12$

  In the original equation, the minus sign indicates subtraction; after subtracting, it changes to mean the opposite of a; and in the answer it means a negative number.

- Opposites (e.g., 8 and $^-8$) are the same distance from zero (in opposite directions) and thus adding opposites results in zero.

- Subtracting n is the same as adding the opposite of n (this is not a "rule," but it is an important concept to be developed using contexts and visuals).

- Some generalizations students have constructed (or been told) are no longer true (e.g., subtracting makes smaller) (Bishop et al., 2014).

ALGEBRAIC EQUATIONS

Like rational numbers, algebraic equations involve new notations. Beyond notations, students must be able to apply properties and the order of operations in new ways to determine missing values. Significant conceptual foundations include:

- The equal sign represents a balance between two quantities. It does not mean "compute," which is a common interpretation by students that affects the development of algebraic thinking (Byrd, McNeil, Chesney, & Matthews, 2015; Knuth, Alibali, Hattikudur, McNeil, & Stephens, 2008).

- There are multiple ways to notate multiplication and division, and there are situations in which one form is preferred over others:

Multiplication:	4×5	$4 \cdot 5$	$(4)(5)$	$4x$
Division:	$24 \div 6$	$\frac{24}{6}$	$24 \cdot \frac{1}{6}$	

- The order of operations is a convention for evaluating expressions, but it is not a rule for solving equations. For example, to *evaluate* 3(4) − 2, one would subtract last, but to *solve* 3x − 6 = 12, one could "add 6" first or "divide by 3" first (these basic transformations are the focus of Module 6).

- Collecting like terms—for example, that 7a + 3a = 10a—is an application of the distributive law (not adding seven apples and three apples). An unknown factor, a, has been factored out: (7 + 3)a.

- A variable can be a missing value or represent infinite options. Compare the meaning of x in these situations:

| $5x + 12$ | $^-10 = 6x + 15$ | $y = 6x + 15$ | $2x + y = 10$ |
| | | | $^-x - y = 3$ |

- When exploring equations with two variables, the variables co-vary. In the case of $^-x - y = 3$, as x goes up by 1, y goes down by 1. And this relationship can be represented in graphs, tables, equations, and situations.

- Solving equations or solving systems of equations has more to it than "solving." As illustrated in Figure 7, developing fluency with systems of linear equations also attends to conceptualizing, representing systems, and interpreting the results.

FIGURE 7 ● Concept Map for Systems of Linear Equations

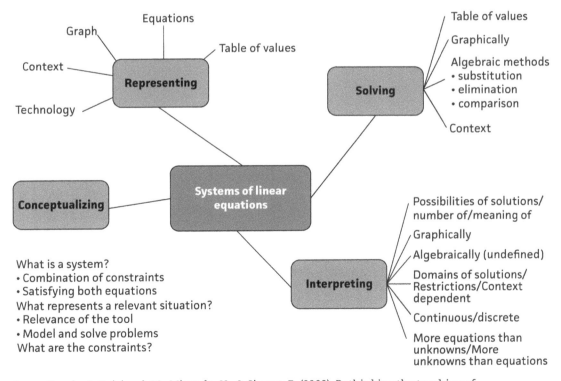

Source: Proulx, J., Beisiegel, M., Miranda, H., & Simmt, E. (2009). Rethinking the teaching of systems of equations. *Mathematics teacher, 102*(7), 526–533.

WHAT AUTOMATICITIES DO STUDENTS NEED?

Automaticity is the ability to complete a task with minimal attention to process. Automaticities help students select strategies, move between strategies, and carry out a strategy. To begin, automaticity with basic facts warrants special attention. Students must know their facts (i.e., be automatic) *and* know the strategies that come with basic fact fluency (Bay-Williams & Kling, 2019). These strategies grow into useful strategies for rational numbers, including whole numbers, fractions, and decimals. Figure 8 shows this relationship for addition and subtraction fact strategies.

FIGURE 8 ● How Addition and Subtraction Fact Strategies Grow Into General Strategies

WHOLE NUMBER EXAMPLES	DECIMAL & FRACTION EXAMPLES	NEGATIVE NUMBER EXAMPLES
REASONING STRATEGY: MAKING 10 [BASIC FACTS] → **MAKE TENS** (HUNDREDS, ETC.) [WHOLE NUMBERS] → **MAKE A WHOLE** (TENTHS, ETC.) [FRACTIONS AND DECIMALS] AND MAKE A ZERO (NEGATIVE NUMBERS).		
$8 + 6 = 10 + 4$ $= 14$ $39 + 28 = 40 + 27$ $= 67$ $395 + 787 = 400 + 782$ $= 1{,}182$	$9.7 + 3.5 = 10.0 + 3.2$ $= 13.2$ $3\frac{3}{4} + 2\frac{1}{2} = 4 + 2\frac{1}{4}$ $= 6\frac{1}{4}$	$15 + {}^-18 = 15 + ({}^-15 + {}^-3)$ $= (15 + {}^-15) + {}^-3$ $= {}^-3$
REASONING STRATEGY: PRETEND-A-TEN BECOMES **COMPENSATION**, IN GENERAL PRETENDING THERE IS ONE WHOLE NUMBER OR MORE AND THEN COMPENSATING.		
$39 + 28 \to 40 + 30$ $\to 70 - 3$ $= 67$	$5.7 + 9.8 \to 6 + 10$ $\to 16 - 0.5$ $= 15.5$	${}^-5.9 + 17.5 \to {}^-6 + 17.5$ $\to 11.5 + 0.1$ $= 11.6$ ${}^-62 - {}^-49 = {}^-63 - {}^-50$ $= {}^-13$
REASONING STRATEGY: THINK ADDITION BECOMES **COUNTING UP**, IN GENERAL, FINDING THE DIFFERENCE BETWEEN THE TWO NUMBERS.		
$615 - 582 \to 582$ to $600\ (18)$ $\to 600$ to $615\ (15)$ $\to$ jumps add to 33	$2\frac{3}{8} - 1\frac{7}{8} \to 1\frac{7}{8}$ to $2\left(\frac{1}{8}\right)$ $\to 2$ to $2\frac{3}{8}\left(\frac{3}{8}\right)$ $\to$ jumps add to $\frac{4}{8}$ or $\frac{1}{2}$	${}^-3.5 - 5.2 \to 5.2$ to $0\ ({}^-5.2)$ $\to 0$ to $-3.5\ ({}^-3.5)$ $\to$ jumps add to ${}^-8.7$
REASONING STRATEGY: DOWN UNDER 10 BECOMES **COUNTING BACK**.		
$3{,}450 - 1{,}650 \to$ $3{,}450 - 1{,}450$ (to $2{,}000$) $\to$ $2{,}000 - 200 = 1{,}800$	$5.2 - 0.8 \to 5.2 - 0.2$ (to 5) $\to 5 - 0.6$ $= 4.4$	${}^-3.5 - 5.2 \to {}^-3.5 - 5$ (to ${}^-8.5$) $\to {}^-8.5 - 0.2$ (to ${}^-8.7$)

Multiplication fact strategies also generalize, as shown in Figure 9. Negative numbers fall across these categories and simply have an additional step of determining the sign of the answer.

FIGURE 9 ● How Multiplication Fact Strategies Grow Into General Reasoning Strategies

WHOLE NUMBER EXAMPLES	DECIMAL EXAMPLES	FRACTION EXAMPLES
REASONING STRATEGY: ADD-A-GROUP [BASIC FACTS] → **BREAK APART (BY ADDENDS)** AND **PARTIAL PRODUCTS.**		
$42 \times 6 = (40 \times 6) + (2 \times 6)$ $= 240 + 12$ $= 252$	$4.2 \times 6 = (4 \times 6) + (0.2 \times 6)$ $= 24 + 1.2$ $= 25.2$	$3 \times 2\frac{1}{4} = (3 \times 2) + \left(3 \times \frac{1}{4}\right)$ $= 6 + \frac{3}{4}$ $= 6\frac{3}{4}$
REASONING STRATEGY: SUBTRACT-A-GROUP BECOMES **COMPENSATION (ALSO PARTIAL PRODUCTS).**		
$79 \times 5 = 80 \times 5 - 1 \times 5$ $= 400 - 5$ $= 395$	$9.8 \times 7 = 10 \times 7 - 0.2 \times 7$ $= 70 - 1.4$ $= 68.6$	$7 \times 6\frac{7}{8} = 7 \times 7 - 7 \times \frac{1}{8}$ $= 49 - \frac{7}{8}$ $= 48\frac{1}{8}$
REASONING STRATEGY: DOUBLING BECOMES **HALVE AND DOUBLE**, IN GENERAL, **BREAK APART TO MULTIPLY** (BY FACTORS).		
$45 \times 6 = 45 \times 2 \times 3$ $= 90 \times 3$ $= 270$	$4\frac{1}{2} \times 6 = 9 \times 3$ double and halve: $= 27$	$24 \times 7.5 = 12 \times 15$ halve and double. Repeat: $= 6 \times 30$ $= 180$

There are automaticities beyond the basic facts that students need to be able to employ reasoning strategies: for example, using 25s, 15s, and 30s; doubling; halving; using fraction equivalents within fraction families (e.g., halves, fourths, and eighths); and making conversions between common decimals, percentages, and fractions.

See Chapter 5 (pp. 107–129) of the anchor book, *Figuring Out Fluency,* for more about automaticities for fluency.

WHAT PROPERTIES AND UTILITIES SUPPORT STRATEGIC COMPETENCE?

All strategies and algorithms are based on properties of the operations. And navigating strategies requires adeptness at various skills.

PROPERTIES

It is important to note that knowing properties does not equal using properties. It is *not* useful to have students name the associative property. It is absolutely necessary that students *use* properties in solving problems efficiently. For example, in the problem −8 × 3.5, it is not important that students say, "I am going to factor −8 into −4 × 2 and apply the associative property." What *is* important is that they realize they *can* reassociate numbers and get the same

TEACHING TAKEAWAY

Knowing properties does not equal using properties. Instruction must focus on applying properties, not identifying them.

product: $(^-4 \times 2) \times 3.5 = {^-4} \times (2 \times 3.5) = {^-4} \times 7 = {^-28}$. This is the Halve and Double strategy, which *uses* the associative property.

The distributive property is critical for fluency with multiplication. The examples in Figure 10 show Break Apart to Multiply (left) and Compensation (right). Both are based on the distributive property.

FIGURE 10 ● Using the Distributive Property to Solve Multiplication Problems

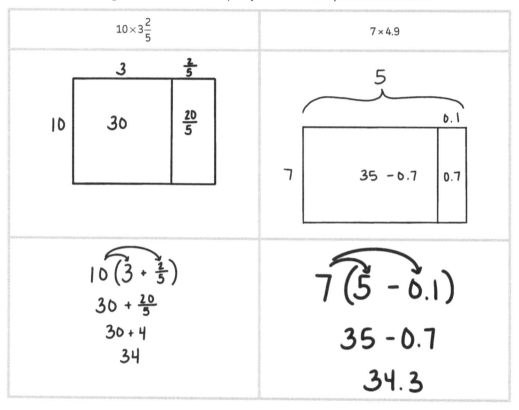

The distributive property is at the heart of algebraic reasoning. Consider the relationship between these two visuals to make sense of the distributive property:

In the first case, the result is unknown, and the distributive property is used to multiply partial products. In the second case, the result is typically given. For example: $4(x + 7) = 120$ and the goal is to figure out the missing part. Important for algebraic reasoning is to know that the distributive property is bidirectional. It is often presented as multiplication: $4(x + 7) = 4x + 28$, but it is often useful going the other direction (Ramful, 2015). For example, consider how a student might solve this problem:

$$4x + 28 = 4(2x + 6)$$

One option is to factor on the left side:

$$4(x + 7) = 4(2x + 6)$$

$$\text{Thus, } x + 7 = 2x + 6 \text{ and } x = 1$$

In other words, the distributive property doesn't just mean "distribute"; it means distribute or factor.

TEACHING TAKEAWAY

The distributive property doesn't just mean "distribute"; it means distribute or factor.

The identity property is also central to procedural fluency. The multiplicative identity (1) is useful in multiplicative situations. For example, to solve $1.28 \div 0.4$, you can think of it as the fraction $\frac{1.28}{0.4}$ and multiply by $\frac{10}{10}$ in order to have a whole number divisor: $\frac{1.28}{0.4} \times \frac{10}{10} = \frac{12.8}{4}$ and from this fraction, see that the answer is 3.2. Both the additive identity (0) and the multiplicative identity (1) are utilized in solving equations. For example, multiplying by the reciprocal is an efficient way to solve the equation $\frac{2}{3}(8 - 7x) = 24$:

$$\frac{3}{2} \cdot \frac{2}{3}(8 - 7x) = 24 \cdot \frac{3}{2}$$

$$(8 - 7x) = 36$$

$$8 - 7x = 36$$

$$-7x = 28$$

$$x = -4$$

UTILITIES AND OTHER FOUNDATIONS

Beyond utility with the properties of the operations, there are a few other special relationships that are utilized extensively. They include knowing: (1) distance from a 10, (2) flexible decomposition, and (3) part–part–whole relationships.

See Chapter 3 (pp. 47–75) of the anchor book for more about foundations and good beginnings for fluency.

In addition to knowing these utilities, there are other foundations that support reasoning. These skills are not to be gatekeepers, though when students are not adept at these skills, that is what they become. Thus, students must have adequate time for quality practice—practice that is focused, varied, processed, and connected. Figure 11 briefly summarizes important foundations and offers a list of games and routines, included online, that you can use for ongoing, meaningful experiences with the whole class, or for interventions with a subset of students.

TEACHING TAKEAWAY

Becoming automatic with select skills supports reasoning strategies, and thus should be taught before and alongside strategy instruction.

FIGURE 11 ● Foundations and Activity List for Quality Practice

FOUNDATION	OVERVIEW	ONLINE ACTIVITIES FOR QUALITY PRACTICE
Flexible Decomposition	Decomposing numbers and expressions flexibly and with automaticity helps students select and carry out a strategy. This is needed for implementing reasoning strategies with whole numbers, decimals, fractions, ratios, proportions, and equations. For example, when finding $128 \div {}^-8$, one might recognize that 128 can be decomposed into $64 + 64$ so that a known fact can be used to solve the problem.	1. *Five Ways, Most Ways* (Game) 2. *Lose It* (Game) 3. "Common or Unique" (Routine)
Number Relationships and Distance From Zero	Recognizing how numbers are related to each other (e.g., that 8 is 2 less than 10, 4 is one-fourth of 16, and $4x$ is also one-fourth of $16x$) helps students to notice efficient strategies. Distance from zero is important to computing positive and negative numbers. Number lines are effective models for developing number relations.	4. *Cover the Line* (Game) 5. *Combinations* (Game) 6. *Farthest From* (Game)
Factors and Multiples	Knowing factors and multiples begins with basic facts. Recognizing multiples and factors is useful for many skills in mathematics and is necessary to enact reasoning strategies. For example, knowing factors helps to find unit rates and simplify fractions; knowing multiples helps to find common denominators or simplify an algebraic expression. Exploring factors and multiples through a rote process (i.e., listing out all the multiples) is not effective in helping students *use* factors and multiples adeptly.	7. *Six Charts* (Game) 8. "The Stand" (Routine) 9. *Multiple Cover Up* (Game)
Impact of Operations	To be flexible thinkers, students need to understand the impact of operations—in particular, recognizing equivalent operations. This requires understanding such things as subtracting a negative is equivalent to adding a positive, dividing by 2 is the same as multiplying by $\frac{1}{2}$, and multiplying a number by a fraction equivalent to 1 (e.g., $\frac{5}{5}$) results in an equivalent number.	10. *Another Way to Say It* (Game) 11. *PoNeg Products Three by Three* (Game) 12. "The Truth" (Routine) 13. "The One and Done" (Routine)
Unit Fractions	Automaticity with multiplying and dividing with unit fractions supports reasoning strategies. For example, in solving $\frac{2}{5} \times 25$ a student can first think of it as a unit fraction problem: $\frac{1}{5} \times 25$. (What is one-fifth of 25?) That is 5, which means two-fifths is 10.	14. "The Missing" (Routine) 15. "If I Know This" (Routine)

 These games (and this chart) can all be found at this book's companion website at **resources.corwin.com/FOF/ rationalnumbersalgequations**.

WHAT ARE STRATEGIES FOR COMPUTATIONAL ESTIMATION?

Just like computation, estimation has strategies and the use of those strategies should be *flexible*. For multiplication and division of fractions or decimals, students might use any of these methods:

1. *Rounding.* Flexible rounding includes choosing which numbers should be rounded, and then deciding how best to round those numbers given the context of the problem and types of numbers and operations involved. For 24.4 + 34.452, rounding both down to the nearest whole number will

give a low estimate, whereas rounding one up and one down gives a closer estimate.

2. *Front-end estimation.* This method focuses on the largest (absolute) place value to perform the operation, adjusting as needed. For example, for 57.5 × 2.67, multiply 50 × 2. As you can see in this case, that estimate is going to be quite a bit less than the actual answer. More flexibly, then, students may multiply 60 × 2 or 50 × 3. With division, front-end estimation focuses on compatibles (an overlap to the next strategy).

3. *Compatible numbers.* With flexibility in mind, change one or more of the numbers involved to nearby numbers (e.g., whole numbers, in the case of fractions) that make the operations easier to perform. For example, to divide 9.7 ÷ 0.22, thinking about how many quarters (0.25) are in $10 (40).

WHAT ARE SIGNIFICANT REASONING STRATEGIES?

Teaching strategies beyond the standard algorithms is necessary for fluency, but time is limited. Thus, we must ask ourselves, which strategies are worthy of attention? Let's just take some pressure off here. The list is short, and we must help students see that they are not necessarily learning a new strategy, but they are applying a strategy they learned with basic facts or whole numbers and transferring it to fractions or decimals. In the anchor book, we propose Seven Significant Strategies for the operations, which are shared in Figure 12.

FIGURE 12 ● Reasoning Strategies for Rational Numbers and Algebraic Equations

STRATEGIES FOR THE OPERATIONS	STRATEGIES FOR COMPARING RATIOS AND SOLVING PROPORTIONS	STRATEGIES FOR SOLVING EQUATIONS FOR AN UNKNOWN	STRATEGIES FOR SOLVING SYSTEMS OF LINEAR EQUATIONS
1. Count On/Count Back	1. Build Up/Break Down	1. Use Relational Reasoning	1. Identify the Point of Intersection on a Graph
2. Make Tens, Make a Whole, Make a Zero	2. Find a Unit Rate	2. Choose a Basic Transformation: ● Combine like terms	2. Identify Values in a Table
3. Break Apart to Multiply	3. Use Scale Factor	● Add or subtract like terms on both sides of the equation	3. Use Substitution
4. Halve and Double	4. Use $y = kx$		4. Use Elimination
5. Compensation	5. Find Cross Product	● Multiply or divide on both sides of the equation	
6. Use Partials		● Use distributive property	
7. Use an Inverse Relationship			

Notice that these are ways to reason and not representations. Representations are not strategies—representations support the use of strategies! For example, with proportional reasoning, ratio tables, tape diagrams, and double number lines are *representations*. These representations support reasoning. Reasoning strategies include generating equivalent ratios, using unit rates, and using scale

TEACHING TAKEAWAY

Representations are not strategies. When a student says, "I used a ratio table" ask *How did you use it?* to learn what reasoning they used.

factor (or within/between ratio). When a student says, "I used a ratio table," ask *how* they used it—then you will learn what reasoning they used.

HOW DO I TEACH, PRACTICE, AND ASSESS STRATEGIES?

The answer to this question is the focus of Parts 2 and 3. Here, we offer general background and guidance to support implementation of the activities in Parts 2 and 3.

EXPLICIT STRATEGY INSTRUCTION

TEACHING TAKEAWAY

Explicitly teaching a strategy does not mean turning the strategy into an algorithm.

Let's unpack the phrase *explicit strategy instruction*. The *Merriam-Webster* dictionary defines *explicit* as "fully revealed or expressed without vagueness" ("Explicit," 2021). In mathematics teaching, being *explicit* means making mathematical relationships visible. A *strategy* is a flexible method to solve a problem. *Explicit strategy instruction*, then, is engaging students in ways to clearly see why and how a strategy works, eventually learning when it is a useful strategy. Learning how and when to use strategies *empowers* students, developing a positive mathematics identity and a sense of agency. Importantly, explicitly teaching a strategy does not mean turning the strategy into an algorithm. Strategies require flexible thinking.

QUALITY PRACTICE

Quality practice is not a worksheet! Quality practice is *focused* on enacting a strategy, *varied* in the type of activity, *processed* by the student to make sense of what they did, and *connected* to what they are learning. The variety of practice in this book includes worked examples, routines, games, and independent tasks. Worked examples are excellent opportunities for students to attend to the thinking involved with a strategy. Three types of worked examples are useful and focus on different aspects of fluency:

See Chapter 6 (pp. 130–153) of the anchor book for more about quality practice.

1. *Correctly worked example*: Efficiency (selects an appropriate strategy) and flexibility (applies strategy to a new problem type).

2. *Partially worked example*: Efficiency (selects an appropriate strategy) and accuracy (completes steps accurately; gets correct answer).

3. *Incorrectly worked example*: Accuracy (completes steps accurately; gets correct answer).

Also, comparing two correctly worked examples is effective in helping students become flexible in choosing methods (Durkin, Star, & Rittle-Johnson, 2017; Star et al., 2020). Throughout the modules are dozens of examples, which can be used as worked examples (and adapted to other similar worked examples). Your worked examples can be from a fictional "student" or be authentic student work.

Routines are 5- to 10-minute whole-class interactions that can be repeated many times with different numbers. Routines in one section of this book can often be applied to other sections/topics, so when you find one that your students love, adapt it! Games provide enjoyable practice but are particularly valuable because they invite discussion and peer teaching. Independent activities are designed for individuals to work at their own pace and have independent think time. Collectively, these four ways to practice provide ongoing opportunities for students to become adept at using the strategies.

Most of these activities can be adapted to use for other numbers, strategies, operations, or topics. For example, a routine can be changed from adding integers to adding fractions, or a game that focuses on adding can be adapted to multiplication. Resources like game boards and recording sheets are downloadable and editable files. Knowing this means that you have many more activities than you find on a first count.

ASSESSING STRATEGY USE

Assessing strategy use is hard to do with traditional quizzes and tests. Here are three effective alternatives.

1. *Journal prompts* provide an opportunity for students to write about their thinking process. Each module provides a collection of prompts that you might use for journaling. You can modify those or craft your own. The prompt can specifically ask students to explain how they used the strategy:

Explain and show how you can use scale factors to solve this proportion: $\dfrac{2.5}{4} = \dfrac{10}{?}$

Or a prompt can focus on identifying when that strategy is a good idea:

Circle the equations in which you would first eliminate parentheses. For one that you would use a different first step, explain why:

$4(x - 3) = 9$ $\dfrac{1}{2}(3x + 5) = 7$

$4(x - 2) - 3(x - 2) = 10$ $3(x + 1) = 4(x - 3)$

---

2. *Observations* help you keep track of students and monitor progress (see Figure 13). For example, you can tally which strategies you see students using as they play a game or engage in a routine or independent task. Or you can qualify how well students are using a strategy by using codes:

+ Is implementing the strategy adeptly

✔ Understands the strategy, takes time to think it through

– Is not implementing the strategy (yet)

FIGURE 13 ● Observation Tool for Proportional Reasoning Strategies

Observation Tool: Solving Missing Value Proportions

Names	Proportional Reasoning Strategies				
	Build Up/ Break Down	Unit Rate	Scale Factor	$y = kx$	Cross Products

online resources | This resource can be downloaded at **resources.corwin.com/FOF/ rationalnumbersalgequations**.

3. *Interviewing* is an excellent way to really understand student thinking. Pick one to three problems that lend to a strategy/topic you are working on and write each on a note card. While students are engaged in an instructional or practice activity, have students rotate to see you, or you can do a quick check at their desk. Show the student a problem and ask them to (1) solve it and (2) explain how they thought about it. Pair this with an observation tool to keep track of how each student is progressing.

With interviews and observations, you don't need to assess every student the same day. Some days, you collect data on some students; other days, you collect data on other students. For instructional planning, you don't need to talk to every student to gain important insights to inform what strategies need more attention.

HOW DO I SUPPORT STUDENTS' FLUENCY OVER TIME?

As soon as students know more than one strategy for a given operation, it is time to integrate routines, tasks, independent activities, and games that focus on choosing when to use a strategy. That is where Part 3 of this book comes in. As you read in Fluency Action 1, students need to be able to choose efficient strategies based on those they've learned.

Do not wait until after all strategies are learned to focus on when to use a strategy—instead, weave in Part 3 activities regularly. Each time a new strategy is learned, it is time to revisit activities that engage students in making choices from among the strategies in their repertoire. Students must learn what to look for in a problem to decide which strategy they will use to solve the problem *efficiently* based on the numbers in the problem. This is *flexibility* in action, and thus leads to fluency.

IN SUM, WAYS TO SUPPORT "REAL" FLUENCY

Part 1 has briefly described factors that are important in developing fluency, and these factors are necessary for implementing the modules. We close Part 1 with five key factors to figuring out fluency:

1. Be clear on what fluency means (three components and six actions). This includes communicating it to students and their parents.

2. Attend to foundational skills: conceptual understanding, properties, utilities, computational estimation, and, of course, basic fact fluency.

3. Help students connect the features of a problem to appropriate strategy selection.

4. Reinforce student reasoning and choice selection, rather than focus on speed and accuracy.

5. Assess fluency, not just accuracy.

Time invested in strategy work has a big payoff: confident and fluent students (and that is the "best product"). That is why we have so many activities in this book. Teach the strategies as part of core instruction *and* continue to practice throughout the year, looping back to strategies that students might be forgetting to use (with Part 2 activities) and offering ongoing opportunities to choose from among strategies (with Part 3 activities).

TEACHING TAKEAWAY

Teaching for fluency means teaching strategies as core instruction, routinely practicing them, and offering opportunities for students to choose among strategies.

NOTES

PART 2

STRATEGY MODULES

BONUS CONTENT:

In addition to the strategy modules here, a Good Beginnings Module is available online, which includes necessary understandings and skills to enact the reasoning strategies in this book, along with 15 more activities. Consider checking it out!

Topics in the Good Beginnings Module:

- Flexible Decomposition

- Number Relationships and Distance From Zero

- Factors and Multiples

- Operation Sense

- Unit Fractions

 This resource can be downloaded at **resources.corwin.com/FOF/rationalnumbersalgequations**.

Reasoning Strategies for Addition

In this module we highlight four significant strategies for addition:

- Count On

- Make Tens (Extended to Make Hundreds etc., Make a Whole, and Make a Zero)

- Compensation

- Partial Sums

The focus of each section is on developing an understanding of how the strategy works and when it is a good choice. In Part 3 of this book, we offer activities that focus on choosing among these significant addition strategies.

STRATEGY OVERVIEW:
Count On

What Is the Count On Strategy? This strategy starts at one of the numbers and uses efficient jumps to add the other number. Because adding negative numbers means you may be moving in either direction, this strategy name can be adapted accordingly—for example, Using Counting or Using Jumps.

How Does Count On Work? The strategy is based on partial sums, keeping track of partial results as you add. *The thinking process:*

1. Decide which number to start with.

2. Decide how to break apart the other number to convenient and efficient "jumps."

3. Count on using the chunks you chose.

Examples Across Number Types

Whole Numbers

$$3{,}450 + 1{,}360$$

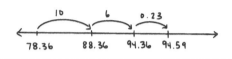

1,300   50   10

3,450 + 1,300 = 4,750
4,750 + 50 = 4,800
4,800 + 10 = 4,810

Fractions

$$3\tfrac{7}{8} + 5\tfrac{1}{2}$$

$$5\tfrac{1}{2} + 3 = 8\tfrac{1}{2}$$

$$8\tfrac{1}{2} + \tfrac{1}{2} = 9$$

$$9 + \tfrac{3}{8} = 9\tfrac{3}{8}$$

Decimals

$$16.23 + 78.36 = 94.59$$

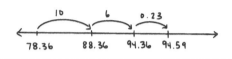

78.36   88.36   94.36   94.59

Negative Numbers

$$^-64 + {}^-59 = {}^-123$$

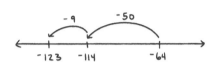

$^-123$ $^-114$ $^-64$

WHEN DO YOU CHOOSE COUNT ON (USE JUMPS)?

The Count On strategy is useful when one of the addends is relatively small or when you can easily break apart one of the addends into convenient chunks.

MODULE 1 Strategies for Addition

MODULE 2 Strategies for Subtraction

MODULE 3 Strategies for Multiplication

MODULE 4 Strategies for Division

MODULE 5 Strategies for Ratios and Proportions

MODULE 6 Strategies for Solving Equations for an Unknown

MODULE 7 Strategies for Solving Systems of Linear Equations

TEACHING ACTIVITIES FOR COUNT ON

Count On is the first strategy students learn with whole numbers, but it is a useful strategy across number types, and often overlooked as an option. These teaching activities illustrate how the strategy works. The number line is a very useful tool for this strategy. The teaching goal is that students (1) become adept at using Count On efficiently and accurately and (2) know when they will want to use the Count On strategy.

ACTIVITY 1.1
NUMBER LINE COMPARISONS WITH WORKED EXAMPLES

Using Jumps works well with negative numbers, though it looks different than counting on with positive numbers. A great way to highlight the differences is by comparing worked examples on number lines. To do this, create a set of related problems, as shown below. Have students work together to compare the examples. Then, bring the class together to share their observations, highlighting points such as how the direction of jumps is connected to the sign of the second addend.

$$137 + 45 = 182$$

+40   +5

137   177   182

$$137 + {}^-45 = 92$$

+ ⁻5   + ⁻40

92   97   137

$$^-137 + 45 = {}^-92$$

+40   +5

⁻137   ⁻97   ⁻92

$$^-137 + {}^-45 = {}^-182$$

+ ⁻5   + ⁻40

⁻182   ⁻177   ⁻137

Notice that in these examples students recognize they can count on in chunks, which is more efficient than counting by ones or tens. When negative numbers are introduced, students need to revisit the idea of chunking their jumps. To support such thinking, provide a collection of different ways to count on to solve a given equation.

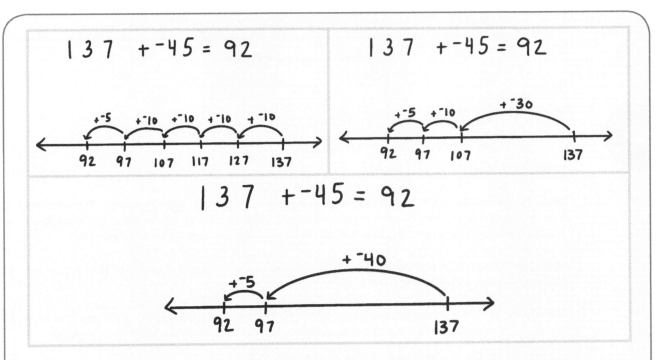

Again, ask students to compare how the worked examples, number lines, and counts are similar and different. Notice that these examples start from the first addend, but students can also compare two problems in which one example starts from the first addend and the second problem starts from the second addend. Discussion can help students think about which number is the better "start."

ACTIVITY 1.2
CONNECTING BONDS AND NUMBER LINES

Number bonds help students think about the different ways a number can be decomposed, which is necessary for using the Count On strategy. In this activity, students identify an addend to decompose with a number bond and break it apart in a way that is useful for solving the problem. Then, students use that decomposition to count on a number line. Highlight flexibility and efficiency as you discuss options.

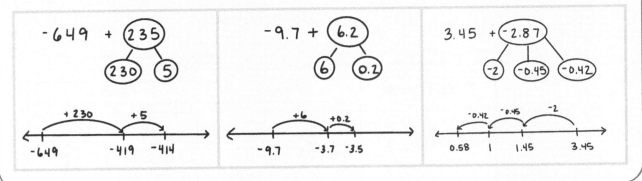

See Part 1, page 20, for an overview about quality practice.

ACTIVITY 1.3

Name: Make It Close   **Type:** Game

About the Game: The goal of *Make It Close* is to create a sum as close to a target as possible. The twist in this game is that the target changes from round to round. The example described here is adding a negative and a positive integer, but this game can be modified to other numbers (e.g., two negative numbers or two decimals).

Materials: Four decks of digit cards (0–9) or playing cards (queens = 0, aces = 1; remove 10s, kings, and jacks); *Make It Close* placemats and recording sheet (optional)

Directions:

1. To set the target, one player draws four cards and creates an addition problem (two-digit negative number + two-digit positive number). This sum is the target number for the round.

2. One player deals four digit cards to each player.

3. Players arrange their digit cards to create an addition problem with a sum as close to the target as possible (using the two-digit negative number + two-digit positive number format).

4. Each player shows (e.g., using a number line) or tells how they counted on (used jumps) to find their sum.

5. The player closest to the target earns a point for the round.

6. Repeat Steps 1–5.

7. The first player to earn five points wins the game.

> **TEACHING TAKEAWAY**
> Have students record their reasoning on a number line. This creates a record of their work, increases accountability, and provides a formative assessment.

In this example, the target is 7. The first player is dealt 2, 4, 5, and 5 and makes −45 + 52. The second player is dealt 2, 1, 7, and 6 and makes −62 + 71. Player 1 wins the round.

Make It Close

Directions: Use digit cards to make an addition problem. The sum of the problem is the target. Deal new digit cards to make an addition problem that is close to the target. The player closest to the target gets a point.

Target Problem	Player 1 (give yourself a ✓ if you are closest to the target)	Player 2 (give yourself a ✓ if you are closest to the target)
−37 + 44 = 7	−45 + 52 = 7 ✓	−62 + 71 = 9

Make It Close

Directions: Use digit cards to make an addition problem. The sum of the problem is the target. Deal new digit cards to make an addition problem that is close to the target. The player closest to the target gets a point.

Target Problem	My Problem (give yourself a check if you are closest to the target)

ACTIVITY 1.4

Independent Task: Greatest Sum, Smallest Sum   **Type:** Task

About the Task: This activity strengthens number sense and reasoning. It is readily adapted to play as a game in which students try to find the largest or smallest sum (e.g., pairs compete in a group of four). This activity can be modified to feature two-digit addends, decimals, or fractions.

Materials: Two sets of digit cards (0–9) or playing cards (queens = 0, aces = 1; remove 10s, kings, and jacks); *The Largest Sum, The Smallest Sum* recording sheet

Directions:

1. Students choose a situation for their addends (positive + positive, positive + negative, or negative + negative). Alternatively, you can direct them to use a specific situation.

2. Students choose six cards to make two three-digit addends matching the situation they select.

3. Students arrange the digit cards to make the greatest sum and find it by counting on.

4. Students then rearrange the same digit cards to make the smallest sum and then find it by counting on.

5. Students record their thinking on the recording sheet or in their math journals.

6. Students shuffle cards and repeat the activity.

RESOURCE(S) FOR THIS ACTIVITY

1	2	3	4
5	6	7	8
9	1	2	3
4	5	6	7
8	9	0	0

The Largest Sum, The Smallest Sum

Directions: Choose a condition for the addends. Pull digit cards to make an addend. Pull digit cards to make another addend. Arrange the digits in each number to make the largest sum. Count on to show the sum. Then rearrange the digits in each number to make the smallest sum.

Condition of the addends:	Positive + Positive		Positive + Negative	Negative + Negative
	Largest Sum		Smallest Sum	
First Addend:	Second Addend:		First Addend:	Second Addend:
Show how you added:			Show how you added:	

online resources 🔗 This resource can be downloaded at **resources.corwin.com/FOF/rationalnumbersalgequations**.

STRATEGY OVERVIEW:
Make Tens (Extended)

What Is the Make Tens Strategy (and Its Extensions)? Make Tens begins with basic facts as Making 10, as students move over the amount needed from one addend to make the other addend a 10: 9 + 6 = 10 + 5. It becomes **Make Tens** with multidigit sums like 49 + 43 = 50 + 42. It extends to **Make Hundreds, Thousands, etc.** With fractions and decimals the strategy becomes **Make a Whole**—for example, rethinking 6.9 + 17.4 as 7 + 17.3. Finally, with negative numbers, this strategy includes **Make a Zero**—for example, thinking of 43 + ⁻52 as 43 + ⁻43 + ⁻9.

HOW DOES MAKE TENS (EXTENDED) WORK?

The strategy is based on breaking apart one addend to form a benchmark number with the other addend with the goal of creating a simpler problem to add. *The thinking process for positive numbers:*

1. Decide which number is close to a benchmark of ones, tens, hundreds, etc.
2. Determine how far from the benchmark that number is.
3. Break apart the other number to move over the amount needed to "make" that benchmark.
4. Add.

The thinking process for negative and positive numbers:

1. Notice that the two addends have different signs.
2. Break apart the one that has the larger absolute value such that one part will "make a zero" with the other addend.
3. The remaining part is the sum.

Examples Across Number Types

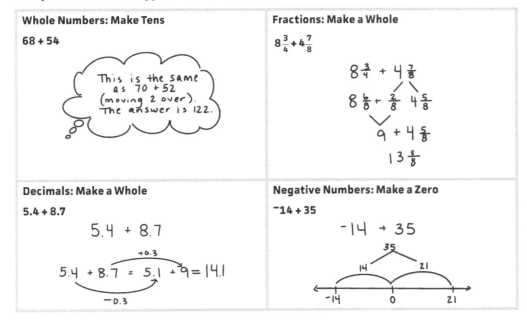

Whole Numbers: Make Tens	Fractions: Make a Whole
68 + 54	$8\frac{3}{4} + 4\frac{7}{8}$

Decimals: Make a Whole	Negative Numbers: Make a Zero
5.4 + 8.7	⁻14 + 35

WHEN DO YOU CHOOSE MAKE TENS (EXTENDED)?

Make Tens and Make a Whole are useful when either or both addends are close to, but less than, a benchmark. For sums like 3,457 + 6,349—where neither addend is close to a benchmark—this strategy is not useful. Make a Zero is useful when one addend is negative and the other is positive.

TEACHING ACTIVITIES for Make Tens

Make Tens strategy is a very useful place value strategy. Make a Zero supports student reasoning with negative numbers as they consider the magnitude and direction of each addend. These teaching activities illustrate how the strategy works. The teaching goal is that students (1) become adept at using Make Tens (and Make a Whole and Make a Zero) strategy efficiently and accurately and (2) know when they will want to use this strategy.

ACTIVITY 1.5
SAME AND DIFFERENT

In this activity, pose two equivalent expressions in which one shows the expression re-thought as Make Tens, Hundreds, or Make a Whole works. Ask students to notice what is the same and what is different across the set of problems. There are several ways to form a set: Use a set with same number types (one column in the table below), use a mixed set (provide a mix of statements across columns), or include statements with missing values (e.g., a fourth statement in the set).

MAKE TENS	MAKE HUNDREDS	MAKE A WHOLE	MAKE A WHOLE
57 + 64 is the same as 60 + 61	288 + 335 is the same as 300 + 323	5.7 + 6.4 is the same as 6.0 + 6.1	$3\frac{7}{8} + 2\frac{5}{8}$ is the same as $4 + 2\frac{1}{2}$
39 + 77 is the same as 40 + 76	725 + 676 is the same as 800 + 601	3.9 + 7.7 is the same as 4.0 + 7.6	$4\frac{1}{3} + 6\frac{2}{3}$ is the same as $4 + 7$
55 + 87 is the same as 52 + 90	744 + 566 is the same as 710 + 600	5.5 + 8.7 is the same as 5.2 + 9.0	$9\frac{1}{4} + 5\frac{7}{8}$ is the same as $9\frac{1}{8} + 6$

ACTIVITY 1.6
EXPRESSION MATCH

Provide students with a collection of cards with expressions and related Make a Zero expressions recorded on them. Students work with partners to find cards with equivalent expressions. The table provides some examples you might use. There are two "Matches With" cards for each expression to focus on flexible and efficient decompositions.

EXPRESSION	MATCHES WITH	MATCHES WITH
⁻14 + 16	10 + ⁻10 + ⁻4 + 6	⁻14 + 14 + 2
15 + ⁻21	15 + ⁻15 + ⁻6	10 + 5 + ⁻10 + ⁻11
⁻100 + 47	⁻47 + ⁻53 + 47	⁻40 + ⁻60 + 40 + 7
62 + ⁻13	49 + 13 + ⁻13	50 + 12 + ⁻12 + ⁻1
3.1 + ⁻8.5	3.1 + ⁻3.1 + ⁻5.4	3 + 0.1 + ⁻3 + ⁻5.5
⁻2.5 + 9.1	⁻2 + ⁻0.5 + 2 + 7.1	⁻2.5 + 2.5 + 6.6

TEACHING TAKEAWAY

Expression cards can be made on index cards or cardstock. Ask volunteers or students to make sets for you.

PRACTICE ACTIVITIES for Make Tens

See Part 1, page 20, for an overview about quality practice.

ACTIVITY 1.7

Name: "Say It as Make a Zero"   **Type:** Routine

About the Routine: This routine challenges students to rename expressions in a variety of ways (SanGiovanni, 2019). In this particular version, the focus is on an equivalent expression that lends itself to the Make a Zero strategy, but it works well with the Make a Whole, Compensation, and other strategies as well. You may want to begin with a Make Tens version to build background (example follows).

Materials: Prepared sets of expressions (examples follow)

Directions: 1. Pose three expressions to students and have them discuss other ways to say them. When you first launch this routine or when this strategy is new, pose the expressions one at a time. Later, you can pose them together.

2. Give students time to think about a way to rewrite the expressions (or rethink the expressions) to Make a Zero.

3. Pair students to compare and discuss their new expressions, then discuss options as a whole group.

4. Record options on the board and ask students (a) the answer and (b) which expression they used to find the answer.

Examples for Make a Zero:

"SAY IT AS MAKE A ZERO"		
38 + $^-$75	$^-$23 + 45	$^-$57 + 43

In this example, students might think of renaming the first expression as 38 + $^-$38 + $^-$37 where the opposites combine for zero. Students won't necessarily think of a decomposition that neatly creates a zero. In 38 + $^-$75, students might decompose $^-$75 as $^-$38 + $^-$2 + $^-$35, ultimately finding the sum to be $^-$2 + $^-$35 or $^-$37.

"SAY IT AS MAKE A ZERO"		
1.45 + $^-$4.4	$^-$6.5 + 7.7	3.02 + $^-$1.75

"SAY IT AS MAKE A ZERO"		
$\frac{3}{8} + -5\frac{2}{8}$	$-3\frac{1}{4} + 6\frac{3}{4}$	$-6\frac{1}{2} + 7\frac{3}{4}$

Additional examples for Make Tens (Extended)

"SAY IT AS MAKE TENS"		
47 + 37	28 + 56	63 + 19

"SAY IT AS MAKE HUNDREDS"		
219 + 313	475 + 233	119 + 526

"SAY IT AS MAKE A WHOLE"		
$3\frac{3}{4} + 5\frac{2}{4}$	$\frac{6}{8} + 4\frac{7}{8}$	$2\frac{5}{6} + 3\frac{2}{6}$

ACTIVITY 1.8

Name: Make Zero a Hero   **Type:** Game

About the Game: *Make Zero a Hero* is designed to focus students' attention on decomposing an addend in order to use the Make a Zero strategy for adding positive and negative numbers.

Materials: *Make Zero a Hero* game board per pair, digit cards (0–9) or playing cards (queens = 0, aces = 1; remove 10s, kings, and jacks), or two 10-sided dice; counters in two different colors

Directions: 1. Players take turns generating two digits with cards or dice and decide if they want the number to be negative or positive.

2. Players look for an available space on the game board wherein the number that they created can be used to Make a Zero to solve the given problem.

3. Players state the revised expression to show the Make a Zero strategy.

4. If enacted correctly, the player places their marker on the game board.

5. The player with the most 3-in-a-rows wins.

For example, Jackson rolls a 3 and a 1. He decides to make ⁻13 with the two digits because he sees that he can use it to solve ⁻49 + 13. He states that ⁻49 + 13 is the same as ⁻36 + ⁻13 + 13 so it equals ⁻36 and places his piece on the board (left example). On his next turn, Jackson rolls a 1 and a 7 and decides to make it 17. He states that he can solve 67 + ⁻17 as 50 + 17 + ⁻17, which equals 50, and puts his game piece on the board (right example).

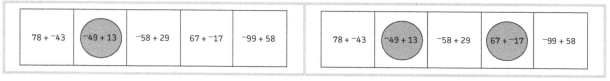

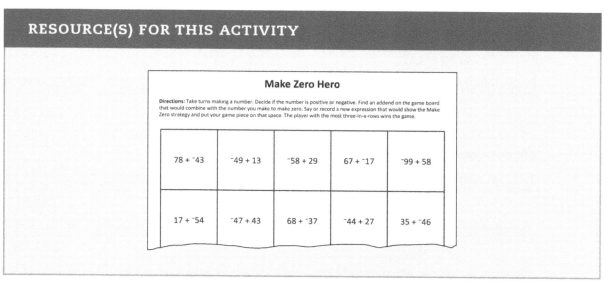

RESOURCE(S) FOR THIS ACTIVITY

Make Zero Hero

Directions: Take turns making a number. Decide if the number is positive or negative. Find an addend on the game board that would combine with the number you make to make zero. Say or record a new expression that would show the Make Zero strategy and put your game piece on that space. The player with the most three-in-a-rows wins the game.

78 + ⁻43	⁻49 + 13	⁻58 + 29	67 + ⁻17	⁻99 + 58
17 + ⁻54	⁻47 + 43	68 + ⁻37	⁻44 + 27	35 + ⁻46

online resources → This resource can be downloaded at **resources.corwin.com/FOF/rationalnumbersalgequations**.

STRATEGY OVERVIEW:
Compensation

What Is the Compensation Strategy? This strategy involves *adjusting* one or both of the addends to make the expression easier to add, and then *compensating* in order to preserve equivalence.

HOW DOES COMPENSATION WORK?

The strategy is based on the zero property of addition (if you add *n* and then subtract *n*, the change is 0). *The thinking process:*

1. Select a number close to one or more addends that is easier to add.

2. Add the revised problem.

3. Compensate by undoing whatever was done in Step 1 (e.g., if you added 5, take 5 away or if you added ⁻2, add 2).

Examples Across Number Types

Whole Numbers	Fractions
485 + 648	$3\frac{7}{8}+8\frac{7}{8}$
Adjust: Add 15 to 485	Adjust: Add $\frac{1}{8}$ to both addends
Compensate: Subtract 15 from sum	Compensate: Subtract $\frac{2}{8}$ from sum

$$485 + 648$$
$$+15\downarrow$$
$$500 + 648$$
$$1148$$
$$-15\downarrow$$
$$1133$$

$$3\tfrac{7}{8} + 8\tfrac{7}{8}$$
$$+\tfrac{1}{8}\downarrow \qquad \downarrow+\tfrac{1}{8}$$
$$4 + 9$$
$$13$$
$$13 - \tfrac{2}{8} = 12\tfrac{3}{4}$$

Decimals	Negative Numbers
35.14 + 18.9	**⁻6.8 + ⁻9.9**
Adjust: Add 1.1 to 18.9 resulting in 20 and then add 20 to 35.14	Adjust: Add ⁻0.2 to ⁻6.8 and ⁻0.1 to ⁻9.9
Compensate: Subtract 1.1	Compensate: Add 0.3 to sum

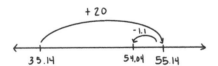

$$35.14 + 20 = 55.14$$
$$55.14 - 1.1 = 54.04$$

$$-6.8 + -9.9$$
$$-0.2\downarrow \qquad \downarrow-0.1$$
$$-7 + -10$$
$$-17$$
$$-17 + 0.3 = -16.7$$

WHEN DO YOU CHOOSE COMPENSATION?

Compensation is a very versatile strategy. It is a particularly good choice when one or both numbers are near a benchmark. It is not as easy to use when neither number is near a benchmark—for example, 52.6 + 77.5.

TEACHING ACTIVITIES for Compensation

This strategy is all about choice. Which addend might you change—or do you want to change both? As students explore Compensation with negative numbers, they must attend to doing the opposite to preserve equivalence. These teaching activities illustrate how Compensation works to help students become adept at using it and knowing when they will want to use it.

ACTIVITY 1.9
ONE OR BOTH AND I PREFER

Compensation can be carried out by adjusting either or both addends. In this activity, partners apply the strategy all three ways, recording their thinking like in this table and noting which one they prefer. One idea is to have students fold a blank piece of paper into fourths (columns) to record the problem in one section, and each option in a different section.

EXPRESSION	CHANGE FIRST ADDEND THEN COMPENSATE	CHANGE SECOND ADDEND THEN COMPENSATE	CHANGE BOTH ADDENDS THEN COMPENSATE
5.7 + 3.8	6 + 3.8 = 9.8 9.8 − 0.3 = 9.5	5.7 + 4 = 9.7 9.7 − 0.2 = 9.5	6 + 4 = 10 10 − 0.5 = 9.5

After students have explored three to five problems, discuss each problem separately. Ask, "What do you notice about the three ways to solve [5.7 + 3.8]?" Ask students to vote on which one they like best and have them explain why. Stress that there is no "correct" choice, but if they know why they like one option over another, then that will help them use the strategy. In sum, ask, "When might you change only one addend and when might you change both?" This activity can be modified for any type of number. The table shows an example for adding mixed numbers.

EXPRESSION	CHANGE FIRST ADDEND THEN COMPENSATE	CHANGE SECOND ADDEND THEN COMPENSATE	CHANGE BOTH ADDENDS THEN COMPENSATE
$6\frac{2}{3} + 7\frac{1}{6}$ $6\frac{4}{6} + 7\frac{1}{6}$	$7 + 7\frac{1}{6} = 14\frac{1}{6}$ $14\frac{1}{6} - \frac{2}{6} = 13\frac{5}{6}$	$6\frac{4}{6} + 7 = 13\frac{4}{6}$ $13\frac{4}{6} + \frac{1}{6} = 13\frac{5}{6}$	$7 + 7 = 14$ $14 - \frac{2}{6} + \frac{1}{6} = 13\frac{5}{6}$

RESOURCE(S) FOR THIS ACTIVITY

One or Both and I Prefer

Directions: Record an addition problem. Complete the chart to show the different ways you can think about adding it using Compensation. Star the approach you prefer.

Expression	ADD EXTRA TO BOTH ADDENDS, THEN TAKE IT BACK	ADD EXTRA TO FIRST ADDEND, THEN TAKE IT BACK	ADD EXTRA TO SECOND ADDEND, THEN TAKE IT BACK
5.5 + 3.8	6 + 4 = 10 10 − 0.5 = 9.5 9.5 − 0.2 = 9.3, so 5.5 + 3.8 = 9.3	6 + 3.8 = 9.8 9.8 − 0.5 = 9.3, so 5.5 + 3.8 = 9.3	5.5 + 4 = 9.5 9.5 − 0.2 = 9.3, so 5.5 + 3.8 = 9.3

This resource can be downloaded at **resources.corwin.com/FOF/rationalnumbersalgequations**.

ACTIVITY 1.10
FOUR COMPENSATIONS

As students learn strategies, it is important that they learn both how a strategy works and when it works well. This activity helps students think about how to compensate when adding negative numbers, compared to what happens when adding positive numbers. In this activity, you present four expressions with similar addends, as shown in the table. Begin by sharing worked examples adjusting either addend, as illustrated here.

289 + 475	⁻289 + ⁻475
Change: 289 to 300 [add 11]	Change: ⁻475 to ⁻500 [subtract 25]
Add: 300 + 475 = 775	Add: ⁻289 + ⁻500 = ⁻789
Compensation: 775 −11 = 764	Compensation: ⁻789 + 25 = ⁻764
⁻289 + 475	289 + ⁻475
Change: ⁻289 to ⁻300 [subtract 11]	Change: 289 to 300 [add 11]
Add: ⁻300 + 475 = 175	Add: 300 + ⁻475 = ⁻175
Compensation: 175 + 11 = 186	Compensation: ⁻175 − 11 = ⁻186

Ask students what they notice about how each expression was solved. The key is attending to whether the change leads to subtracting (thus, adding is needed to compensate) or vice versa. Number lines can help students reason through these decisions. Discuss options for compensating, along with when it seems to work the best (which addend or both). After examining the set, give students their own set to explore. Examples are provided in the table. Extend the activity by asking students to create new expressions that work well with Compensation and expressions that don't.

POSSIBLE PROBLEMS FOR STUDENTS TO EXPLORE ON THEIR OWN			
78 + 97	512 + 544	398 + 612	4.3 + 7.8
⁻78 + ⁻97	⁻512 + ⁻544	⁻398 + ⁻612	⁻4.3 + ⁻7.8
⁻78 + 97	⁻512 + 544	⁻398 + 612	4.3 + ⁻7.8
78 + ⁻97	512 + ⁻544	398 + ⁻612	⁻4.3 + 7.8

PRACTICE ACTIVITIES for Compensation

See Part 1, page 20, for an overview about quality practice.

ACTIVITY 1.11

Name: "Or You Could . . ."   **Type:** Routine

About the Routine: This routine is applied to various strategies throughout this book. In this section, the focus is on ways to use Compensation. You can focus solely on ways to compensate or include other strategies students have learned. Using the cards, this can be a partner or small-group activity where each person shares in a different way.

Materials: "Or You Could . . ." cards or other expressions for students to adjust into friendlier problems

Directions:
1. Pose a few expressions to students.

2. Place students with partners and ask them to brainstorm options for how to use Compensation to create a simpler problem to add.

3. Bring the class together to discuss and record the different ways an expression might be considered.

4. The first student to share says, "You could rethink this problem as . . . [teacher records the revised expression].

5. The next student(s) say, "Or you could . . ." and offer other ways to use Compensation.

6. After recording a few different ideas, prompt students to consider which option they think is easier to solve.

For example, you pose $^-46 + {}^-98$. After working in groups, one student shares, "You could change the expression to $^-46 + {}^-100$." Another student says, "Or you could change the expression to $^-50 + {}^-100$." A third student says, "Or you could change the expression to $^-50 + {}^-98$." After recording ideas, have students select the one they like best and solve the problem. Expressions to consider for the routine are provided on cards, as shown.

RESOURCE(S) FOR THIS ACTIVITY

$^-36 + {}^-18$	$^-55 + {}^-17$	$^-1.99 + {}^-1.46$	$6.23 + 4.29$	$^-58 - {}^-22$	$^-22 - 64$
$^-35 + {}^-17$	$89 + {}^-29$	$22.5 + 13.7$	$83.5 + {}^-21.9$	$^-45 - 49$	$56 - {}^-88$
$^-48 + 16$	$^-78 + 18$	$^-80.15 + {}^-10.95$	$^-70.5 + {}^-70.3$	$^-87 - {}^-76$	$^-34 - 37$
$^-74 + {}^-59$	$^-65 + {}^-17$	$67.1 + {}^-22.9$	$^-51.3 + 33.6$	$^-44 - 39$	$^-42 - {}^-17$
$^-57 + 19$	$^-68 + 25$	$^-5.37 + {}^-4.29$	$^-199.9 + {}^-199.9$	$35 - {}^-18$	$34 - {}^-59$

online resources ↘ This resource can be downloaded at **resources.corwin.com/FOF/rationalnumbersalgequations**.

ACTIVITY 1.12

Name: Estimation Cover   **Type:** Game

About the Game: Determining reasonableness is part of being fluent. Students need to practice estimating and comparing their estimates to actual answers. *Estimation Cover* is a game to do just that. The downloadable game board and expression cards can be modified for use with a variety of number types.

Materials: *Estimation Cover* game board (one per pair of players), *Estimation Cover* expression cards, two-sided counters for game pieces

Directions: 1. Players shuffle the expression cards and stack them face down.

2. Players take turns flipping an expression card and estimating the sum.

3. Players put their game piece on the corresponding estimate.

4. Then, both players find the actual sum using the Compensation strategy and confirm that the estimate was reasonable. Note that you and your students will have to come to an agreement about what is reasonable. We suggest within 10 of the actual sum (in either direction).

5. The first player to make four-in-a-row wins the game.

RESOURCE(S) FOR THIS ACTIVITY

Estimation Cover-Up

Directions: Players take turns pulling an estimation cover-up card. Players estimate the sum and place their marker on a corresponding space. Then, players use the Compensation strategy to find the exact sum. The game continues until one player gets four in a row.

+/-150	+/-140	+/-130	+/-120	+/-110
+/-100	+/-90	+/-80	+/-70	+/-60
+/-50	+/-40	+/-30	+/-20	+/-10
+/-10	+/-20	+/-30	+/-40	+/-50
+/-60	+/-70	+/-80	+/-90	+/-100
+/-110	+/-120	+/-130	+/-140	+/-150

53 + ⁻42	19 + ⁻72
⁻42 + 27	⁻17 + ⁻44
⁻82 + ⁻36	⁻89 + 17
17 + ⁻45	12 + ⁻98
⁻102 + 58	⁻74 + ⁻17

online resources — This resource can be downloaded at **resources.corwin.com/FOF/rationalnumbersalgequations**.

STRATEGY OVERVIEW:
Partial Sums

What Is the Partial Sums Strategy? This strategy refers to a process of adding place values, starting with the *largest* place value and moving to the smallest (the reverse of standard algorithms). When no regrouping is involved, the Partial Sums strategy is straightforward—just add or subtract each place value. In other cases, the regrouping is captured when combining the partial sums.

HOW DOES PARTIAL SUMS WORK?

In this strategy, you break one or more of the numbers into parts to add them, then combine the partial sums to get the total sum. *The thinking process:*

1. Choose how to break apart one or both of the addends.
2. Add the parts to find each partial sum (using vertical or horizontal recording).
3. Add the partial sums to get the sum.

Examples Across Number Types

Whole Numbers	Fractions
1,258 + 477	$13\frac{4}{5} + 2\frac{1}{10}$
Vertical Record	**Horizontal Record**
$$\begin{array}{r} 1,258 \\ +\ \ 477 \\ \hline 1,600 \\ 120 \\ +\ \ \ \ 15 \\ \hline 1,735 \end{array}$$	$13\frac{4}{5} + 2\frac{1}{10}$ $13 + 2 = 15$ $\frac{4}{5} + \frac{1}{10} = \frac{9}{10}$ $15 + \frac{9}{10} = 15\frac{9}{10}$
Horizontal Record $477 + 1,258$ $400 + 1,200 = 1,600$ $70 + 50 = 120$ $7 + 8 = 15$ $1,600 + 120 + 15 = 1,735$	

Decimals	Negative Numbers
7.7 + 12.58	**⁻482 + ⁻369**
Horizontal Record	**Horizontal Record**

Decimals

7.7 + 12.58

Horizontal Record

$$7.7 + 12.58$$

$$7 + 12 = 19$$
$$0.7 + 0.5 = 1.2$$
$$0 + 0.08 = 0.08$$

$$19 + 1.2 + 0.08 = 20.28$$

Vertical Record

$$
\begin{array}{r}
7.7 \\
+\ 12.58 \\
\hline
19.00 \\
1.20 \\
+\ \ 0.08 \\
\hline
20.28
\end{array}
$$

Negative Numbers

⁻482 + ⁻369

Horizontal Record

$$-400 + -300 = -700$$
$$-80 + -60 = -140$$
$$-2 + -9 = -11$$

$$-700 + -140 + -11 = -851$$

Vertical Record

$$-482 + -369$$

$$
\begin{array}{r}
-482 \\
-369 \\
\hline
-700 \\
-140 \\
-\ 11 \\
\hline
-851
\end{array}
$$

WHEN DO YOU CHOOSE PARTIAL SUMS?

Partial Sums is what we do when no regrouping is needed. This strategy is almost always applicable (like the standard algorithm) but perhaps not most efficient (e.g., 998 + 1,345 is more efficiently solved with Make a Thousand or Compensation). It is an effective replacement for standard algorithms (the front-end, left-to-right approach and lack of "tick-mark" notations make it more accessible). With negative numbers, this strategy makes sense when both numbers are negative and no other, more efficient strategy, is apparent.

TEACHING ACTIVITIES for Partial Sums

While Partial Sums is often interpreted as strictly "by place value," that is not necessarily the case—it should be thought of more flexibly, finding partials that make adding easier to do. These teaching activities illustrate how the Partial Sums strategy works to help students become adept and flexible at using it.

ACTIVITY 1.13
PLACE VALUE DISCS FOR PARTIAL SUMS

This activity can be used with whole numbers, decimals, or negative numbers. First, create numbers and place the corresponding number of place value discs in different paper or plastic bags. In the image on the left, Bag A has ⁻376 and Bag B has ⁻134. On the right, the student shows the expression shown in the bag (⁻376 + ⁻134) and then records the partial sums used to find the sum in both bags (⁻510).

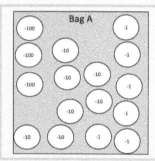
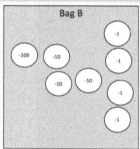

$$-376 + -134$$
$$-300 + -100 = -400$$
$$-70 + -30 = -100$$
$$-6 + -4 = \underline{-10}$$
$$-510$$

The two examples below show the partial sums recording for two other problems to illustrate what the process looks like with one negative addend and one positive addend, or with decimals. Paper discs are available for download in the online resources, or you can create your own by labeling colored plastic chips.

TEACHING TAKEAWAY

Use a permanent black marker to add a negative sign to physical place value discs.

$$^-273 + 417$$
$$-200 + 400 = 200$$
$$-70 + 10 = -60 \bigg\} 140$$
$$^-3 + 7 = 4$$
$$\underline{144}$$

$$4.43 + ^-7.32$$
$$4 + -7 = ^-3$$
$$0.4 + ^-0.3 = 0.1$$
$$0.03 + ^-0.02 = 0.01$$
$$\overline{-2.89}$$

ACTIVITY 1.14
MISSING PARTIALS, MISSING PROBLEM

In this activity, students try to determine your secret problem by using clues about partials. You share a partial sum and then students write down the addends they think might have generated it. Have some students share their thoughts. Then, tell the next partial sum. Again, students record what might have generated the second partial sum and you solicit some of their ideas. Repeat for each partial. Then, have students record what they think the original problem might have been. Record ideas on the board, asking other students if they are accurate options. Then, reveal your problem! Ask students to compare your problem to the ones they created.

For example, a teacher creates the problem ⁻528 + ⁻237 and tells students her addends are both negative numbers. The table shows what the teacher shares and what two students in the class guess.

TEACHER SHARES	GINA GUESSES	CHRISTOPHER GUESSES
The first partial sum is ⁻700	⁻100 + ⁻600	⁻200 + ⁻500
The second partial is ⁻50	⁻30 + ⁻20	⁻40 + ⁻10
The last partial is ⁻15	⁻8 + ⁻7	⁻6 + ⁻9

After the last partial in this example is shared, students determine what they think the original problem was. Gina shares ⁻138 + ⁻627. Christopher shares ⁻246 + ⁻519. The teacher reveals the original problem and the class discusses what they notice across the expressions. A fun option in this activity is to set constraints—for example, that all digits are different.

PRACTICE ACTIVITIES for Partial Sums

See Part 1, page 20, for an overview about quality practice.

ACTIVITY 1.15

Name: "Complex Number Strings"   **Type:** Routine

About the Routine: Students benefit from opportunities to look for patterns across similar problems. This activity starts with simpler problems and grows to more complicated ones.

Materials: Prepare a matrix of related expressions

Directions: 1. Post a matrix of related number strings with one known sum.

2. Explain to students that they will use the known sum to work across the rows and down the columns.

3. After students signal that they know the sums of each, hold a class discussion or ask small groups of students to discuss these questions:

   a. How does the first known problem relate to others in the complex string?

   b. What patterns do you notice within a column?

   c. What relationships do you see between the columns?

4. Summarize by asking students to generalize about what they learned (whatever the focus of the string was).

Negative integers example:

$^-8 + ^-8 = ^-16$	$^-80 + ^-80 =$	$^-800 + ^-800 =$	$^-8,000 + ^-8,000 =$
$^-8 + ^-6 =$	$^-80 + ^-60 =$	$^-800 + ^-600 =$	$^-8,000 + ^-6,000 =$
$^-8 + ^-3 =$	$^-80 + ^-30 =$	$^-800 + ^-300 =$	$^-8,000 + ^-3,000 =$
$^-8 + ^-2 =$	$^-80 + ^-20 =$	$^-800 + ^-200 =$	$^-8,000 + ^-2,000 =$

Decimal example:

$0.8 + 0.8 = 1.6$	$0.08 + 0.08 =$	$0.008 + 0.008 =$	$0.88 + 0.88 =$
$0.8 + 0.7 =$	$0.08 + 0.07 =$	$0.008 + 0.007 =$	$0.88 + 0.77 =$
$0.8 + 0.6 =$	$0.08 + 0.06 =$	$0.008 + 0.006 =$	$0.88 + 0.66 =$
$0.8 + 0.3 =$	$0.08 + 0.03 =$	$0.008 + 0.003 =$	$0.88 + 0.33 =$

ACTIVITY 1.16

Name: Take 5 Target   **Type:** Game

About the Game: *Take 5 Target* involves estimation and reasoning as students try to get close to the target number they have created. This game is slightly different than other target games in two ways: (1) both players can score if they are both close to the target and (2) the target can be created using two-digit or three-digit numbers. This can be played with positive or negative numbers. Here the target is a negative number. Encourage students to use Partial Sums or other reasoning strategies as they play.

Materials: Four decks of digit cards (0–9) or playing cards (queens = 0, aces = 1; remove 10s, kings, and jacks); *Take 5 Target* recording sheet (optional), 10 counters (optional)

Directions: 1. Players shuffle the cards and place them face down.

2. Two cards are pulled to determine the target for the round—a negative number.

3. Players take 5 cards and use as many of their cards as they can (e.g., a one-digit + one-digit or a three-digit + two-digit), arranging the digits and determining the sign to get a sum close to the target.

   Scoring: Sum within 5 of the target scores as many cards as the player used. Closest sum scores 2 bonus points.

4. The first player to 40 wins the game (or highest score after 5 rounds wins).

5. After the game, tell which problems were best solved with Partial Sums and which were better solved with other strategies.

For example, a player flips over a 1 and a 4, making a target of ⁻14. Xander pulls 3, 5, 2, 9, and 1. He makes ⁻53 + 35 = ⁻18. Latrenda pulls 0, 1, 8, 4, and 7. She makes ⁻104 + 87 = ⁻17. Xander scores 4 points (he is within 5 of the target and used 4 cards); Latrenda uses all of her cards (5 points) and is the closest (+2 points), so she scores 7 points.

RESOURCE(S) FOR THIS ACTIVITY

Take 5 Target Recording Sheet

Directions: Pull two cards to make a two-digit negative number that is the target for the round. Then take 5 cards and use as many as you can to get a sum close to the target. Sum within 5 of the target scores as many cards as you used (5 points if you used all 5 cards). Closest sum scores 2 bonus points. First to 40 wins.

Target	My Problem Solved With Partial Sums	Target	My Problem Solved With Partial Sums

online resources — This resource can be downloaded at **resources.corwin.com/FOF/rationalnumbersalgequations**.

Reasoning Strategies for Subtraction

In this module, we highlight four significant strategies for subtraction:

- Count Back (Separate Interpretation)
- Think Addition (Find the Difference Interpretation)
- Compensation
- Partial Differences

The focus of each section is on developing an understanding of how the strategy works and when it is a good choice. In Part 3, we offer additional activities that can be used to focus on choosing among subtraction strategies.

STRATEGY OVERVIEW:
Count Back

What Is the Count Back Strategy? This strategy uses efficient jumps to subtract the subtrahend (second number) from the minuend (first number). The Count Back strategy is used for both separate (take away from the minuend) and compare (difference between minuend and subtrahend) problem situations. This section focuses on the separate interpretation. Because subtracting negative numbers means you are moving in a positive direction, this strategy label can be adapted to "Use Counting" or "Use Jumps."

HOW DOES COUNT BACK WORK?

This strategy involves decomposing the subtrahend in convenient chunks to eventually take away the entire quantity. *The thinking process:*

1. Decide how to break apart the subtrahend into chunks that can easily be subtracted from the minuend.
2. Count back from the minuend by the chunks.
3. The location after the last jump (count) is the answer.

Examples across number types:

Whole Numbers

683 – 167

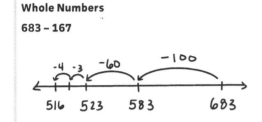

683 – 167 = 516

Fractions

$11\frac{1}{4} - 3\frac{3}{8}$

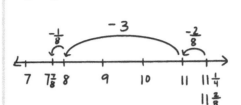

$11\frac{1}{4} - 3\frac{3}{8} = 7\frac{7}{8}$

Decimals

56.5 – 18.3

$$56.5 - 16 = 40.5$$
$$40.5 - 2.3 = 38.2$$

56.5 – 18.3 = 38.2

Negative Numbers

−3.4 – 5.8

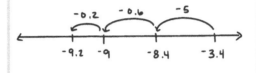

−3.4 – 5.8 = −9.2

WHEN DO YOU CHOOSE COUNT BACK?

Count Back is often a good choice when the subtrahend is relatively small (e.g., 436.3 – 14.2 or −72 – 14). Importantly, when the subtraction problem involves two numbers that are relatively close together (e.g., 436 – 388 or $7\frac{1}{2} - 6$), then a compare interpretation is more efficient than a separate interpretation.

MODULE 1 Strategies for Addition
MODULE 2 Strategies for Subtraction
MODULE 3 Strategies for Multiplication
MODULE 4 Strategies for Division
MODULE 5 Strategies for Ratios and Proportions
MODULE 6 Strategies for Solving Equations for an Unknown
MODULE 7 Strategies for Solving Systems of Linear Equations

TEACHING ACTIVITIES for Count Back (Use Jumps)

Count Back (or Use Counting or Jumps) is often the first strategy students learn for subtraction. What begins as count back by ones becomes count back by tens, hundreds, tenths, etc. With negative numbers, jumps can go in either direction, depending on the sign of the subtrahend. This idea of direction in adding and subtracting negative numbers is critical for working with this strategy and other reasoning strategies. This section offers activities for helping students develop efficient ways to use jumps. The goal is that students become adept at using this strategy while also thinking about when they will want to use it.

ACTIVITY 2.1
IT ALWAYS WORKS?

Students might be adept at counting back with whole numbers but struggle to implement the same strategy with fractions or decimals. In this activity, students explore worked examples to make sense of the strategy and then apply it to other types of numbers. Show three or four worked examples that illustrate different ways the problem might be solved using Count Back. Number lines are used here, but a series of equations is another good option.

TEACHING TAKEAWAY

Using worked examples with whole numbers can help students make sense of the strategy that they can then apply to other types of numbers.

Problem: 93 – 48

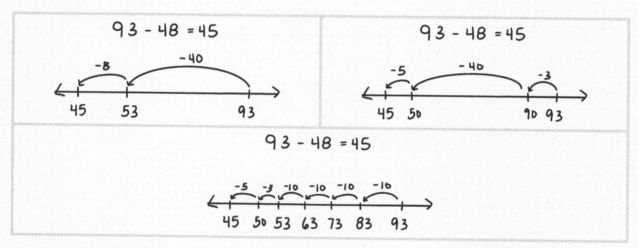

Have students discuss how the strategy is carried out differently in each example. Talk about efficiency and how the size of the count back might change as the numbers in the problem change.

Ask students if this strategy will work well with larger numbers, decimals, or fractions. Solicit initial thoughts. Post or hand out a set of problems with the numbers with which you want them to be working (e.g., decimals). Provide open or marked number lines. Challenge students to use their choice of jumps to solve each problem in the set. Then, compare with peers to see how they implemented their jumps to reach a solution.

POSSIBLE PROBLEMS FOR STUDENTS TO EXPLORE			
DECIMALS		**FRACTIONS**	
13.7 – 5.2	3.45 – 1.08	$3\frac{7}{8} - 5\frac{2}{8}$	$11\frac{3}{4} - 2\frac{3}{8}$
81.4 – 27.8	8.06 – 3.38	$12\frac{1}{4} - 2\frac{3}{4}$	$5\frac{2}{5} - 3\frac{1}{2}$
114.5 – 88.3	55.35 – 16.91	$30 - 13\frac{5}{6}$	$32\frac{3}{16} - 4\frac{5}{8}$

ACTIVITY 2.2
TRUTHS AND LIES

"Two Truths and a Lie" is a familiar get-to-know-you activity. In this mathematized version, students examine representations of the Count Back (Use Jumps) strategy with positive and negative numbers determining which are true and which are not. This activity is an excellent way to help students attend to the direction they are going when subtracting positive and negative numbers. You might begin with giving two truths and a lie but can adapt to two lies and a truth, or simply truth or lie, so that students can think critically about each example.

Problem: 47 – ⁻83

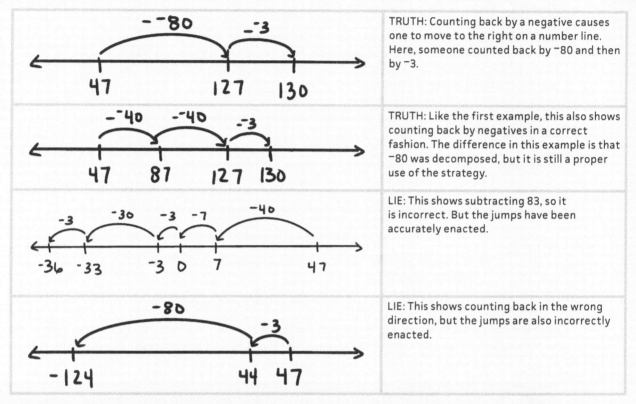

	TRUTH: Counting back by a negative causes one to move to the right on a number line. Here, someone counted back by ⁻80 and then by ⁻3.
	TRUTH: Like the first example, this also shows counting back by negatives in a correct fashion. The difference in this example is that ⁻80 was decomposed, but it is still a proper use of the strategy.
	LIE: This shows subtracting 83, so it is incorrect. But the jumps have been accurately enacted.
	LIE: This shows counting back in the wrong direction, but the jumps are also incorrectly enacted.

Once students have determined which are Truths and which are Lies, you can compare different problems to highlight important ideas. In this case, the two Lies provide an opportunity to discuss how to jump over 0.

As you create examples, use ideas from what you have seen students doing in their individual work. For example, you may find that students make errors when jumping over 0, so a problem like 35 – 52 is a good choice.

PRACTICE ACTIVITIES for Count Back
(Use Jumps)

See Part 1, page 20, for an overview about quality practice.

ACTIVITY 2.3

Name: Pick Your Jumps   **Type:** Game

About the Game: Once students understand the strategy, it is time to work on becoming more efficient with selecting jumps. *Pick Your Jumps* is a game in which students solve a problem by counting back and the player with the fewest, yet practical and doable, jumps earns a point.

Materials: *Pick Your Jumps* expression cards (or expressions recorded on index cards), *Pick Your Jumps* recording page

Directions: 1. Place shuffled *Pick Your Jumps* expression cards face down.

2. Players flip over one card and use Count Back (use counting/jumps) to solve it, recording their ideas on an open number line or with expressions.

3. Players count the number of jumps they used to reach the answer.

4. The player with the fewest jumps wins the round. Both players earn a point if they have the same number of jumps.

5. The player with the most points after four rounds wins.

For example, a student gets the card 71 − 146. Her first move was to count back 71 − 70 to 1 (1 jump). Then, 1 − 71 to ⁻70 (2 jumps). Then, ⁻70 − 5 to ⁻75 (3 jumps). The player made 3 jumps to solve the problem.

> **TEACHING TAKEAWAY**
> Games like *Pick Your Jumps* are great opportunities to play "teacher versus the class." This allows you to highlight different approaches and challenge students to find efficient options.

RESOURCE(S) FOR THIS ACTIVITY

Pick Your Jumps

Directions: Take turns choosing an expression. Count back to solve. Solve the problem and record the number of jumps you needed to solve it. The player with the fewest jumps gets a point for the round. Each player gets a point if they have the same number of jumps. The player with the most points after 4 rounds is the winner.

	Expression	Solve	Total Jumps
Example	71 − 146 =	71 − 70 • 1 1 − 71 • ⁻70 ⁻70 − 5 • ⁻75	3 jumps

44 − 39	25 − 55
81 − 213	17 − 45
⁻32 − 83	⁻44 − 66
⁻16 − 77	71 − 146
⁻29 − 144	90 − 18

$9\frac{1}{3} - 7\frac{2}{3}$	$^-6\frac{5}{6} - 5\frac{2}{3}$
$^-3\frac{2}{5} - 4\frac{1}{5}$	$4\frac{1}{4} - ^-8\frac{3}{4}$
$4\frac{1}{4} - ^-7\frac{3}{8}$	$^-5\frac{1}{3} - 4\frac{5}{12}$
$^-2\frac{1}{2} - ^-9\frac{1}{6}$	$^-7\frac{5}{8} - 6\frac{1}{2}$
$3\frac{2}{3} - 7\frac{7}{12}$	$4\frac{3}{4} - 9\frac{2}{3}$

online resources — These resources can be downloaded at **resources.corwin.com/FOF/rationalnumbersalgequations**.

ACTIVITY 2.4

Name: What's the Difference?　　　　　　　**Type:** Task

About the Task: In What's the Difference, students make a number and subtract minuends with distinct similarities to notice patterns that can be useful in reasoning. For example, taking away 10 more each time creates differences that are 10 less each time.

Materials: Digit cards (0–9) or playing cards (queens = 0, aces = 1; remove 10s, kings, and jacks); *What's the Difference?* recording sheet

Directions:
1. Student flips over two cards to make a two-digit minuend and record it in each blank minuend place on their recording sheet.

2. Student uses the Count Back strategy to solve each problem.

3. Student then reflects on the patterns within the problems and creates a new problem related to the other four.

4. Student draws two new cards and repeats Steps 1–3 with a new minuend.

The resource on the left shows problems that subtract 50 more each time, which highlight interesting patterns, especially as the answers become negative. The resource on the right shows decimal differences, but a similar pattern in the subtrahend. Students can complete both recording sheets using the same digits, uncovering more patterns.

RESOURCE(S) FOR THIS ACTIVITY

What's the Difference?

Directions: Make a number and record it in each blank. Find the difference using a Count Back strategy.

My number minus …	Difference (Count back so find the difference)
____ − 47	
____ − 97	
____ − 147	
____ − 197	

What patterns do you notice in the differences?

Create a new problem that would be related to these and show how you find the difference of the new problem.

What's the Difference?

Directions: Make a decimal and record it in each blank. Find the difference using a Count Back strategy.

My number minus …	Difference (Count back to find the difference)
___.__ − 4.7	
___.__ − 9.7	
___.__ − 14.7	
___.__ − 19.7	

What patterns do you notice in the differences?

Create a new problem that would be related to these and show how you find the difference of the new problem.

online resources　This resource can be downloaded at **resources.corwin.com/FOF/rationalnumbersalgequations**.

STRATEGY OVERVIEW:
Think Addition (Find the Difference)

What Is Think Addition (Find the Difference)? With positive numbers, students rethink the subtraction expression as a missing addend equation and then solve it, asking the question, "How many more?" This is a compare interpretation (not a separate interpretation), which more generally asks the question, "What is the *difference* or *distance* between the two numbers?" With negative numbers, this notion of distance is important, as the distance is from the subtrahend to the minuend (and direction matters).

HOW DOES THINK ADDITION WORK?

Think Addition, or more broadly, **Find the Difference**, focuses on the distance from the subtrahend to the minuend. The question is, "How far away is the subtrahend from the minuend (and which direction)?" Another way to word this question is, "What do I need to add to the subtrahend to reach the minuend?" Number lines can support this reasoning.

The thinking process:

1. Think about the subtraction problem as a compare situation (i.e., How far apart are these numbers?).

2. Find how far apart the two numbers are (and which direction).

3. The distance and direction is the answer to the subtraction problem.

Examples Across Number Types

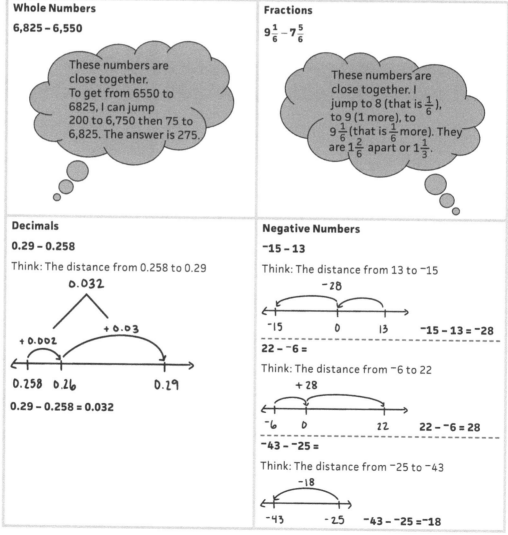

Whole Numbers

6,825 – 6,550

These numbers are close together. To get from 6550 to 6825, I can jump 200 to 6,750 then 75 to 6,825. The answer is 275.

Fractions

$9\frac{1}{6} - 7\frac{5}{6}$

These numbers are close together. I jump to 8 (that is $\frac{1}{6}$), to 9 (1 more), to $9\frac{1}{6}$ (that is $\frac{1}{6}$ more). They are $1\frac{2}{6}$ apart or $1\frac{1}{3}$.

Decimals

0.29 – 0.258

Think: The distance from 0.258 to 0.29

0.029 – 0.258 = 0.032

Negative Numbers

⁻15 – 13

Think: The distance from 13 to ⁻15

⁻15 – 13 = ⁻28

22 – ⁻6 =

Think: The distance from ⁻6 to 22

22 – ⁻6 = 28

⁻43 – ⁻25 =

Think: The distance from ⁻25 to ⁻43

⁻43 – ⁻25 = ⁻18

WHEN DO YOU CHOOSE THINK ADDITION (FIND THE DIFFERENCE)?

This strategy is useful when the two numbers are relatively close together (e.g., 17.3 − 15.8) or when both are near a benchmark (e.g., for 805 − 398; both are near a hundred). For negative values, this strategy is very useful in making sense of subtraction and can be useful across problems. In general, finding the difference is not an efficient option when the subtrahend is easy to take away (e.g., $12\frac{1}{2} - 2\frac{3}{4}$).

NOTES

TEACHING ACTIVITIES for Think Addition

Think Addition is a useful strategy across number types. It is particularly useful when solving problems where both numbers are negative. For example, in ⁻75 − ⁻42, the difference (distance and direction) from ⁻42 to ⁻75 is ⁻33. This makes more sense than explaining that you need to add the opposite, ⁻75 + 42, then subtract and take the sign of the larger numeral. Teaching this strategy includes attending to why it works and when it is a good idea to choose it.

ACTIVITY 2.5
TEACHING PROMPTS FOR THINK ADDITION

Use the following prompts as opportunities to develop understanding of and reasoning with the strategy. Have students use representations and tools to justify their thinking, including base-10 models, number lines, and so on. After students work with the prompt(s), bring the class together to exchange ideas. These prompts are also useful for assessing student understanding. Any prompt can be easily modified to feature different numbers.

- Tell how you can use addition to solve a subtraction problem. Use examples to support your explanation.

- Does Think Addition work with negative numbers? Create an example or illustration to convince others that it does or does not work.

- How are these two problems alike and different?

    1. A ditch that is $4\frac{1}{3}$ feet long needs to be $7\frac{1}{2}$ feet long. How much longer does the ditch need to be?
    2. Angel has a goal to ride their bike $7\frac{1}{2}$ miles. They have gone $4\frac{1}{3}$ miles. How many miles do they have left?

- Jeremy says that 6.14 − 3.71 can be solved by thinking 3.71 + 6.14. Do you agree or disagree with Jeremy? Explain your thinking.

- Use a number line to show how 210 − ⁻355 = ? is related to ⁻355 + ? = 210.

- Leo used Find the Difference (Think Addition) to solve a subtraction problem. He added 3, then 0.4, then 0.07. What subtraction problem might he have solved?

ACTIVITY 2.6
THE MATCH

Prepare a set of cards for each group of students. The examples in the table are available as an online resource, or you can create your own. Give a set of cards to each group of students and ask them to find the matches. Then, have students solve the problems using number lines or equations using Find the Difference (Think Addition) thinking. You might focus solely on one number type or select across various types of numbers. After solving, ask students to select from their set and solve it using Count Back and compare the two ways of reasoning.

WHOLE NUMBERS		DECIMALS	
• $950 - 675 = ?$	• $675 + ? = 950$	• $5.1 - 3.2 = ?$	• $3.2 + ? = 5.1$
• $714 - 690 = ?$	• $690 + ? = 714$	• $9.65 - 6.9 = ?$	• $6.9 + ? = 9.65$
• $239 - 182 = ?$	• $182 + ? = 239$	• $21.7 - 18 = ?$	• $18 + ? = 21.7$
• $1,201 - 799 = ?$	• $799 + ? = 1,201$	• $30 - 27.97 = ?$	• $27.97 + ? = 30$
• $375 - 263 = ?$	• $263 + ? = 375$	• $7.15 - 6.675 = ?$	• $6.675 + ? = 7.15$

FRACTIONS		NEGATIVE NUMBERS	
• $2\frac{3}{4} - 1\frac{1}{4} = ?$	• $1\frac{1}{4} + ? = 2\frac{3}{4}$	• $^-4 - 6 = ?$	• $6 + ? = ^-4$
• $7\frac{7}{12} - 4\frac{11}{12} = ?$	• $4\frac{11}{12} + ? = 7\frac{7}{12}$	• $^-4 - {}^-6 = ?$	• $^-6 + ? = ^-4$
• $12\frac{5}{8} - 9\frac{3}{4} = ?$	• $9\frac{3}{4} + ? = 12\frac{5}{8}$	• $11 - 23 = ?$	• $23 + ? = 11$
• $13\frac{3}{10} - 10\frac{4}{5} = ?$	• $10\frac{4}{5} + ? = 13\frac{3}{10}$	• $^-11 - 23 = ?$	• $23 + ? = ^-11$
• $22\frac{1}{6} - 20\frac{1}{2} = ?$	• $20\frac{1}{2} + ? = 22\frac{1}{6}$	• $17 - {}^-14 = ?$	• $^-14 + ? = 17$

TEACHING TAKEAWAY

You can extend activities that have students focus on a strategy by asking them to revisit problems and look for those that might also be solved efficiently with another strategy.

RESOURCE(S) FOR THIS ACTIVITY

$950 - 675 = ?$	$675 + ? = 950$
$714 - 690 = ?$	$690 + ? = 714$
$239 - 182 = ?$	$182 + ? = 239$
$1,201 - 799 = ?$	$799 + ? = 1,201$
$375 - 263 = ?$	$263 + ? = 375$

online resources ⌖ This resource can be downloaded at **resources.corwin.com/FOF/rationalnumbersalgequations**.

PRACTICE ACTIVITIES for Think Addition

See Part 1, page 20, for an overview about quality practice.

ACTIVITY 2.7
WORKED EXAMPLES

Worked examples are excellent as teaching activities or for independent practice. Correctly worked examples and partially worked examples help students make sense of a strategy and incorrectly worked examples attend to common errors. (See Part 1, p. 20, for more on worked examples.)

SAMPLE WORKED EXAMPLES FOR COUNT ON/COUNT BACK	
Correctly Worked Examples (make sense of the strategy) What did _____ do? Why does it work? Is this a good method for this problem?	Scott and Rosa solved $2\frac{1}{4} - \frac{3}{4}$. Both got $1\frac{1}{2}$ as an answer. Compare their thinking. Scott: 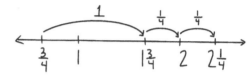 Rosa: 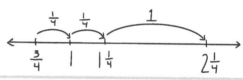
Partially Worked Examples (implement the strategy accurately) Why did _____ start the problem this way? What does _____ need to do to finish the problem?	Mindy worked to solve 7,418 – 5,750. Why did she start the problem like this? What does she need to do next? 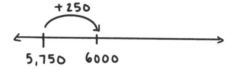 Lacey started to use Think Addition to solve 1.57 – 0.82. What did she do to finish the problem? 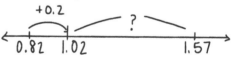
Incorrectly Worked Example (highlight common errors) What did _____ do? What mistake does _____ make? How can this mistake be fixed?	**To solve** $3\frac{5}{8} - 1\frac{7}{8}$, Jonah counted up from $1\frac{7}{8}$ and got 2 as his answer. What did he do correctly? What mistake did he make? 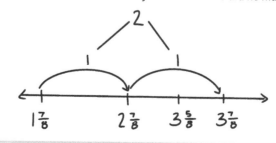

ACTIVITY 2.8

Name: All Lined Up   **Type:** Game

About the Game: *All Lined Up* is a game of strategy that promotes fluency, number sense, and reasoning. In this version, ask students to use Find the Difference thinking to solve the problems. You can change it to practice any strategy or give students choice as they work to become flexible and efficient.

Materials: *All Lined Up* game board per player, four sets of digit cards (0–9) or playing cards (queens = 0, aces = 1; remove 10s, kings, and jacks)

Directions: 1. Players pull digit cards to generate two numbers for which they will find the difference.

2. Players find the difference between their two numbers, recording their thinking on paper or in their math journals.

3. Each player selects a box on their game board to place their answer. The challenge: Differences must be placed in order from least to greatest.

4. If a difference cannot be placed in a box, the player loses their turn.

5. The first player to fill each of their six boxes wins the game.

In this example, students are creating two three-digit decimal numbers with ones, tenths, and hundredths. On his first turn, Tre created 3.86 – 4.12. He placed the difference of ⁻0.26 in the third box. On his next turn, he created 7.18 – 3.93, placing the difference in the fifth box. Then, he made 6.41 – 8.05, placing the difference ⁻1.64 to the left of ⁻0.26. On his fourth turn, Tre made 4.72 – 5.58, which has a difference of ⁻0.86. There is no space to place it between ⁻1.64 and ⁻0.26, so Tre loses his turn.

All Lined Up

Directions: Create a subtract problem. Find the difference. Place the difference in one of the boxes so that the numbers in the boxes are in order from least to greatest. Record your work and star the problems that were best solved with Think Addition.

	– 1.64	– 0.26		3.25	

RESOURCE(S) FOR THIS ACTIVITY

All Lined Up

Directions: Create a subtraction problem. Find the difference. Place the number in one of the boxes so that the numbers in the boxes are in order from least to greatest. Record your work and star the problems that were best solved with Think Addition.

online resources 🔎 This resource can be downloaded at **resources.corwin.com/FOF/rationalnumbersalgequations**.

STRATEGY OVERVIEW:
Compensation

What Is Compensation? This strategy involves *adjusting* the expression to make it easier to subtract, and then *compensating* to preserve equivalence. The quantities tend to be adjusted to convenient benchmark numbers or changed in order to avoid regrouping.

HOW DOES COMPENSATION WORK WITH SUBTRACTION?

Like addition, Compensation with subtraction can involve adjusting either or both numbers, but with subtraction, the way in which the related Compensation occurs varies with each type. It is worth the time invested to explore the different options and to sort out the correct way to compensate in each case. The table below illustrates the three options for **267 – 185.**

WHAT IS BEING ADJUSTED	ADJUSTED PROBLEM AND SOLUTION	COMPENSATION JUSTIFICATION
Minuend: Add 20	**287** – 185 = 102 102 – 20 = 82	20 was added into the problem, so 20 must be subtracted.
Subtrahend: Add 15	267 – **200** = 67 67 + 15 = 82	15 too much was taken away, so 15 must be added back to the answer.
Both: Add 15	**282 – 200** = 82	15 too much will be taken away, so add 15 to the minuend. Alternately: Think of this as a difference and slide up the number line 15.

TEACHING TAKEAWAY

One way to think about Compensation is as a slide on the number line—slide both numbers the same distance to create an easier-to-compute equivalent subtraction problem.

Notice that changing both can be interpreted as take away or find the difference. The difference between the numbers being subtracted is a *constant difference*. Thus, you can "slide" on the number line to make an easier-to-solve equivalent subtraction problem. The table of examples includes each of these types. *The thinking process:*

1. Decide which value(s) you will adjust.
2. Adjust the original problem.
3. Solve the new problem.
4. Compensate for how the original problem was adjusted, as needed.

Examples Across Number Types

Whole Numbers	Fractions
62 – 48	$9\frac{1}{6} - 7\frac{5}{6}$
Adjust subtrahend:	Adjust both (going up $\frac{1}{6}$):
$62 - 50 = 12$ $12 + 2 = 14$	$9\frac{1}{6} \quad - \quad 7\frac{5}{6}$ $+\frac{1}{6}\downarrow \qquad \downarrow +\frac{1}{6}$ $9\frac{2}{6} - 8 = 1\frac{2}{6}$ $1\frac{1}{3}$
Decimals	**Negative Numbers**
15.6 – 5.9	⁻35 – 18
Adjust minuend:	Adjust subtrahend
$15.9 - 5.9 = 10$ $10 - 0.3 = 9.7$	$^-35 - 20 = {}^-55$ $^-55 + 2 = {}^-53$

WHEN DO YOU CHOOSE COMPENSATION?

Compensation is very versatile, so it works well in many problems. The slide is an excellent strategy for fraction subtraction when regrouping would otherwise be necessary—just slide the subtrahend to the nearest integer value and compensate by moving the minuend the same amount.

Example: $6\frac{4}{12} - 3\frac{9}{12}$

TEACHING ACTIVITIES for Compensation

Compensation with subtraction "behaves" differently than addition, but like addition, there are options for which number(s) to adjust. These activities give students opportunities to make sense of Compensation as it is used for subtraction.

ACTIVITY 2.9
COMPENSATION LANE

This activity uses a graphic organizer to help students think about how they changed the subtraction problem, and consequently, how they need to compensate. If the minuend is increased, for example, the answer must be decreased, but if the subtrahend is increased (too much is taken away) the answer needs to be increased, as shown here. For finding the common difference, no Compensation is required. Thus, there is no need for the third box. To scaffold this activity, you can begin by exploring problems that only change the minuend or only change the subtrahend. But it is important that eventually students ask themselves, "Which number should I change to make this easier to subtract, or should I change both?"

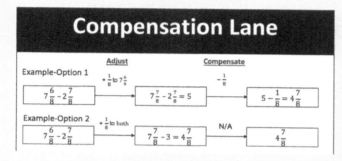

The same ideas apply to working with negative numbers.

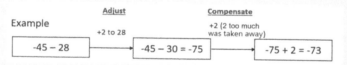

RESOURCE(S) FOR THIS ACTIVITY

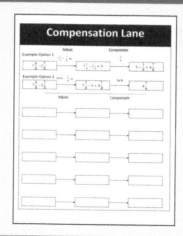

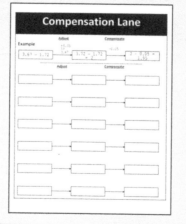

online resources ➤ This resource can be downloaded at **resources.corwin.com/FOF/rationalnumbersalgequations**.

ACTIVITY 2.10
CONSTANT DIFFERENCE PROOFS

Constant difference is an effective way to subtract all kinds of numbers, avoiding regrouping and the related errors. With positive and negative numbers, directionality can make this strategy a little more difficult to understand, so students benefit from convincing themselves this strategy works. In this activity, students are tasked with proving that the concept of constant difference holds true with positive and negative numbers. Pose a single problem adjusted in different ways like those shown below. For example, in A the new expression has been shifted left three places, by adding −3 to both values.

A	B
⁻36 − ⁻17	⁻36 − ⁻17
+⁻3 + ⁻3	⁻4 − 4
⁻39 − ⁻20 = ⁻19	⁻40 − ⁻21 = ⁻19
C	D
⁻36 − ⁻17	⁻36 − ⁻17
+ 7 + 7	+ 6 + 6
⁻29 − ⁻10 = ⁻19	⁻30 − ⁻11 = ⁻19

Have students prove that the four are indeed true, using physical representations or number lines, or other representations:

- A number line drawn on centimeter grid paper and two strips of paper cut to the length between the numbers (e.g., 19 cm for examples A through D in the table) can be used to show the constant difference, sliding the paper strip.

- Cuisenaire rods and similar tools would also work well, using an open number line. For example, (a) can be illustrated like this:

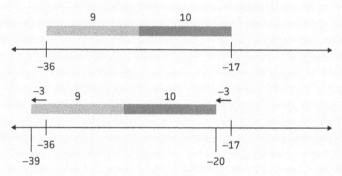

After proving/showing they each work, ask which constant difference they think is the best for making the subtraction easier to solve.

Pose a new problem and ask partners to discuss ways they can apply constant difference (e.g., ⁻61 − ⁻48), finding at least two options. Then, ask students to select which option they think is best and complete the problem. To generalize these ideas, ask students to create new problems and prove that constant difference is still viable (or challenge them to find an example where it will not work).

Note that this first investigation involves a negative minus a negative, but other problem types can be explored. For example, you might begin with both numbers being positive, then both negative, and then one of each.

PRACTICE ACTIVITIES for Compensation

See Part 1, page 20, for an overview about quality practice.

ACTIVITY 2.11

Name: "Why Not???"　　　　　　　　　　　**Type:** Routine

About the Routine: When learning about a strategy, it is important to think about when it is a good choice and when another strategy might be better. This routine helps students determine if a problem is a good choice for Compensation.

Materials: Prepared expressions (see examples)

Directions: 1. Have students briefly think–pair–share what it means to use the Compensation strategy.

2. Pose a set of three to five expressions.

3. Ask partners to consider and discuss which expressions are good choices for solving with a Compensation strategy and which are not.

4. Bring the whole group together to explain which ones are not (and why not).

For example, you might pose these problems if working with negative numbers:

Problem	Possible Student Response to "Is this a good fit for Compensation?"
⁻318 – 40	No, because you can just subtract 40 easily.
⁻815 – ⁻618	Yes, because changing ⁻815 to ⁻818 is an easier problem to solve.
⁻4.84 – 2.57	No, because neither number is close to a benchmark.
7.17 – 9.25	Yes, because you can add 0.08 to 7.17 to get 7.25. That is ⁻2. Then, you can subtract 0.08 from ⁻2 to get ⁻2.08.

Problem examples to use with the routine:

WHOLE NUMBERS	DECIMALS	FRACTIONS	NEGATIVE NUMBERS
• 697 – 400	• 5.3 – 2.8	• $1\frac{11}{15} - \frac{7}{15}$	• ⁻65 – ⁻17
• 1,863 – 350	• 3.63 – 1.7	• $2\frac{5}{16} - \frac{13}{16}$	• ⁻47 – 29
• 1,214 – 517	• 9.14 – 7.17	• $4\frac{3}{5} - 2\frac{7}{10}$	• 14 – ⁻27
• 617 – 519	• 5.24 – 3.19	• $3\frac{1}{6} - 4\frac{5}{6}$	• ⁻34 – 41
• 1,350 – 762	• 6 – 2.85	• $6\frac{8}{11} - 1\frac{10}{11}$	• 92 – 118

ACTIVITY 2.12

Name: The Absolute Difference   **Type:** Game

About the Game: This game focuses on subtraction with integers. While many strategies can be used to compute the problems, students can be encouraged to use Compensation. Because the numbers are the same, but the signs are changing, this game also helps students notice patterns in subtracting negative and positive numbers.

Materials: Digit cards (0–9) or playing cards (queens = 0, aces = 1; remove 10s, kings, and jacks); *The Absolute Difference* recording sheet

Directions:
1. Players draw four cards and make 2 two-digit numbers.

2. The position of the digits will remain constant in the four problems; only the signs change in each new problem.

3. Players find the difference of the two numbers in each problem and record it (using Compensation as appropriate).

4. Players record the absolute value of the difference as the score (number of points) for that problem.

5. After the four problems are complete, the sum of the absolute values is found and the player with the highest score wins.

6. After the game, students show (or write) how they solved one of the problems using Compensation.

For example, Hope generated a 3, 8, 6, and 3. She made 63 and 38 with the digits. She then recorded the four different problems, found the differences, and added their absolute values. After the game, she selected the second problem to show Compensation thinking:

Change: I changed ⁻63 - ⁻38 to = ⁻63 + 38 and adjusted to ⁻63 + 40 (add 2)

Solve: ⁻63 + 40 = ⁻23

Compensate: (subtract 2) ⁻23 - 2 = ⁻25.

Problem			Difference	Absolute Value of Difference (Points)
⁺63	−	⁺38	= 25	25
⁻63	−	⁻38	= -25	25
⁻63	−	⁺38	= -101	101
⁺63	−	⁻38	= 101	101
Score (add the absolute values to find your points) ---------->				252

 This resource can be downloaded at **resources.corwin.com/FOF/rationalnumbersalgequations**.

STRATEGY OVERVIEW:
Partial Differences

What Is Partial Differences? Partial Difference strategy involves decomposing both values and subtracting parts, starting with the largest values and moving to the smallest. While the Partial Differences is often by place value, there are usually good alternatives. For example, 2,456 – 1,267 can be solved these ways:

2,000 – 1,000 = 1,000	2,400 – 1,200 = 1,200	2,400 – 1,200 = 1,200
400 – 200 = 200	50 – 60 = ⁻10	56 – 67 = ⁻11
50 – 60 = ⁻10	6 – 7 = ⁻1	
6 – 7 = ⁻1		
Total Difference:	Total Difference:	Total Difference:
1,000 + 200 + ⁻10 + ⁻1 = 1,189	1,200 + ⁻10 + ⁻1 = 1,189	1,200 + ⁻11 = 1,189
OR	OR	OR
1,000 + 200 – 10 – 1 = 1,189	1,200 – 10 – 1 = 1,189	1,200 – 11 = 1,189

HOW DOES PARTIAL DIFFERENCES WORK?

Both numbers are decomposed, the parts are subtracted, and differences are then combined. When each place value in the minuend is greater than the corresponding place value in the subtrahend, all the partial differences are positive and the process is straightforward (e.g., 45.7 – 23.5). When any place value in the subtrahend has the larger value than the minuend, negative numbers occur. Before students learn about negative numbers, the process focuses on subtracting partials, as needed, but once students learn to add negatives, they can think about partial differences as adding positive and negative values.

The thinking process:

1. Choose how to break apart both numbers.
2. Subtract the parts to find each partial difference.
3. Add or subtract the partial differences to get the total difference.

Examples Across Number Types

Whole Numbers	Fractions	Decimals
824 – 359	$14\frac{5}{8} - 7\frac{3}{4}$	**24.08 – 15.5**
$\begin{array}{r} 824 \\ -359 \\ \hline 500 \\ -30 \\ +\underline{-5} \\ \hline 465 \end{array}$	$14 - 7 = 7$ $\frac{5}{8} - \frac{6}{8} = \frac{-1}{8}$ $6\frac{7}{8}$	$24 - 15 = 9$ $0.0 - 0.5 = {}^{-}0.5$ $0.08 - 0 = 0.08$ $9 - 0.5 + 0.08 = 8.58$

Notice there is not a negative numbers box here. While it is possible to use this strategy when the numbers in the problem are negative, it can become confusing for students to consider the directions of each of the parts, and it is generally not a useful strategy.

WHEN DO YOU CHOOSE PARTIAL DIFFERENCES?

With whole numbers and decimals, partials are an effective replacement for standard algorithms (the front-end, left-to-right approach and lack of "tick mark" notations make it more accessible). This method is not a good choice when a more efficient method is possible (e.g., 13.45 – 4.9 is more efficiently solved with Compensation). As noted above, this is not generally useful when one or both of the numbers is negative.

TEACHING ACTIVITIES for Partial Differences

Partial Differences can require more steps than other strategies shared in this module. Yet it is a good option when the numbers in the problem don't lend to the other strategies. And it can make more sense than subtraction algorithms. Teaching this strategy, then, attends to how it works and when it is (and is not) a good choice.

ACTIVITY 2.13
YEAH ... BUT ...

In this activity, students use Partial Differences to solve problems and then reflect on whether or not it was a good option for those problems. To begin, pose a correctly worked example solved using Partial Differences and ask students to discuss what they did to solve the problem. Then, ask students if another strategy would have been more efficient for that problem. Next, pose two to three subtraction problems and ask students to solve them using Partial Differences (some lend to Partial Differences and some do not). After students have solved the set, ask them how they used Partial Differences and what might have been challenging. Ask students to revisit the problems and determine which would be more efficiently solved a different way. To extend or summarize the activity, ask students to explain when Partial Differences is a good option and generate example problems to support their explanation. Alternatively, ask students to create three problems that are good for solving with Partial Differences and three that are not.

WORKED EXAMPLE	POSSIBLE PROBLEMS FOR STUDENTS TO WORK AND DISCUSS	POINTS TO NOTE ABOUT PROBLEMS
$658 - 242$ $600 - 200 = 400$ $50 - 40 = 10$ $8 - 2 = 6$ $400 + 10 + 6 = 416$	a. $3,455 - 1,328$ b. $4,005 - 879$ c. $5,761 - 4,350$	Problems a and b create negative partials that students have to attend to, whereas Problem c does not, like the worked example.
$87.55 - 12.03$ $87 - 12 = 75$ $0.55 - 0.03 = 0.52$ $75 + 0.52 = 75.52$	a. $45.06 - 21.08$ b. $68.99 - 43.02$ c. $45.71 - 5.80$	These problems lend to breaking apart by whole number part and decimal part. Or students can do each place value separately and discuss which is more efficient.

ACTIVITY 2.14
THE MISSING PROBLEM

This activity engages students in figuring out what the original problem was. You pose a set of partial sums or partial differences with missing values, and students find the unknowns and determine the original problem. After doing several of these, challenge students to create their own Missing Problems and then have students exchange and solve each other's examples.

The Missing Problem: Fractions

A **Partial Differences** example of The Missing Problem:

$23 -$ _____ $= 16$ $\frac{7}{8} -$ _____ $= \frac{1}{8}$

Original Problem (Answer): $23\frac{7}{8} - 7\frac{3}{4}$.

A **Partial Differences** example of The Missing Problem:

$15 -$ _____ $= 6$ $\frac{1}{6} -$ _____ $= -\frac{1}{6}$

Original Problem (Answer): $15\frac{1}{6} - 9\frac{1}{3}$.

The Missing Problem: Decimals

A **Partial Sums** example of The Missing Problem:

$11 +$ _____ $= 17$ $0.7 +$ _____ $= 1.2$

Original Problem (Answer): $11.7 + 6.5$.

A **Partial Differences** example of The Missing Problem:

$23 -$ _____ $= 16$ $0.7 -$ _____ $= 0.1$ $0.05 -$ _____ $= 0.02$

Original Problem (Answer): $23.75 - 7.63$.

A **Partial Differences** example of The Missing Problem:

$15 -$ _____ $= 15$ $0.3 -$ _____ $= -0.1$ $0.07 -$ _____ $= 0.04$ $0.005 -$ _____ $= -0.001$

Original Problem (Answer): $15.375 - 0.436$.

PRACTICE ACTIVITIES for Partial Differences

See Part 1, page 20, for an overview about quality practice.

ACTIVITY 2.15

Name: "Over/Under"　　　　　　　　　　**Type:** Routine

About the Routine: We place this routine here because estimation is essentially adding or subtracting the front parts of the numbers. Estimation and reasonableness are always important, but they are particularly critical when using strategies or algorithms with numerous steps because of the increased chance of errors. You can vary the difficulty of this routine with the "Over/Under" target number and examples you select.

Materials: Identify a target number for comparison and prepare a few subtraction expressions that are not easy to compute mentally.

Directions:

1. Share the "Over/Under" number.

2. Pose each expression, one at a time, asking students to decide if the answer is "Over" or "Under" the given number.

3. Provide a few seconds of think time; then have students share their decision with the class (e.g., thumbs up for over, thumbs down for under).

4. Ask students how they decided. Collect several ideas. Reinforce simple and quick methods.

5. Optional: Solve the problem and compare to the "Over/Under" number.

"OVER/UNDER 2.5"			
79.7 – 77.9	9 – 6.2	6.22 – 3.9	5.14 – 2.8

"OVER/UNDER 0"			
⁻47 – 50	89 – ⁻50	⁻617 – 507	⁻14 – ⁻25

In the first example, students should notice it will be under 0 because they are taking away 50 from a negative number. The same is true for the third expression. The other two are both over 0. These next two examples are more challenging:

"OVER/UNDER 50"			
93.1 – 61.9	⁻27.16 – ⁻95.4	31 – ⁻6.34	16.8 – ⁻62.2

"OVER/UNDER 25"			
28.70 – 7.19	30.60 – 3.89	8.422 + ⁻43.78	⁻20.89 + ⁻1,737

ACTIVITY 2.16

Name: For Keeps—Subtraction   **Type:** Game

About the Game: *For Keeps* can be used for addition or subtraction (here, we focus on subtraction). The goal is to get the lowest total, keeping two of the four problems that you make. As students play, encourage them to notice if one of their other strategies is a better option or if they will use Partial Differences to subtract.

Materials: *For Keeps—Subtraction* game board; digit cards (0–9) or playing cards (queens = 0, aces = 1; remove 10s, kings, and jacks)

Directions: 1. Players draw four cards and make two 2-digit numbers.

2. Players find the difference and decide whether they want to keep the difference. If so, they write the difference in the "For Keeps" column; if not, they record the difference in the "Not Kept" column. The decision is final; the number cannot be moved once new cards are drawn.

3. Players play a total of four rounds yet can only keep two numbers. At the end of the fourth round, each player adds the two scores in the "For Keeps" column.

4. The player with the lowest score wins.

In the following example, Jacob keeps his first two differences, so he cannot keep the last two (which works out well for him). His score is 10.

For Keeps-Subtraction

Directions: Make two, two-digit numbers. Find the difference and decide if you want to keep the answer as a score or not. You can only keep two of the four rounds. After the fourth round, add the two scores you kept. The player with the lowest score wins.

Round	Numbers Created		Difference For Keeps	Difference NOT Kept
1	44	38	6	
2	21	17	4	
3	75	53		22
4	40	29		11
		Sum of Keeps:	10	

For Keeps can be adapted to larger whole numbers or decimals by simply stating what the numbers created need to look like and adjusting how many cards are drawn. *For Keeps* can also be played with negative numbers; for example, Jacob could have switched order of the numbers in Round 2 (17 – 21) to get ⁻4, resulting in a final score of 2.

RESOURCE(S) FOR THIS ACTIVITY

For Keeps—Subtraction

Directions: Make 2 two-digit numbers. Find the difference and decide if you want to keep the answer as a score or not. You can only keep two of the four rounds. After the fourth round, add the two scores you kept. The player with the lowest score wins.

Round	Numbers Created		Difference for Keeps	Difference Not Kept
1				
2				
3				
4				

online resources ▶ This resource can be downloaded at **resources.corwin.com/FOF/rationalnumbersalgequations**.

NOTES

_____

_____

_____

_____

_____

_____

_____

_____

_____

_____

_____

_____

_____

_____

_____

_____

Reasoning Strategies for Multiplication

In this module we highlight these significant strategies for multiplication:

- Break Apart by Addends (including Partial Products strategy)
- Break Apart by Factors (including Halve and Double strategy)
- Compensation

The focus of each section is on developing an understanding of how each of these strategies works and when it is a good choice. In Part 3 of this book, we offer activities that focus on choosing among these significant strategies for multiplication (as well as the related standard algorithms).

STRATEGY OVERVIEW:
Break Apart by Addends

In our anchor book, *Figuring Out Fluency in Mathematics, K–8*, we address Break Apart and Partial Products separately. We differentiate these strategies with Break Apart involving decomposing one factor (in various ways, not always by place value) and Partial Products involving decomposing both factors by place value. With fractions and decimals, using Partial Products is rarely efficient, though it does help students make sense of related algorithms. Thus, here we blend these strategies together.

What Is Break Apart by Addends? Break Apart strategy involves breaking apart one or both factors into addends, finding the product of the parts, and then adding together the parts to get the total product. The term *Break Apart* can refer to breaking apart into addends (e.g., 12 into 10 + 2) or into factors (e.g., 12 into 2 × 6). Either option (or both options) can be useful for solving a problem like 12 × 2.5. We separate these two ideas into separate sections. This section is about addends, and the next section is about factors.

HOW DOES BREAK APART BY ADDENDS WORK?

Break Apart by Addends utilizes the distributive property. An area visual helps to see how this strategy works. *The thinking process*:

1. Decide which number to break apart (or choose both) and how you will break it apart into a sum.
2. Use the distributive property, multiplying the parts of each factor by each of the parts of the other factor.
3. Add each of the partial products together to get the total product.

As with all multiplication and division problems involving negative numbers, the problem has an added step of considering what the sign of the answer must be.

Whole Numbers

26 × 47

Break apart with area model:

$$\underset{\text{Factor}}{26} \times \underset{\text{Factor}}{47}$$

Break apart with equations:

$$\underset{\text{Factor}}{26} \times \underset{\text{Factor}}{47}$$

Fractions

$6 \times 2\frac{1}{4}$

Break apart the mixed number:

$$12 + 1\frac{1}{2}$$
$$13\frac{1}{2}$$

Break apart the whole number:

$$\left(4 \times 2\frac{1}{4}\right) + \left(2 \times 2\frac{1}{4}\right)$$
$$9 + 4\frac{1}{2} = 13\frac{1}{2}$$

Decimals

14.3 × 12

Break apart the first factor:

$$12(10 + 4 + 0.3)$$
$$120 + 48 + 3.6$$
$$171.6$$

Break apart the second factor:

$$171.6$$

WHEN DO YOU CHOOSE BREAK APART BY ADDENDS?

Break Apart is a good choice when you can break apart a factor and compute the parts mentally. For two-digit by one-digit multiplication, Break Apart by Addends is almost always a good option. As problems get larger, Break Apart may not be an efficient strategy. With fractions and decimals, this strategy is often useful when one of the numbers is a whole number. For example, when multiplying a whole number and a mixed number, Break Apart is almost always more efficient than changing the mixed number into a fraction. For any type of number, breaking apart both numbers (Partial Products) is a good option when (1) breaking apart just one factor doesn't work and (2) the fractions or decimals lend to mental math.

MODULE 1 Strategies for Addition

MODULE 2 Strategies for Subtraction

MODULE 3 Strategies for Multiplication

MODULE 4 Strategies for Division

MODULE 5 Strategies for Ratios and Proportions

MODULE 6 Strategies for Solving Equations for an Unknown

MODULE 7 Strategies for Solving Systems of Linear Equations

TEACHING ACTIVITIES for Break Apart by Addends

Breaking apart by addends supports students' place value concepts and can be an effective alternative to standard algorithms. In teaching Partial Products, the key is that students see that it is flexible—students choose how to break apart the problem, deciding which number they want to break apart (or if they want to break apart both numbers). These activities focus on explicitly teaching Break Apart and exploring when it is useful.

 ## ACTIVITY 3.1
MODELS AND PARTIALS

Students learned about how they can use area models to represent the distributive property for multiplying whole numbers in fourth and fifth grade. This activity builds on that understanding connecting to other number types. First, pose a multiplication problem with 2 two-digit factors like 36 × 64. Have students work together to complete the area model and then write the related equations, as shown in the example.

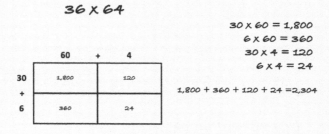

After sharing student work, focus the discussion on how the numbers were decomposed, how the equations relate to the model, and how they are used to establish the product. Then, ask students if this strategy would work with decimals (or fractions). Provide sets of problems to explore and discuss (see examples here):

FRACTIONS	DECIMALS	DECIMALS
$15 \times 3\frac{3}{4}$	23×5.4	43×75
	4.6×7	43×7.5
$8\frac{1}{3} \times 6$	2.3×0.8	4.3×7.5
		0.43×0.75
$6\frac{1}{2} \times 8\frac{1}{4}$		

Notice that each expression highlights different learning opportunities. In the first fraction problem, one might decompose 15 into 10 and 5, or leave it as 15. The second and third are opportunities to discuss the strategy and reinforce multiplication with like and unlike denominators.

Anticipate that students may decompose the numbers in different ways (and encourage them to do so). For example, 23 × 5.4 can be decomposed 23 into 10, 10, and 3 or 20 and 3.

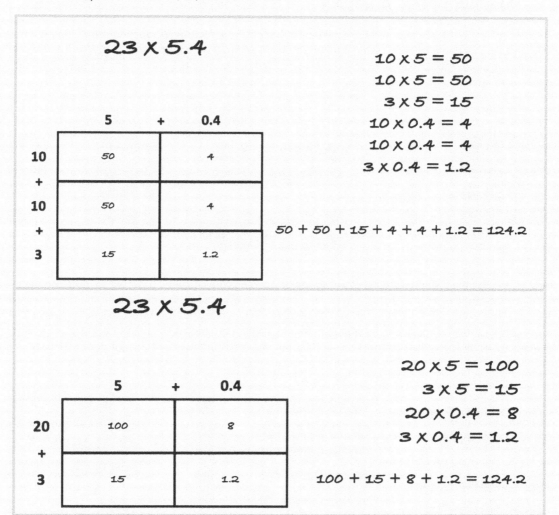

23 X 5.4

	5	+	0.4
10	50		4
+			
10	50		4
+			
3	15		1.2

10 x 5 = 50
10 x 5 = 50
3 x 5 = 15
10 X 0.4 = 4
10 X 0.4 = 4
3 X 0.4 = 1.2

50 + 50 + 15 + 4 + 4 + 1.2 = 124.2

23 X 5.4

	5	+	0.4
20	100		8
+			
3	15		1.2

20 x 5 = 100
3 X 5 = 15
20 X 0.4 = 8
3 X 0.4 = 1.2

100 + 15 + 8 + 1.2 = 124.2

ACTIVITY 3.2
NEGATIVE ARRAYS

Before decomposing multidigit negative factors, students benefit from focusing on decomposing single-digit negative factors. Begin with positive numbers, asking students to build an array for a given total (e.g., 24). Then, ask students to decompose the arrays into two smaller arrays and record related expressions. The example shows different ways to break apart a 4 × 6 array.

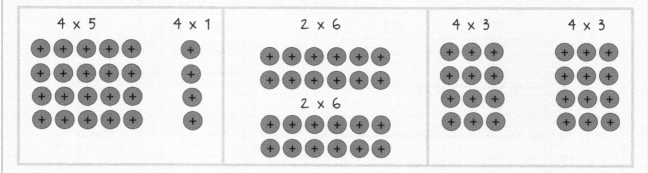

Have the class discuss the different ways that arrays can be decomposed and work together to generate the equations that would go with these examples. To explore negative numbers, ask students to determine what the array for 5 × −6 would look like (left example). Once created, ask students to decompose this array into two smaller arrays. The middle and right examples show two possible decompositions. Ask students to record the related expressions and generalize how the Break Apart by Addends strategy works in the same way with negative factors as it does with positive factors.

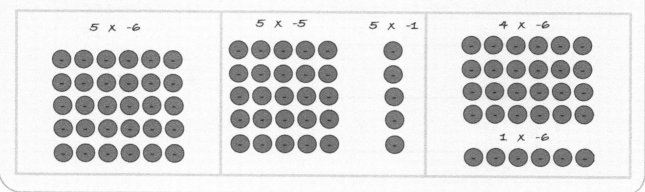

PRACTICE ACTIVITIES for Break Apart by Addends

See Part 1, page 20, for an overview about quality practice.

ACTIVITY 3.3

Name: "The Breaks"

Type: Routine

About the Routine: This routine engages students in comparing different ways to break apart factors and then determine which option(s) are most advantageous. "The Breaks" can be adapted to compare the Break Apart by Addends and Break Apart by Factors strategies. To do this, use one column to record ways to Break Apart by Addends and use the other column for ways to record Break Apart by Factors.

> **TEACHING TAKEAWAY**
> Many practice activities can be adapted to have students use and compare different strategies.

Materials: Prepare expressions for which there are several options for how to use Break Apart by Addends.

Directions:
1. Pose a multiplication expression to students (e.g., 45 × ⁻6).

2. Ask students to decide how they might break apart the first factor.

3. Students share ideas with a partner.

4. Record ideas in the first column.

5. Repeat Steps 2–4 for the second factor (using the second column to record ideas).

6. Ask students which break(s) they prefer.

7. *Optional:* Add a third choice of breaking apart both factors.

"The Breaks": 45 × ⁻6

BREAK APART 45	BREAK APART ⁻6
40 × ⁻6 + 5 × ⁻6	45 × ⁻3 + 45 × ⁻3
10 × ⁻6 + 10 × ⁻6 + 10 × ⁻6 + 10 × ⁻6 + 5 × ⁻6	45 × ⁻2 + 45 × ⁻2 + 45 × ⁻2
15 × ⁻6 + 15 × ⁻6 + 15 × ⁻6	45 × ⁻5 + 45 × ⁻1
20 × ⁻6 + 20 × ⁻6 + 5 × ⁻6	

In this example, the teacher posed 45 × ⁻6. The teacher recorded student ideas for breaking apart 45 in the first column and ideas for breaking apart 6 in the second column. Many of the students preferred the first expression in the left column. Some preferred the middle expression on the right, noticing that they could find 45 × 2 and then multiply that by 3 (break apart by factors).

ACTIVITY 3.4

Name: Lucky Highs and Lows　　　　**Type:** Game

About the Game: Players use digits to create expressions with the greatest or least possible product. You can determine high or low in advance, or, for a twist, reveal high or low after players have made their product. *Lucky Highs and Lows* can feature different types of numbers for factors. Students can use whole numbers (e.g., 35 × 26, 3 × 526), fractions or mixed numbers (e.g., $\frac{5}{3} \times \frac{6}{2}$, $3 \times 5\frac{2}{6}$), decimals (e.g., 3.5 × 2.6, 0.35 × 0.26), or integers (e.g., ⁻35 × 26).

Materials: 10-sided dice, four decks of digit cards (0–9), or playing cards (queens = 0, aces = 1; remove 10s, kings, and jacks); *Lucky Highs and Lows* recording sheet (optional)

Directions:
1. Players flip a coin or two-sided counter to determine the goal for the round (make the greatest product or the least product).

2. Players draw four cards (or roll the die four times) and arrange the digits to create two factors aligned to the setup of the game.

3. Players attempt to make the highest product or the lowest product using Break Apart by Addends to solve their problem, as appropriate.

4. The player with the product that best meets the goal for the round wins a point.

5. Repeat Steps 1–4. The first player to score 5 points wins the game.

TEACHING TAKEAWAY
You can direct students to use a specific strategy while playing a game to focus their practice on becoming adept at using the strategy.

RESOURCE(S) FOR THIS ACTIVITY

Lucky Highs and Lows

Directions: Use four digits to make two factors. Arrange the digits to make the greatest or least product possible. Flip a coin or counter to determine the goal (greatest or least). The player with the best product for the goal wins a point.

Round 1:	Round 4:

Goal:　　　　　　　　　　　Win the round?
❑ Greatest product　　　　❑ Yes
❑ Least product　　　　　　❑ No

Goal:　　　　　　　　　　　Win the round?
❑ Greatest product　　　　❑ Yes
❑ Least product　　　　　　❑ No

Round 2:	Round 5:

online resources　This resource can be downloaded at **resources.corwin.com/FOF/rationalnumbersalgequations**.

ACTIVITY 3.5

Name: Backward Breaks   **Type:** Task

About the Task: Reversing an activity is a good way to enrich a task (SanGiovanni, Katt, & Dykema, 2020). In this task, students are given a decomposed multiplication problem and they find the product and recompose the original expression.

Materials: *Backward Breaks* cards, *Backward Breaks* recording sheet

Directions:
1. Students choose a card and record the information.

2. Students find the product and record it.

3. Students determine the original problem.

4. Students determine if the decomposed expression card was the most efficient way (for them) to think about the problem, or they write another way that the problem might have been solved.

RESOURCE(S) FOR THIS ACTIVITY

⁻10 × 4 + ⁻10 × 4 + ⁻8 × 4	20 × ⁻15 + 4 × ⁻15
⁻20 × ⁻12 + ⁻4 × ⁻12	20 × ⁻20 + 7 × ⁻20
10 × ⁻14 + 10 × ⁻14 + 2 × ⁻14	20 × ⁻25 + 6 × ⁻25
10 × ⁻8 + 5 × ⁻8	50 × ⁻30 + 5 × ⁻30 + 4 × ⁻30
⁻60 × ⁻9 + ⁻7 × ⁻9	⁻10 × ⁻72 + ⁻2 × ⁻72

Backward Breaks

Directions: Select a decomposed expression card. Find the product. Write the original problem. Tell if there is a more efficient way to think about the problem.

Decomposed problem	Product	Original problem	Is there a more efficient way to think about the problem?
10 × 4 + 10 × 4 + 8 × 4	10 × 4 = 40 10 × 4 = 40 8 × 4 = 32 So, the product is 112.	28 × 4	I could do it this way: 25 × 4 + 3 × 4

This resource can be downloaded at **resources.corwin.com/FOF/rationalnumbersalgequations**.

STRATEGY OVERVIEW:
Break Apart by Factors (Including Halve and Double)

What Is Break Apart by Factors? In this strategy, one factor is decomposed into factors and the factor is reassociated with the other factor. For example, for 25 × 16 the 16 can be factored into 4 × 4. Then, the expression is 25 × 4 × 4, which can then be solved as 100 × 4 = 400. Whenever a factor is even, a 2 can be factored out (halving it) and multiplied by the other number (doubling it)—the Halve and Double strategy. When multiplying by a fraction, students can break apart a fraction that is *not* a unit fraction into a unit fraction to support their reasoning. For example, to solve $\frac{2}{5} \times 25$ a student might reason, "I know one-fifth of 25 is 5. I multiply that by 2 and get 10." This thinking can be recorded showing how the fraction was broken apart into factors and reassociated:

$$\frac{2}{5} \times 25$$

$$2 \times \left(\frac{1}{5} \times 25\right)$$

$$2 \times 5 = 10$$

HOW DOES BREAK APART BY FACTORS WORK?

Breaking apart into factors utilizes the associative property. *The thinking process:*

1. Look to see if there is a way to factor one of the numbers such that multiplying that factor by the other number creates an easier problem.
2. Rethink the problem with the factor associated with the other factor.
3. Multiply the adapted problem.

As with all multiplication problems involving negative numbers, the problem has an added step of considering what the sign of the answer needs to be.

Whole Numbers	Fractions	Decimals
Factor Factor 15 × 8 3 × 5 3 × 5 × 8 3 × 40 120	$12 \times \frac{1}{4}$ $3 \times 4 \times \frac{1}{4}$ 3×1	2.5×1.6 $2.5 \times 4 \times 0.4$ 10×0.4 4

A common use of Break Apart by Factors is to Halve and Double. *The thinking process*:

1. Look for a problem with an even factor and a factor ending in a 5 (or $\frac{1}{2}$ or 0.5).
2. Halve the even factor (divide it by 2).
3. Double the other factor (multiply it by 2).
4. Multiply the adapted problem.

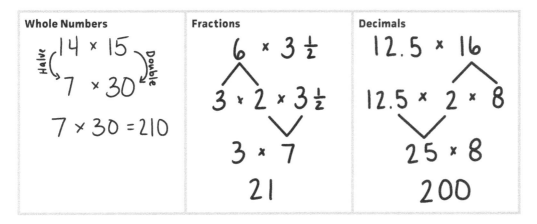

Whole Numbers	Fractions	Decimals
Halve $\left(\begin{array}{c} 14 \times 15 \\ 7 \times 30 \end{array}\right)$ Double $7 \times 30 = 210$	$6 \times 3\frac{1}{2}$ $3 \times 2 \times 3\frac{1}{2}$ 3×7 21	12.5×16 $12.5 \times 2 \times 8$ 25×8 200

WHEN DO YOU CHOOSE BREAK APART BY FACTORS?

Break Apart by Factors is useful when you can make a benchmark or whole number and create an easier problem. It is useful for thinking through multiplication by fractions that are not unit fractions. Halve and Double is useful when the ending of one number is 5, 0.5, or $\frac{1}{2}$ and the other number is even.

NOTES

_____

_____

_____

_____

_____

_____

_____

_____

TEACHING ACTIVITIES for Break Apart by Factors

Teaching Break Apart by Factors begins with understanding why it works. Area models can be useful, or you can challenge students to prove why it works, choosing their own visuals or models. A key to using this strategy is recognizing when the opportunities arise. Halve and Double is useful across whole numbers, fractions, and decimals and thus a good place to begin. A key is to look at each factor and consider whether (1) one can be decomposed into factors that can make the other number a benchmark number or whole number or (2) you can make reasoning about the problem manageable (i.e., by using unit fractions).

ACTIVITY 3.6
EQUAL GROUP ARGUMENTS

In this activity, students represent two expressions (e.g., 8 × −12 and 8 × 3 × −4) with an equal groups model to prove if the two expressions are equivalent. Begin by posing two problems for students to model with equal groups. Give students time to create representations, being sure to label them appropriately. Have groups compare their representations. You should see representations that look similar to these:

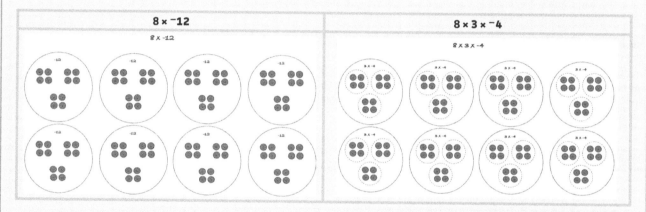

During discussion, it should become clear to students that 8 × 3 × −4 is the same as 8 × −12. Ask students to determine if they believe that breaking apart by factors will always work. Explore other problems such as 15 × 14; 36 × −25; or decimal or fraction examples, like 3.5 × −6. Summarize by discussing why it works, and when it is useful. This will help students be on the lookout for problems that lend to this strategy.

ACTIVITY 3.7
HALVE AND DOUBLE PROOFS WITH CUISENAIRE RODS

This activity uses Cuisenaire rods to prove that the Halve and Double strategy still works with decimals and fractions. Cuisenaire rods are versatile and quite useful for developing an understanding of fractions and decimals. There are 10 rods, each 1 cm longer than another, with white being the smallest (1 cm) and orange the longest (10 cm).

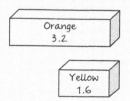

First, ask students to find the value of the yellow rod if the orange rod has a value of 3.2. Then, ask them to predict which of the expressions below would be equivalent and why they think that is so.

| 10 × 3.2 and 5 × 1.6 | 5 × 3.2 and 10 × 1.6 | 14 × 3.2 and 7 × 1.6 | 7 × 3.2 and 14 × 1.6 |

Next, have students use their Cuisenaire rods to show the equivalent expressions.

5 x 3.2 is the same as 10 x 1.6

You can extend this exploration by asking students if it is possible to Halve and Double repeatedly (they can use brown, purple, and red rods to explore). An example of that proof might look something like this:

5 x 3.2 is the same as 10 x 1.6
5 x 3.2 is the same as 20 x 0.8

 # ACTIVITY 3.8
ADDENDS OR FACTORS?

Break Apart by Addends applies the distributive property, whereas Break Apart by Factors applies the associative property. This activity has students explore both. Present students with a problem (e.g., 6.25 × 40) and statements that briefly describe ways to break apart the problem:

- Break 6.25 into 6 + 0.2 + 0.05 and multiply each by 40.

- Break 6.25 into 6 + 0.25 and multiply each by 40.

- Break 40 into 10 × 4 and multiply 10 × 6.25 and then multiply by 4.

- Break 40 into 4 × 10 and multiply 4 × 6.25 and then multiply by 10.

Have groups of students work together to analyze each option to see if (1) it would lead to an equivalent answer and (2) if it is a good way to solve the problem. As a whole group, discuss which Break Apart strategy(ies) they like better and why. Pose new problems and repeat the process. Summarize by asking students when they might choose "by addends" and when they might choose "by factors."

PRACTICE ACTIVITIES for Break Apart by Factors

See Part 1, page 20, for an overview about quality practice.

ACTIVITY 3.9

Name: "About or Between"   **Type:** Routine

About the Routine: There are different ways to estimate. In this routine, students have an opportunity to use different approaches for estimating results. (SanGiovanni, 2019). This routine supports reasonableness and works with any number types, so it is a good routine to use frequently.

Materials: Prepare two or three expressions (examples follow).

Directions: 1. Pose a set of expressions to students.

2. Ask students to choose whether they will give an "about" or a "between" estimate:

   a. About: Use an estimation strategy to find a close product.

   b. Between: Use multiplication to find a range in which the answer lies.

      3. Students share their choice and the way they implemented their approach with partners.

      4. Discuss ideas with the entire class. As you discuss estimates, stress that estimates give an idea of the final result and that there is no one correct way to estimate. Remind students that an efficient method is one that can be done relatively quickly.

5. *Optional:* Have students choose one expression to tell a partner how they might find the exact product.

See Part 1, page 18, for a list of estimation strategies.

"ABOUT OR BETWEEN"		
$4.6 \times {}^-6.3$	${}^-19.1 \times {}^-7$	${}^-3.5 \times 8$

In the first expression, a student might pick "about" and say, "It's about ${}^-24$," using front-end estimation. Another student might pick "between," explaining that the answer is between $4 \times {}^-6$ and $5 \times {}^-7$. This routine is effective with any numbers. Here is a fraction set:

"ABOUT OR BETWEEN"		
$7\frac{1}{4} \times 6$	$4\frac{1}{2} \times 32$	$18 \times 2\frac{1}{3}$

ACTIVITY 3.10

Name: "A String of Halves"   **Type:** Routine

About the Routine: Making use of the Halve and Double strategy relies on students' ability to double and find halves. Often, students do well with doubling, but finding a half proves more challenging. "A String of Halves" aims to help students improve their skill with halving. This routine uses a set of numbers to help students see how numbers are halved.

Materials: Prepare a set of numbers that are intentionally related.

Directions: 1. Post a set of three or more related numbers, as shown.

2. Ask students to mentally find the halves of as many numbers as possible.

3. If students are unable to find all of the halves, have them talk with partners about how they can use the relationships between numbers and the known halves to find the unknown half. If students find all of the halves, have them discuss with partners how the numbers and their halves are related. To extend this situation (when all halves are known), have students generate a new number and its half that is related to the set.

A				B		
8	1.4	9.4		9	0.5	9.5
4	0.7			4.5	0.25	

In Examples A and B, the routine is designed to focus on halving decimals. The teacher started with A because students could find half of 8 and half of 1.4, but not half of 9.4. After completing the first two, the teacher asked students to look for patterns and relationships between the numbers and the halves to solve the third number in the string.

Halving numbers like $6\frac{1}{4}$ or even $4\frac{5}{12}$ can be challenging for students as they think about halving the fractional amount. Like with decimals, this routine develops skill at how to think through halving.

C				D		
6	$\frac{1}{4}$	$6\frac{1}{4}$		5	$\frac{5}{6}$	$5\frac{5}{6}$
3	$\frac{1}{8}$			$2\frac{1}{2}$	$\frac{5}{12}$	$2\frac{11}{12}$

In Examples C and D, the routine has been modified to help students practice halving mixed numbers. Notice that in Example D students have the opportunity to think about how to halve a fraction with an odd numerator. With more examples like this one, students develop the powerful idea in that to halve a fraction one can simply double the denominator.

STRATEGY OVERVIEW:
Compensation (for Multiplication)

What Is Compensation? This strategy involves adjusting one of the factors to make an easier problem, multiplying that new problem, and then compensating for whatever change was made. For example, 99 × 43 can be adjusted to 100 × 43, mentally multiplied (4,300) and that answer is one group of 43 too much, so subtract 43 and the answer is 4,257. With fractions and decimals, the benchmark is a nearby whole number.

HOW DOES COMPENSATION WORK?

This strategy uses the distributive property, just like breaking apart into addends, but in this case subtraction is typically used. *The thinking process:*

1. Decide on a factor to change to create a mental problem or easier problem to multiply.

2. Find the product of your adjusted expression.

3. Determine how much too much (or too little) the answer is and make the appropriate Compensation.

As with all multiplication and division problems involving negative numbers, the problem has an added step of considering what the sign of the answer needs to be.

Whole Numbers	Fractions	Decimals
23 × 8	$5 \times 4\frac{7}{8}$	**9.9 × 35**
Adjust: Change 23 to 25 to get 25 × 8	**Adjust:** Add $\frac{1}{8}$ to $4\frac{7}{8}$ to get 5	**Adjust:** Change 9.9 to 10
Multiply: 25 × 8 = 200	**Multiply:** 5 × 5 = 25	**Multiply:** 10 × 35 = 350
Compensate: 200 is 2 × 8 too much; subtract 16: 200 − 16 = 184. The product of the original problem is 184.	**Compensate:** 25 is $5 \times \frac{1}{8}$ too much, so subtract $\frac{5}{8}$. The product of the original problem is $24\frac{3}{8}$.	**Compensate:** 350 is 0.1 × 35 too much; subtract 350 − 3.5 = 346.5. The product of the original problem is 346.5.

WHEN DO YOU CHOOSE COMPENSATION?

This strategy is useful when one of the factors is close to a benchmark, such as the examples in the table. Notice that in these examples, Break Apart to Multiply is also a reasonable option. However, because the digits are larger (e.g., 9.9), Compensation may be easier.

TEACHING ACTIVITIES for Compensation

Compensation with multiplication requires understanding that when you change a factor (e.g., the multiplier) by adding one, the resulting product is one *group* larger. Thus, Compensation involves subtracting one *group,* not just subtracting 1 unit. The following teaching activities help students to make sense of Compensation.

ACTIVITY 3.11
SEEING IS BELIEVING

In this activity, students are charged with creating visual models to justify Compensation statements. For example, state that $3 \times 4\frac{5}{6}$ is the same as $3 \times 5 - 3 \times \frac{1}{6} = 15 - \frac{3}{6}$ or $14\frac{1}{2}$, having students prove it to be true. In this example, students used fraction circles to show their thinking. First, they showed three groups of $4\frac{5}{6}$.

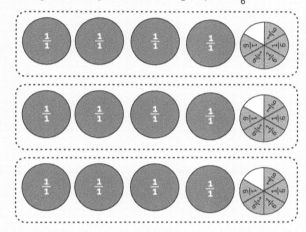

Then, they showed 3 × 5 (on the left) and the amount they would need to take away ($3 \times \frac{1}{6}$) to compensate for their adjustment (on the right).

Students recorded the related equations: $3 \times 4\frac{5}{6} = 3 \times 5 - 3 \times \frac{1}{6}$. Repeat with new problems.

ACTIVITY 3.12
TRUE OR FALSE STATEMENTS

Students may believe that Compensation for multiplication functions similarly to Compensation with addition. For example, they may think that 38 × 8 is the same as 40 × 8 – 2 because they added 2 to 38. In this activity, you provide students with a collection of statements and students use reasoning to decide if they are true or false. Here are some possible prompts for students to explore:

True or False:

- 69×4 is the same as 70×4, then take away 4

- 6×48 is the same as $6 \times 50 - 2$

- 7×59 is the same as $7 \times 60 - 7$

- $4\frac{7}{8} \times 3$ is the same as $5 \times 3 - \frac{1}{8}$

- $3 \times 6\frac{5}{6}$ is the same as $3 \times 7 - \frac{1}{2}$

- 4×7.99 is the same as $4 \times 8 - 0.04$

- 4.9×4.9 is the same as 5×5, then take away 0.2

NOTES

_____

_____

_____

_____

_____

_____

_____

_____

_____

PRACTICE ACTIVITIES for Compensation

See Part 1, page 20, for an overview about quality practice.

ACTIVITY 3.13

Name: "A Little More, a Little Less"   **Type:** Routine

About the Routine: Compensation can be applied in different ways. This routine helps students consider different ways to adjust a problem in order to solve it efficiently.

Materials: Prepare three or four expressions that fit the Compensation strategy.

Directions:

1. Pose a few expressions to students (one at a time, or the full set).

2. Give students time to think and talk to each other about ways they could adjust a factor to a little more or a little less to create a problem easier to multiply. Students do not solve the expressions, but instead just decide how to adjust the expression.

3. As a whole group, ask how problems were adjusted.

4. For each idea, ask everyone to think about how that change will need to be compensated to address the little more or less that was changed.

5. Have students solve the set of problems using Compensation.

"A LITTLE MORE, A LITTLE LESS"		
26 × 12	11 × 48	19 × 35

"A LITTLE MORE, A LITTLE LESS"		
$5 \times 2\frac{7}{8}$	$9\frac{7}{8} \times 5$	$6 \times 8\frac{3}{4}$

"A LITTLE MORE, A LITTLE LESS"			
5 × 5.8	9.5 × 20	4.9 × 8	3.1 × 16

"A LITTLE MORE, A LITTLE LESS"		
⁻75 × 9	⁻6 × 48	⁻19 × ⁻30

The idea of a little more and a little less can be challenging with negative numbers. For example, if the first expression was positive, we would say the product is a little less than 75 × 10. But, because a factor is negative, the product will actually be a little more than ⁻75 × 10. One option is to solve it as though the problem is whole numbers and then determine the sign of the answer.

ACTIVITY 3.14

Game: *Give Some to Get Some*   **Type:** *Game*

About the Game: *Give Some to Get Some* focuses students' attention on the Compensation strategy as they look for expressions in which they would give some to a factor to create a friendlier problem.

Materials: *Give Some to Get Some* game board per pair, one regular six-sided die per pair

Directions: 1. Players take turns rolling the die to generate a number.

2. The player uses that number to look for an expression in which the amount rolled could be used to adjust one of the factors to make a friendlier problem. For example, a player rolls a 2. She selects ⁻68 × 30 because she could rethink the problem adjusting ⁻68 to ⁻70 (a change of 2), creating ⁻70 × 30.

3. The player solves the problem verbally or in writing. In this case, she explains that her answer is ⁻2 × 30 or ⁻60 off, so she has ⁻2,100 + 60, which is ⁻2,040. Her partner confirms this is correct (e.g., using a calculator). She places a counter on ⁻68 × 30.

4. If a player rolls a 4, 5, or 6, they lose their turn because factors adjusted by these amounts do not typically yield an efficient problem.

5. The game ends when all the spaces are filled or time is up.

6. The player who has the most three-in-a-rows wins (they can overlap).

RESOURCE(S) FOR THIS ACTIVITY

Give Some to Get Some: Fractions

Directions: Take turns rolling a number. Choose a space on the game board where the amount you roll could be given to one factor to make a whole. Solve that problem to claim the space. The game ends when all spaces are covered. The player with the most three-in-a-rows wins.

$3\frac{7}{8} \times 5$	$4 \times 6\frac{3}{4}$	$7\frac{7}{8} \times 4$	$12 \times 2\frac{5}{6}$	$3 \times 4\frac{3}{4}$
$4 \times 2\frac{8}{9}$	$6 \times 4\frac{5}{6}$	$3\frac{7}{9} \times 6$	$3 \times 5\frac{4}{5}$	$8\frac{7}{8} \times 5$
$4 \times 5\frac{3}{5}$	$2\frac{9}{10} \times 4$	$4 \times 2\frac{4}{5}$	$2\frac{3}{4} \times 8$	$7\frac{5}{6} \times 6$
$7\frac{9}{10} \times 8$	$4 \times 2\frac{7}{9}$	$5\frac{8}{10} \times 5$	$5 \times 1\frac{8}{9}$	$10 \times 3\frac{3}{4}$
$\frac{7}{8} \times 24$	$8\frac{5}{6} \times 6$	$2 \times 9\frac{8}{9}$	$3\frac{7}{8} \times 5$	$3\frac{4}{5} \times 10$

Give Some to Get Some: Decimals

Directions: Take turns rolling a number. Choose a space on the game board where the amount you roll could be given to one factor to make a whole. Solve that problem to claim the space. The game ends when all spaces are covered. The player with the most three-in-a-rows wins.

7×6.9	3.7×6	1.7×25	2.8×7	9×2.7
5×9.98	4.9×4	5×1.98	8.8×7	12×3.8
9.9×15	3.9×50	3.8×12	9×3.98	6×7.9
19.8×5	6×2.9	5.9×13	7×1.99	4×5.8
2.9×30	6.8×15	1.7×25	6×2.97	35×1.9

Give Some to Get Some

Directions: Take turns rolling a number. Choose a space on the game board where the amount you roll could be used to adjust one of the factors to use the Compensation strategy. The game ends when all spaces are covered. The player with the most three-in-a-rows wins.

$16 \times ^-77$	$^-39 \times 16$	$^-99 \times ^-98$	$^-38 \times 12$	$79 \times ^-24$
$^-89 \times 26$	$^-38 \times 63$	$37 \times ^-69$	17×25	$48 \times ^-23$
$25 \times ^-38$	$^-47 \times 54$	$97 \times ^-5$	$^-88 \times 17$	$^-89 \times ^-27$
$^-99 \times 58$	$68 \times ^-29$	$^-68 \times 33$	$^-59 \times ^-13$	$^-77 \times 17$
$^-35 \times 46$	$68 \times ^-27$	$^-27 \times 44$	$57 \times ^-43$	$^-46 \times ^-27$

online resources This resource can be downloaded at **resources.corwin.com/FOF/rationalnumbersalgequations**.

ACTIVITY 3.15

Name: Creating Compensations   **Type:** Task

About the Task: This task is a high-order thinking activity for students to create problems that can be adjusted by the given amount. Some problems lend to Compensation and some do not. As students create problems based on their role, they gain important insights about what problems lend to Compensation.

Materials: Regular die, *Creating Compensations* recording sheet

Directions: 1. Students generate a number by rolling the die (6s are wild).

2. Students use the number to generate an expression that they would solve by adjusting one of the factors by the amount they rolled.

3. Students solve the problem on the recording sheet using Compensation.

4. Students note whether Compensation was the best option for their problem, or if another option would have been better.

For example, a student rolls a 2. She creates the expression 5 × ⁻498. She solves it by adjusting ⁻498 to ⁻500, and then compensates by subtracting 5 × ⁻2(⁻10) to get ⁻2,490. She notes that Compensation is a good strategy for this problem.

> **TEACHING TAKEAWAY**
>
> Asking students to reflect on a game or activity improves clarity of purpose for students and provides insight into student thinking for teachers.

RESOURCE(S) FOR THIS ACTIVITY

Creating Compensations

Directions: Roll a regular die. Create and solve a problem that has a factor that you could adjust by that amount. Record your thinking.

Number I rolled	Problem I created	How I use compensation to solve my problem
2	5 × ⁻498	I can adjust to 5 × ⁻500 and then take away ⁻10. The answer is ⁻2,490.

online resources 🔖 This resource can be downloaded at **resources.corwin.com/FOF/rationalnumbersalgequations**.

Reasoning Strategies for Division

In this module we highlight two significant strategies for division:

- Think Multiplication (Use the Inverse Operation)
- Partial Quotients

The focus of each section is on developing an understanding of how these two strategies work and when they are a good choice. In Part 3 of this book, we offer activities that focus on choosing among these significant strategies for division (and the standard algorithms).

STRATEGY OVERVIEW:
Think Multiplication

What Is Think Multiplication? This is a division strategy wherein the problem is reframed as a multiplication problem with a missing factor. Once it is reframed into a multiplication problem, other strategies can come into play to reason toward an answer (e.g., Partial Products).

HOW DOES THINK MULTIPLICATION WORK?

Think Multiplication is an example of using an inverse relationship. Symbolically, this means that if $a \times b = c$, then $c \div b = a$ and $c \div a = b$. Therefore, a division expression can be interpreted as a multiplication expression.

The thinking process:

1. Rethink the division problem as a missing factor multiplication problem.
2. Use multiplication to find the unknown factor. As needed, use reasoning strategies.
3. Once an unknown factor is found, multiply the factors to determine if there is a remainder or not.

As with all division problems involving negative numbers, the problem has an added step of considering what the sign of the answer needs to be.

Depending on which number is the missing factor, there are two ways to interpret the problem—both build number sense and understanding of division. This distinction is particularly useful with fractions:

$3 \div \frac{1}{4} = ?$	$? \times \frac{1}{4} = 3$	How many groups of $\frac{1}{4}$ equal 3 wholes?
	$\frac{1}{4} \times ? = 3$	One-fourth of what number equals 3 wholes?

Whole Numbers	**Fractions**	**Decimals**
240 ÷ 12	$3 \div \frac{1}{4}$	**14.4 ÷ 0.6**
Think: "12 times what number equals 240?"	**Think:** "How many fourths equal 3 wholes?"	**Think:** "How many groups of 6 tenths in 144 tenths? Or, how many 6s in 144?"

Notice that with decimals, using the place value name of tenths builds meaning for thinking of the problem in whole numbers. Also, notice that Partial Products were used to figure out the missing factor.

WHEN DO YOU CHOOSE THINK MULTIPLICATION?

Think Multiplication is useful when division problems have basic fact relationships—for example, $420 \div 60$ or $7.2 \div 0.08$. For fractions, Think Multiplication is particularly useful when dividing a number by a unit fraction (e.g., $5 \div \frac{1}{4}$) and when dividing by a common denominator ($\frac{8}{12} \div \frac{2}{12} = ?$) because this translates to "How many 2 twelfths equal 8 twelfths?" This is the same question as, "How many 2s in 8?" Finally, this strategy is useful when the divisor is a well-known multiple or automaticity (e.g., 15, $\frac{1}{2}$, 0.1, 0.25):

$15 \div 0.1$	$375 \div 25$	$34 \div \frac{1}{2}$	$12.5 \div 0.25$

MODULE 1 Strategies for Addition
MODULE 2 Strategies for Subtraction
MODULE 3 Strategies for Multiplication
MODULE 4 Strategies for Division
MODULE 5 Strategies for Ratios and Proportions
MODULE 6 Strategies for Solving Equations for an Unknown
MODULE 7 Strategies for Solving Systems of Linear Equations

TEACHING ACTIVITIES for Think Multiplication

Think Multiplication relies on understanding how multiplication and division are related. Students are first introduced to the inverse relationship between multiplication and division with basic facts, such as seeing $56 \div 7$ and thinking, "What 7s fact do I know that equals 56?" They then continue with larger problems, such as $560 \div 7$. These basic examples can be a good initial experience in exploring this strategy as it applies to fractions and decimals. Importantly, changing the equation to multiplication is the first step of this strategy. Once translated to a multiplication problem, the answer may be obvious, or a multiplication strategy may be needed to determine the answer.

ACTIVITY 4.1
IS IT THE INVERSE?

This activity is an opportunity for students to revisit the inverse relationship between multiplication and division as it applies to rational numbers. Students are given two related equations, one with a multiplication or division equation and the other, a related equation that uses the inverse operation. Ask students to determine if the two equations express an inverse relationship. If not, have them write the inverse relationship. After exploring several examples, ask students how using an inverse could help them solve division problems. The table shows examples with different number types. The first example for each number type is a true example and the second is false.

TEACHING TAKEAWAY

Encourage students to use manipulatives, drawings, and diagrams to justify thinking, especially when it comes to understanding properties and relationships.

NUMBER TYPE EXAMPLE	EQUATION	TRUE INVERSE-RELATED EQUATION?
Fractions	$\frac{27}{8} \div \frac{3}{8} = 9$	$9 \times \frac{3}{8} = \frac{27}{8}$
	$\frac{15}{8} \div \frac{3}{8} = 5$	$5 + \frac{3}{8} = \frac{15}{8}$
Decimals	$45.5 \div 5 = 9.1$	$5 \times 9.1 = 45.5$
	$37.2 \times 2 = 74.4$	$74.4 = 37.2 \div 2$
Integers	$^-48 \div ^-4 = 12$	$12 \times ^-4 = ^-48$
	$^-175 \div ^-7 = 25$	$^-175 \div 25 = ^-7$
Signed Fractions	$^-64 \times -\frac{1}{4} = 16$	$16 \div -\frac{1}{4} = ^-64$
	$^-9 \times \frac{1}{3} = ^-3$	$^-9 \div 3 = -\frac{1}{3}$
Signed Decimals	$^-5 \times 0.4 = ^-2$	$^-2 \div 0.4 = ^-5$
	$8 \div ^-16 = ^-0.5$	$16 \div ^-0.5 = 8$

You can extend this activity in two different ways:

1. Ask students to generate sets of equations for classmates to consider.

2. Pose a list of equations and ask students to generate a related true equation using the inverse operation.

ACTIVITY 4.2
DECOMPOSING DIVIDENDS

Using the inverse is helpful in division situations beyond known multiplication problems. In some problems, such as 248 ÷ 8 or 24.8 ÷ 0.8, you can decompose the dividend into known multiples of the divisor. For example, 24 is a familiar multiple of 8; 248 can be decomposed into 240 (10 groups of 24 or 30 groups of 8) and 8. Then, it can be reasoned that 248 ÷ 8 is 30 groups of 8 and one more group of 8. This specific use of Think Multiplication is very handy, and it can be used with related problems like 24.8 ÷ 8, but it takes time to develop. You can use worked examples to highlight ideas. For example, you might pose this task:

TEACHING TAKEAWAY

Developing this strategy is built on skill with recognizing factors and multiples. See page 17 for more about this utility with additional online resources.

Marissa thinks she can find 3.72 ÷ 6 by thinking of 3.6 ÷ 6 + 0.12 ÷ 6. Prove why Marissa is correct or incorrect. Create other examples to show how her thinking will or won't work.

As you might imagine, students will embark on proving this in a variety of ways. Here, a student proves Marissa is correct by multiplying and then using the division algorithm.

$$3.6 \div 6 = 0.6$$
$$0.12 \div 6 = \underline{0.02}$$
$$0.62$$

$$3.72 \div 6 = 0.62$$

Marissa is right.

$$\begin{array}{r} .62 \\ 6\overline{)3.72} \\ \underline{-36} \\ 12 \\ \underline{-12} \\ 0 \end{array}$$

The critical question to ask is, "Why would Marissa want to break apart the divisor?" It helps students see that she can then use known multiplication facts (e.g., 6 × 6 = 36) to solve the problem.

With division, only the dividend can be decomposed. Be sure that your students investigate decomposing the divisor to see what happens. Pose a problem like:

Oscar thinks he can find 144 ÷ ⁻6 by thinking 144 ÷ ⁻3 + 144 ÷ ⁻2. Prove why Oscar is correct or incorrect. Create other examples to show if his thinking will or will not work.

$$\begin{array}{r} \boxed{24} \\ 6\overline{)144} \\ \underline{-12} \\ 24 \\ \underline{-24} \\ 0 \end{array} \qquad \begin{array}{r} \boxed{48} \\ 3\overline{)144} \\ \underline{-12} \\ 24 \\ \underline{-24} \\ 0 \end{array} \qquad \begin{array}{r} \boxed{72} \\ 2\overline{)144} \\ \underline{-144} \\ 0 \end{array}$$

$$24 \neq 48 + 72$$

(Continued)

(Continued)

After exploring the two worked examples, provide statements and ask students to determine if they are true:

6.5 ÷ 0.5 is the same as 5.0 ÷ 0.5 + 1.5 ÷ 0.5

⁻42 ÷ 3 is the same as ⁻30 ÷ 3 + ⁻12 ÷ 3

0.84 ÷ 4 is the same as 0.40 ÷ 4 + 0.40 ÷ 4 + 0.04 ÷ 4

48 ÷ ⁻12 is the same as 48 ÷ ⁻3 + 48 ÷ ⁻4

60 ÷ 15 is the same as 60 ÷ 5 and 60 ÷ 3

Conclude by asking (again), "Why is breaking apart the dividend helpful?" Help students make the connection that they can break apart the dividend so that they can see a known multiple to help solve the problem.

ACTIVITY 4.3
PROMPTS FOR TEACHING THINK MULTIPLICATION

The following prompts are good opportunities for developing understanding of and reasoning about this strategy. Have students use representations and tools to justify their thinking, including base-10 models, number lines, arrays, integer chips, and so on. After students work with the prompt(s), bring the class together to exchange ideas.

- Which basic facts help you solve 155 ÷ 5? Explain your thinking.

- Tell how $\frac{3}{4} \times 2 = 1\frac{1}{2}$, $\frac{3}{4} \times 4 = 3$, and $\frac{3}{4} \times 16 = 12$ can help you with

  - $4 \div \frac{3}{4}$ $16 \div \frac{3}{4}$ $2 \div \frac{3}{4}$

  - $8 \div \frac{3}{4}$ $32 \div \frac{3}{4}$ $2 \div \frac{1}{4}$

- Tell how ⁻5 × 7 = ⁻35 can help you with ⁻350 ÷ 5, ⁻350 ÷ 7, ⁻350 ÷ 50, and ⁻350 ÷ 70.

- Tell how 0.5 × ⁻9 = ⁻4.5 can help you with ⁻4.5 ÷ 0.5, ⁻4.5 ÷ ⁻9, ⁻4.5 ÷ 5, and ⁻45 ÷ 0.9.

- What is the missing factor in ⁻70 × __ = ⁻630 that will help you solve ⁻630 ÷ ⁻70?

- What are the related multiplication problems for $9 \div \frac{1}{6} = n$?

- How might you use Think Multiplication to solve 14.5 ÷ 0.25?

- Create three division problems with decimals that could be solved by knowing 6 × 7 = 42.

PRACTICE ACTIVITIES for Think Multiplication

See Part 1, page 20, for an overview about quality practice.

ACTIVITY 4.4

Name: Paper Clip Connections   **Type:** Game

About the Game: *Paper Clip Connections* is a take on the classic *Product Game*, in which students try to find products by moving their paper clips strategically. The game reinforces the relationship between multiplication and division with larger numbers. As students find products, they must share the related division problem in order to place their game piece.

Materials: *Paper Clip Connections* game board, two paper clips, about 40 two-color counters, and calculators

Directions: 1. Player 1 places a paper clip on one of the factors in the left column and one of the factors in the bottom row. Factors are not within the grid.

2. The player finds the product of these two numbers and then tells their opponent the related division problem.

3. If accurate, Player 1 places their counter on the space of the corresponding product of the two factors.

4. Player 2 then chooses to move each paper clip one space in either direction and repeats finding the product and telling the related division problem. Or Player 2 can move one paper clip two spaces in either direction.

5. The game continues with each player choosing to move two paper clips one direction or moving one paper clip two spaces in either direction.

6. The first player to get five counters in a row (horizontally, vertically, or diagonally) wins the game.

For example, Player 1 places paper clips on 40 and ⁻30. They say that 40 × ⁻30 = ⁻1,200 and so ⁻1,200 ÷ 40 = ⁻30. Their opponent confirms, and they place their counter on ⁻1,200. Player 2 moves the paper clip on 40 to 30 and the paper clip on ⁻30 to ⁻20. Player 2 says that 30 × ⁻20 = ⁻600 and so ⁻600 ÷ 30 = ⁻20. Player 2 is correct and places their counter on ⁻600. Player 1 then moves the paper clip on 30 two spaces to 50 and cannot move the other paper clip. They share 50 × ⁻20 = ⁻1,000 and that ⁻1,000 ÷ 50 = ⁻20 and place their counter.

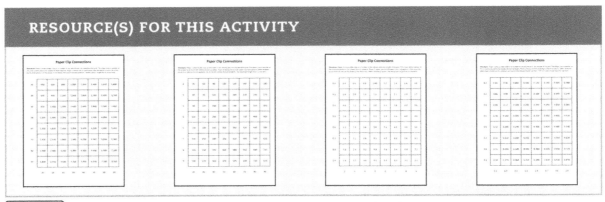

RESOURCE(S) FOR THIS ACTIVITY

online resources — This resource can be downloaded at r**esources.corwin.com/FOF/rationalnumbersalgequations**.

ACTIVITY 4.5

Name: Missing Numbers—Triangle Cards   **Type:** Game

About the Game: Triangle cards are sometimes used in elementary school to learn basic fact-family relationships. Using this familiar tool, this game can help students see how those basic fact relationships extend to other numbers.

Materials: 10-sided dice, digit cards (0–9) or playing cards (queens = 0, aces = 1; 10s, kings, and jacks removed); *Missing Numbers—Triangle Cards* game board (one per player)

Directions: 1. Players take turns generating digits to complete the missing numbers in the triangle cards on their game board.

2. Players lose their turn if the digit they roll/pull can't be used.

3. The first player to complete all four triangle sets wins.

This game offers a unique twist. The triangles in Sets A and B show a specific relationship between the triangles calling for certain digits to complete them. The triangles in Sets C and D are "open" or "wild." A student can use any numbers they want in them, but there is a catch: Each triangle set has to show the same relationship as the one shown in Sets A and B. For example, if Sets A and B show a basic fact (7, 3, 21), a related triangle with a tenths product/dividend (0.7, 3, 2.1) and a related triangle with hundredths product/dividend (0.7, 0.3, 0.21) the student's wild triangles must be similar.

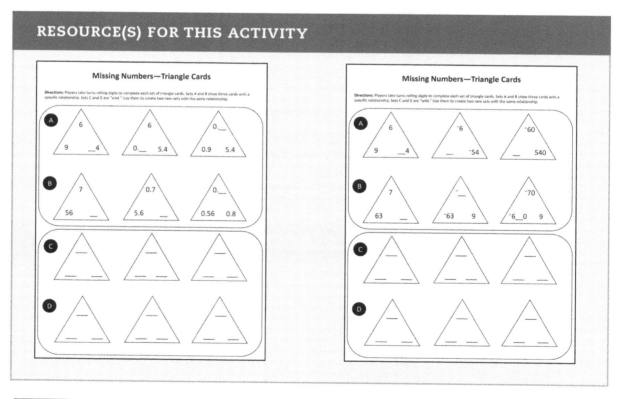

online resources: This resource can be downloaded at **resources.corwin.com/FOF/rationalnumbersalgequations**.

STRATEGY OVERVIEW:
Partial Quotients

What Is Partial Quotients? Partial Quotients is a division strategy in which the dividend is broken apart into convenient parts. While the standard algorithm is also partial products, as a strategy, the partials that are selected are flexible and thus require reasoning. For example, here are three ways to solve $25.2 \div 4$:

$6.3 \times 4 = 25.2$ $6.3 \times 4 = 25.2$ $6.3 \times 4 = 25.2$

HOW DOES PARTIAL QUOTIENTS WORK?

The Partial Quotients strategy is the distributive property in action. The dividend is broken apart; those parts are divided separately; then the quotients of those parts, or partial quotients, are added together. There are at least three ways to represent partial quotients:

REPEATED SUBTRACTION	DECOMPOSING THE DIVIDEND: EQUATIONS	DECOMPOSING THE DIVIDEND: FRACTION BAR	
	$280 \div 14 = 20$ $28 \div 14 = \dfrac{2}{22}$	$280 \div 14 = 20$ $28 \div 14 = \dfrac{2}{22}$	$\dfrac{280 + 28}{14}$ $\dfrac{280}{14} + \dfrac{28}{14}$ $20 + 2 = 22$

The subtract-in-parts thinking process:

1. Select a known product (the divisor times your choice of factor) that will be less than the dividend.
2. Subtract that product from the dividend.
3. Continue selecting products less than what remains of the dividend until the remaining part is smaller than your divisor.
4. Add together your partial quotients.
5. Find the total number of groups taken away.

The decomposing-the-dividend thinking process:

1. Decide how to decompose the dividend into numbers that are easy to divide by your divisor.
2. Record each of those parts separately (as their own equations or as a fraction).
3. Divide each part.
4. Add the partial quotients.

Here are some examples of the partial quotient thinking. Remember that with negative numbers there is the added step of determining the sign of your answer.

Whole Numbers	Fractions	Decimals
$840 \div 35$	$6\frac{1}{2} \div 4$	$26.4 \div 0.6$
$840 \div 35$	$6\frac{1}{2} \div 4$	$26.4 \div 0.6$
$350 \div 35 = 10$	$6 \div 4 = 1\frac{1}{2}$	$\dfrac{26.4}{0.6} \times \dfrac{10}{10} = \dfrac{264}{6}$
$350 \div 35 = 10$	$\frac{1}{2} \div 4 = \frac{1}{8}$	
$140 \div 35 = \dfrac{4}{}$	$1\frac{4}{8} + \frac{1}{8} = 1\frac{5}{8}$	$\dfrac{240 + 24}{6}$
24		$40 + 4 = 44$

WHEN DO YOU CHOOSE PARTIAL QUOTIENTS?

With integers (including whole numbers) and decimals, Partial Quotients always works and is a good choice when Think Multiplication isn't a viable strategy and/or when students are struggling with the standard algorithm. For fractions, Partial Quotients is a good option when dividing by unit fractions (e.g., $8\frac{3}{8} \div \frac{1}{4}$) or by whole numbers (see above).

NOTES

_____

_____

_____

_____

_____

_____

_____

_____

_____

TEACHING ACTIVITIES for Partial Quotients

Partial Quotients strategy has often been taught as an algorithm, giving students a set series of steps to follow. However, it can and should be taught as a reasoning strategy. This distinction as a strategy means there is decision-making involved, such as "Do you want to subtract off partial quotients or decompose the dividend?" If subtracting off partial quotients, "What multiples do you know that will be useful and efficient for this problem?" If decomposing the dividend, "What numbers are good options for the divisor in the problem?" A key to the Partial Quotients strategy is being able to choose partial quotients well, so that there are not too many partials. These considerations and others are the focus of these teaching activities.

 ## ACTIVITY 4.6
ARE THEY THE SAME?

While some partials are more efficient than others, it is important for students to recognize that there are different approaches. Comparing different approaches helps to develop this idea. In this activity, students compare different ways partial quotients were used to find a quotient.

To begin, present three different approaches to partial quotients for the same problem. You might use these examples for 43.8 ÷ 0.6.

Have students discuss how they are the same, how they are different, and which of the three is most like the approach they would take.

0.6 ⟌ 43.8 − 6.0 10 × 0.6 37.8 − 6.0 10 × 0.6 31.8 −30.0 50 × 0.6 1.8 − 0.6 1 × 0.6 1.2 − 1.2 2 × 0.6 0 10 + 10 + 50 + 1 + 2 = 73 43.8 ÷ 0.6 = 73	0.6 ⟌ 43.8 −42.0 70 × 0.6 1.8 − 1.8 3 × 0.6 0 70 + 3 = 73 43.8 ÷ 0.6 = 73	0.6 ⟌ 43.8 − 0.6 1 × 0.6 43.2 − 0.6 1 × 0.6 42.6 − 0.6 1 × 0.6 42.0 − 6.0 10 × 0.6 36.0 −36 60 × 6 0 1 + 1 + 1 + 10 + 60 = 73 43.8 ÷ 0.6 = 73

Next, have students use partial quotients to solve the problem however they like. Then, have the class do a Gallery Walk or compare their approaches in another way. As students examine or discuss others' work, focus attention on which ones are efficient, as well as how the different ways are similar and different.

TEACHING TAKEAWAY

You can promote flexibility by preparing two or more examples using a strategy differently and comparing them.

ACTIVITY 4.7
AREAS AND LISTS

This activity helps students see how Partial Quotients can be found using area models or listing partials beside the division problem. Pose a division problem with or without context. The example here shows 984 ÷ 8.

	100	20	3
8	100 × 8 800 984−800=184	20 × 8 160 184−160=24	3 × 8 24

$$8 \times 123 = 984$$
$$984 \div 8 = 123 \rightarrow 984 \div {}^-8 = {}^-123$$

```
  8 ) 984
    - 800      100 × 8
      184
    - 160      20 × 8
       24
     - 24       3 × 8
        0
                123 × 8
```

$$123 \times 8 = 984$$
so $984 \div 8 = 123$
and $984 \div {}^-8 = {}^-123$

Divide your class in half, charging one half to solve the problem using an area model and the other to keeping a running list. Have each group work separately and come to a consensus about their strategy and recording. Then, pair students from opposite groups to share and compare their strategies. Have students return to their original groups to solve a new problem, this time using the other strategy. Pair the same students to again share and compare.

TEACHING TAKEAWAY

Skill with using the Partial Quotient strategy comes about through flexible decomposition and familiarity with factors and multiples. See Part I, page 18, for a list of activities to develop these skills.

PRACTICE ACTIVITIES for Partial Quotients

See Part 1, page 20, for an overview about quality practice.

ACTIVITY 4.8

WORKED EXAMPLES FOR PARTIAL QUOTIENTS

About Worked Examples: Correctly worked examples, partially worked examples, and incorrectly worked examples each serve different purposes, as illustrated in this table.

SAMPLE WORKED EXAMPLES FOR PARTIAL QUOTIENTS FOR FRACTIONS, DECIMALS, AND INTEGERS
Correctly Worked Example (Make Sense of the Strategy)
What did _____ do? Why does it work? Is this a good method for this problem?

Neil's work for $6\frac{1}{3} \div \frac{1}{6}$	André's work for $372 \div {}^-6$
$6\frac{1}{3} \div \frac{1}{6}$ $6 \div \frac{1}{6} = \boxed{36}$ $\frac{1}{3} \div \frac{1}{6} = \boxed{2}$ 38	$\begin{array}{r} 6\overline{)372} \\ -300 \\ \hline 72 \\ -60 \\ \hline 12 \\ -12 \\ \hline 0 \end{array}$ $\begin{array}{l} 50 \times 6 \\ \\ 10 \times 6 \\ \\ 2 \times 6 \\ \hline 62 \end{array}$ $\begin{array}{l} 6\ 2 \times 6 = 372 \\ 372 \div {}^-6 = {}^-62 \end{array}$

Partially Worked Example (Implement Strategy Accurately)
Why did _____ start the problem this way?
What does _____ need to do to finish the problem?

Dee's work with $^-917 \div {}^-7$	Stan's start for $9.6 \div 8 =$
$\begin{array}{r} {}^-7\overline{){}^-917} \\ -700 \end{array}$ 100×7 $\overline{217}$	$8 \div 8 + 1.6 \div 8$

Incorrectly Worked Example (Highlight Common Errors)
What did _____ do? What mistake does _____ make? How can this mistake be fixed?

Cassie's work for $3\frac{1}{6} \div \frac{1}{3}$	Mia's work for $43.5 \div 6$
$3\frac{1}{6} \div \frac{1}{3} = ?$ $3 \div \frac{1}{3} = \boxed{9}$ $\frac{1}{6} \div \frac{1}{3} = \boxed{2}$ 11	$\begin{array}{r} 6\overline{)43.5} \\ -42 \\ \hline 1.5 \\ -1.2 \\ \hline 0.3 \end{array}$ $\begin{array}{l} 7 \\ \\ 0.2 \\ \hline 7.2 \text{ R } 0.3 \end{array}$

ACTIVITY 4.9

Name: "Breaking Dividends"   **Type:** Routine

About the Routine: This routine explicitly focuses on decomposing the dividend to find friendly computations that make use of the inverse relationship. Using the inverse is efficient for problems that are composites of multiples. That is, $^-72 \div 6$ can be solved by thinking about 72 and that it is composed of multiples of 6 such as 60 + 12 or 30 + 42.

Materials: Prepare a few problems for students to consider.

Directions:

1. Post or state a divisor to students (e.g., 4).

2. Have students identify multiples of the divisor.

3. Pose the division problem and have partners discuss how they might decompose the dividend into multiples of the divisor to take advantage of the Think Multiplication strategy.

For example, a teacher first asks students to think about multiples of 4 and record their ideas. Then, she poses $56 \div 4$, asking students how they might break apart 56 into multiples of 56. Some may offer that 56 can be thought of as 40 and 16, so they can think of it as $40 \div 4 + 16 \div 4$. Others might say that they see 56 as 28 and 28, so they can think of it as $28 \div 7 + 28 \div 7$. Then, the teacher asks students how they might use their ideas about breaking apart for $132 \div 4$ and then $96 \div 4$. Here are some other examples to use in this routine:

- $84 \div 7$ followed by problems like $91 \div 7$, $98 \div 7$, $105 \div 7$, or $112 \div 7$

- $57 \div 3$ followed by problems like $51 \div 3$, $57 \div 3$, $66 \div 3$, or $72 \div 3$

- $70 \div 5$ followed by $75 \div 5$, $80 \div 5$, $95 \div 5$, $110 \div 5$, or $115 \div 5$

- $90 \div 6$ followed by $96 \div 6$, $102 \div 6$, $126 \div 6$, or $132 \div 6$

You can also help students transfer this strategy from thinking about whole numbers to working with decimals or integers. To do this, first pose a whole-number set like those in the first bullet.

START WITH: $84 \div 7$ followed by problems like $91 \div 7$, $98 \div 7$, $105 \div 7$, or $112 \div 7$

(Decimals) CONTINUE WITH: $8.4 \div 7$, $9.1 \div 7$, $9.8 \div 7$, $10.5 \div 7$, or $11.2 \div 7$

(Integers) CONTINUE WITH: $^-84 \div 7$, $^-91 \div 7$, $98 \div ^-7$, $105 \div ^-7$, or $^-112 \div ^-7$

Creating expressions for students to work with may seem challenging. Here is one way to generate problems: First, think of a divisor (like 4 in the example). Then, think of a dividend that is composed of 10 times the divisor (40) and a multiple of the divisor more (16). As students progress, begin to use dividends that use multiples of 10 times the divisor (e.g., 120).

> **TEACHING TAKEAWAY**
>
> To scaffold strategy instruction, first pose whole-number problems; then continue to examples involving more difficult numbers, like decimals or integers.

ACTIVITY 4.10

Name: "Could It Be???" **Type:** Routine

About the Routine: Determining if a solution is reasonable and/or accurate plays a significant role in students' fluency. This skill may be most elusive when dividing numbers. A unique feature of this routine is that students don't have to find a quotient. Instead, a problem has been completed and students have to determine if the solution is reasonable. This approach simulates what we want students to do as they work problems.

Materials: Prepare three to five completed division problems that include correct answers, incorrect but reasonable (close) answers, and incorrect and not reasonable answers.

Directions:
1. Pose a completed problem by showing the problem first and then asking, "Could the Answer Be . . ." (and fill in the answer).

2. Have students think about whether or not the answer is reasonable (without solving it).

3. Ask students to share their thoughts with a partner.

4. Bring the whole group together to share their decision and rationale. Allow students to debate if they disagree (which can happen with reasonable but incorrect answers).

5. Repeat the process for the other problems in the set, as time allows.

6. *Optional:* Solve the reasonable problems to see if they are, in fact, correct.

"COULD IT BE?"				
$4.36 \div 6 = 1.06$	$6.76 \div 6 = 1.21$	$34.8 \div 6 = 5.8$	$9.45 \div 0.9 = 9.6$	$4.85 \div 4.5 = 1.1$

In this example, students first talk about $4.36 \div 6 = 1.06$. The quotient is not reasonable. Students might say so because $1 \times 6 = 6$, which is already too big (Think Multiplication reasoning), or note that 4 divided by 6 will be less than 1 (Partial Quotients reasoning). Listen for students who rely on the rules of moving decimal points without understanding. Help students connect those rules to why they work.

WHOLE-NUMBER EXAMPLES	FRACTION EXAMPLES	INTEGER EXAMPLES
• $560 \div 12 = 50$	• $4\frac{1}{6} \div \frac{1}{2} = 8\frac{1}{3}$	• $^-139 \div 13 = {}^-13$
• $426 \div 60 = 71$	• $36 \div 4\frac{1}{4} = 8\frac{1}{4}$	• $^-72 \div {}^-4 = 18$
• $1{,}680 \div 84 = 20$	• $8\frac{1}{3} \div 2\frac{2}{3} = 3$	• $156 \div {}^-24 = {}^-6$

ACTIVITY 4.11

Name: Quotient Connect   **Type:** Game

About the Game: This game is an engaging way to practice division using Partial Quotients. It is played similarly to the classic board game *Boggle* as students find quotients through connected digits.

Materials: *Quotient Connect* game board; digit cards (0–9), playing cards (queens = 0, aces = 1; remove 10s, kings, and jacks), or division cards; paper for recording work

Directions:
1. Players make a game board by randomly placing digits in each grid, as shown in the example.

2. Players use digit cards to make a division problem. As an alternative, you can provide cards with division problems on them.

3. Both players solve the division problem.

4. Players look for the quotient on the game board they made by finding adjacent digits (similar to the classic board game *Boggle*).

5. Players get 1 point for each example they find. The first player to reach a set goal (e.g., 10 points) or the most points after five problems wins.

For example, two players made the problem ⁻273 ÷ ⁻13. They both found the quotient to be 21. Player 1 found 21 in two places, earning 2 points, as shown. Player 2 found 21 in three places, earning 3 points. Note that when using integers, negative quotients can still be used. The 21s found by these students could be thought of as "⁻21s."

RESOURCE(S) FOR THIS ACTIVITY

⁻273 ÷ ⁻13

Quotient Connect Game Boards

Problem:	Problem:

Quotient Connect
Fill in each square with numbers 1 through 9. You may repeat the numbers and place them in any order.

7	5	4	9	8
4	2	3	8	3
1	2	9	6	4
5	5	9	3	2
6	1	1	3	7

Quotient Connect
Fill in each square with numbers 1 through 9. You may repeat the numbers and place them in any order.

1	3	6	4	8
9	1	2	3	8
5	6	4	4	1
3	8	7	2	1
3	7	9	4	8

online resources | This resource can be downloaded at **resources.corwin.com/FOF/rationalnumbersalgequations**.

NOTES

_____

_____

_____

_____

_____

_____

_____

_____

_____

_____

_____

_____

_____

_____

_____

_____

_____

Reasoning Strategies for Ratios and Proportions

In this module, we highlight five significant strategies for ratios and proportions:

- Build Up/Break Down
- Find a Unit Rate
- Use a Scale Factor
- Use $y = kx$
- Find Cross Products

This module focuses on how each of these strategies works as well as when each is a good choice. In Part 3, we offer additional activities that focus on choosing among strategies. Before diving into the strategies themselves, it's important to understand some basics both about the strategies as well as how representations can be used. While representations (e.g., a ratio table or double number line) are not strategies, they are very useful in supporting proportional reasoning as we look through the lens of multiplicative comparison.

WHAT ARE GOOD REPRESENTATIONS FOR RATIOS AND PROPORTIONS?

Proportional reasoning is developmental. The sequence of representations we discuss here supports students' emerging proportional reasoning as they move from early reasoning strategies, to transitional strategies, and then to proportional strategies (Petit et al., 2020; Van de Walle et al., 2023).

VISUALS OR CONCRETE OBJECTS

Visuals and manipulatives are a good beginning, in part because they can help students make sense of and compare additive and multiplicative comparisons.

Problem 1: Which houses have the same ratio of dogs to dog bones?

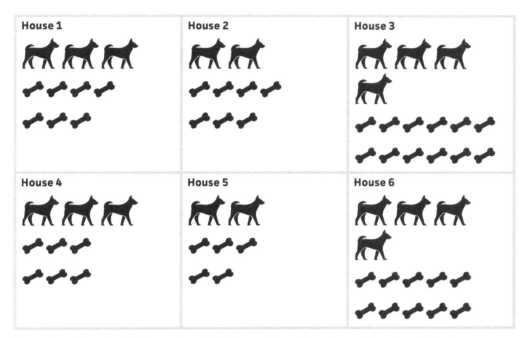

Source: dogs from Stock Illustrations/iStock.com; bones from Iryna Shancheva/iStock.com

The visuals may be drawings that represent the situation, as illustrated here. Or they may be manipulatives, such as colored tiles or Cuisenaire rods that allow for visual comparisons.

For the remaining representations, we will use the following context:

The Mayo Clinic offers this recommendation for weekly exercise (Laskowski, 2021):

Aerobic activity: Get at least 150 minutes of moderate aerobic activity or 75 minutes of vigorous aerobic activity a week, or a combination of moderate and vigorous activity.

Strength training: Exercise all major muscle groups at least two times a week. Aim to do a single set of each exercise using a weight to tire your muscles after about 12 to 15 repetitions.

RATIO TABLES

Ratio tables can be written in horizontal or vertical orientation. To use ratio tables for reasoning, each new pair of values is *up to the solver*. Too often, ratio tables are set up like t-charts in algebra, with the independent variable increasing by 1 each row (or column). That is inefficient. Students are learning to coordinate two values that covary. Thus, they should use convenient pairs to reach a solution.

Problem 2: Using the Mayo Clinic recommendations, a person choosing to exercise moderately will need to exercise how many minutes in eight weeks?

Student A:

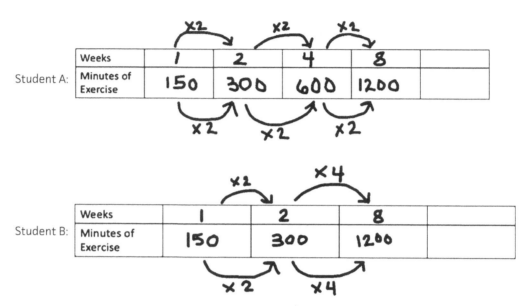

Weeks	1	2	4	8	
Minutes of Exercise	150	300	600	1200	

Student B:

Weeks	1	2	8	
Minutes of Exercise	150	300	1200	

TAPE DIAGRAMS
. . . .

Tape diagrams (sometimes called strip diagrams or bar models) are drawings that look like segments of tape. They are used to illustrate and iterate ratios. They are useful for part-to-part situations (e.g., part aerobic exercise and part rigorous). For example, the ratio of aerobic to strength is reflected in these bars:

Aerobic:

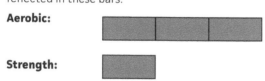

Strength:

Problem 3: Kris decides to have a 3-to-1 ratio of aerobic to strength training. Their goal is 120 minutes of exercise a week. How many minutes of each type of exercise will they need?

A student is not going to want to iterate this ratio from 1 to 120, so one idea is to assign 10 to each piece of tape:

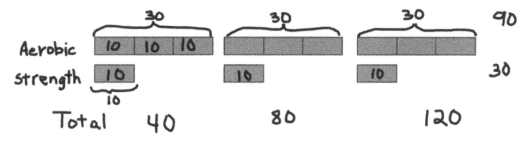

DOUBLE NUMBER LINES

Let's revisit Problems 2 and 3 using a double number line.

Problem 2:

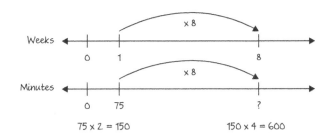

Problem 3:

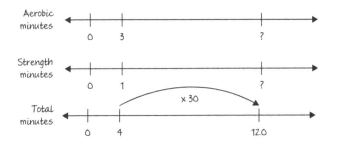

I multiply each part by 30. Aerobic minutes is 90 and strength minutes is 30.

STRATEGIES FOR COMPARING RATIOS AND SOLVING PROPORTIONS

Ratios can be thought of as a multiplicative comparison (e.g., there are twice as many chairs as tables) or as a coordinated unit (e.g., for every table there are two chairs) (Lobato et al., 2010). These two ways of thinking support ratio reasoning. Comparing ratios asks the questions, "Are these ratios equal?" and if not, "Which ratio has more (or less) [context]?" When solving for missing value proportions, the generalizable question is, "What value results in two equivalent ratios?"

Let's now explore the five reasoning strategies (Build Up/Break Down, Find a Unit Rate, Use a Scale Factor, Use $y = kx$, and Find Cross Products) for ratios and proportions, by using the following mixing context:

MIXING PAINT TO MAKE GREEN

Green paint can be made by mixing yellow and blue paint. Will these create the same shade of green? Which one(s) are the bluest?

Mix 1: 9 teaspoons of yellow to 6 teaspoons of blue
Mix 2: 15 teaspoons of yellow to 10 teaspoons of blue
Mix 3: 25 teaspoons of yellow to 15 teaspoons of blue

STRATEGY OVERVIEW:
Build Up/Break Down

WHAT IS THE BUILD UP/BREAK DOWN STRATEGY?

This strategy is an early ratio reasoning strategy. Students look at units in a ratio (e.g., 9 t. yellow to 6 t. blue) as a coordinated unit and use additive or multiplicative thinking to find more equivalent pairs.

HOW DOES BUILD UP/BREAK DOWN WORK?

By adding 9 t. of yellow and 6 t. of blue each time, it is like having the same recipe, just more paint. If you want less paint, you break down; in this case, that could be 3 t. yellow to 2 t. blue. Ratio tables and tape diagrams are commonly used to support thinking. This ratio table shows a student figuring out various equivalent recipes in order to find the one with 10 t. of yellow.

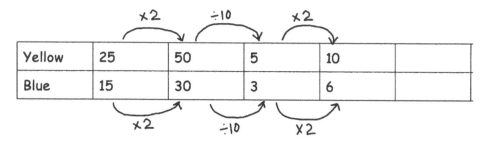

When comparing ratios, one option is to build up/break down to find a common numerator or denominator. To compare Mix 2 to Mix 3, one option is to find a common denominator (same blue), building up each ratio:

$$\textbf{Mix 2: } \frac{15}{10} = \frac{45}{30} \qquad \textbf{Mix 3: } \frac{25}{15} = \frac{50}{30}$$

Now that the mixes have the same amount of blue, the amount of yellow can be compared.

WHEN DO YOU CHOOSE BUILD UP/BREAK DOWN?

This strategy is the most intuitive and is a good initial strategy. It works well with simpler ratios (i.e., ratios that have a noticeable common factor). As numbers get messy, this strategy is not as efficient.

STRATEGY OVERVIEW:
Find a Unit Rate

What Is the Find a Unit Rate Strategy? A unit rate tells how much of one quantity is associated with 1 unit of the other quantity. In the case of the paint, you can find out how much yellow paint for one teaspoon of blue (or vice versa). The unit rates of yellow : blue for each mix are:

$$\textbf{Mix 1: } \frac{9}{6} = \frac{1.5}{1} \qquad \textbf{Mix 2: } \frac{15}{10} = \frac{1.5}{1} \qquad \textbf{Mix 3: } \frac{25}{15} = \frac{1.67}{1}$$

Once the unit rate is found, it can be used to find a missing value in another ratio (multiplying or dividing by the rate), or it can be used to compare ratios. In this case, Mix 1 and Mix 2 are equivalent because they have the same unit rate.

HOW DOES FIND A UNIT RATE WORK?

Find a Unit Rate leverages a partitive understanding of division to find how much of one quantity (e.g., yellow paint) is associated with 1 unit of the other quantity (e.g., blue paint). To solve for a missing value proportion, you find the unit rate for the ratio in which both values are known and apply it to the ratio with the missing value. For example, if you are using Mix 2 and want to know how much yellow paint is needed for 6 units of blue paint, you multiply by the unit rate (1.5).

WHEN DO YOU CHOOSE TO FIND A UNIT RATE?

If you are simply deciding if two ratios are equal or not, this method is efficient—simply divide both and see if they are the same or not. For missing values, this is often efficient (in fact, it uses similar steps to Find Cross Products, but in a different order).

STRATEGY OVERVIEW:
Use a Scale Factor

WHAT IS THE USE A SCALE FACTOR STRATEGY?

This strategy involves noticing a between or within relationship and using that to find a missing value. A ratio of two measures in the same situation is a *within* ratio. A *between* ratio is a ratio of two corresponding measures in different situations:

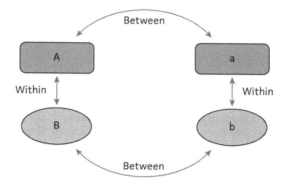

Source: Van de Walle, J. A., Karp, K. S., & Bay-Williams, J. M. (2023). *Elementary and middle school mathematics: Teaching developmentally* (11th ed.). Pearson.

In the paint example, the *A*s represent yellow paint units and *B*s represent the blue paint.

HOW DOES USE A SCALE FACTOR WORK?

This strategy is based on the fact that when two ratios are equal, the *between* and *within* ratios are also equal. Using the strategy involves looking for an obvious multiple within the fraction or between the fractions. If so, look to see if the same relationship holds in the other case. For example, compare the fractions for Mix 1 and Mix 2:

$$\frac{9}{6} \text{ and } \frac{15}{10}$$

You might notice that the *within* ratio from the denominator (blue) to the numerator (yellow) is times × 1.5:

$$\times 1.5 \left(\frac{9}{6} \text{ and } \frac{15}{10} \right) \times 1.5$$

For missing value proportions, you find one scale factor and use it to find the missing value. For example, for the paint problem, imagine you wanted to use Mix 3, but only have 3 teaspoons of blue paint. The missing value proportion looks like this:

$$\frac{25}{15} = \frac{x}{3}$$

Notice that there is a *between* ratio of ÷ 5; apply this to the numerator and we find $x = 5$.

WHEN DO YOU CHOOSE TO USE A SCALE FACTOR?

Many times, there is a whole-number multiple either between or within the fractions, which allows for mentally comparing or finding a missing value. Therefore, this is a good option every time a within or *between* ratio can be identified.

STRATEGY OVERVIEW:
Use $y = kx$

What Is the Use y = kx Strategy? While an equation is a representation, it is also a way to reason about a missing value proportion. Thus, we include it on the strategy list. This strategy extends the idea of unit rates to finding *any* missing value for a ratio using the multiplicative relationship between the values (k).

HOW DOES USE $Y = KX$ WORK?

To use this strategy, you determine the unit rate, or the constant of proportionality (k), and write an equation: **y = kx**. For example, in Mix A, the unit rate is 1.5 because there are 1.5 teaspoons of yellow for 1 teaspoon of blue. Thus, for any recipe in the same ratio, you use the formula $y = 1.5x$, where x is the amount of blue paint and y is the amount of yellow paint. The equation allows you to easily determine the amount of one color of paint, given any amount of the other color.

WHEN DO YOU CHOOSE TO USE $Y = KX$?

This strategy is always useful. But the beauty in it is when you need to determine a number of values. For example, with the paint, if you are making up various batches of different sizes, it is worthwhile to use an equation.

ALGORITHM OVERVIEW:
Find Cross Products

What Is the Find Cross Products Algorithm? This method is not a strategy but an algorithm because it consists of a set of established steps.

For comparing ratios, this algorithm involves multiplying across the diagonals and comparing to see if the products are the same or not.

Comparing Mix 1 to Mix 2:

$$\overset{90}{9} \underset{6}{\diagup\kern-1.2em\diagdown} \overset{90}{\underset{10}{15}}$$

Comparing Mix 2 to Mix 3:

$$\overset{225}{15} \underset{10}{\diagup\kern-1.2em\diagdown} \overset{250}{\underset{15}{25}}$$

Here we see that Mix 1 and Mix 2 have the same cross product, so the ratios are equal. Mix 2 and Mix 3 have different cross products, so those ratios are not equal.

To find an equivalent ratio to Mix 2: $\frac{15}{10} = \frac{40}{b}$

The cross product results in $15b = 400$, which means $b = 26\frac{2}{3}$

HOW DOES FIND CROSS PRODUCTS WORK?

This strategy grows from multiplying by one whole. In essence, a common denominator is found:

$$\frac{10}{10} \times \frac{9}{6} = \frac{15}{10} \times \frac{6}{6}$$

$$\frac{10 \times 9}{60} = \frac{15 \times 6}{60}$$

Once a common denominator is found, then the focus is on the numerators. In other words, if you multiply both sides by 60, you are left with 10 × 9 = 15 × 6. If one of those values is unknown, you then have a linear equation to solve.

WHEN DO YOU CHOOSE TO FIND CROSS PRODUCTS?

As with many algorithms, it always works but requires more steps than reasoning strategies. Thus, the time to use this method is after recognizing that there isn't an obvious scale factor or other way to reason to solve the problem.

NOTES

_____

_____

_____

_____

_____

_____

_____

_____

_____

TEACHING ACTIVITIES for Ratios and Proportions

A key to fluently knowing when to choose a strategy is being able to fully use and understand it. Too often, students are only taught Find Cross Products, which is the least intuitive of the options for comparing ratios. Exploring each of the strategies strengthens students' skills at multiplicative comparisons. Furthermore, each of the strategies is sometimes the most efficient method. Thus, the activities in this section focus on making sense of these strategies and exploring when to use them, developing students' flexibility and efficiency with ratios and proportions.

ACTIVITY 5.1
COMPARING RATIOS IN CONTEXT

A good way to begin reasoning about ratios is to determine if two or more ratios are the same or different. For example, pose any or all of these prompts:

Problem A: Which of these mixtures lead to the same shade of green icing?

FOOD COLORING RECIPES FOR GREEN ICING	
Mix 1:	**Mix 2:**
Yellow: 5 drops	Yellow: 9 drops
Blue: 2 drops	Blue: 6 drops
Mix 3:	**Mix 4:**
Yellow: 15 drops	Yellow: 25 drops
Blue: 10 drops	Blue: 15 drops

Problem B: Do these macaroni and cheese recipes have the same ratio of cheese to milk?

Easy mac and cheese

8 oz pasta

$\frac{1}{3}$ cup butter

$1\frac{1}{2}$ cups of cheddar cheese

2 cups of milk

salt and pepper

Best mac and cheese

12 oz pasta

$\frac{1}{2}$ cup butter

2 cups cheddar cheese

$2\frac{1}{2}$ cups of milk

salt and pepper

Problem C: Which of these options is the better deal if you need 60 oz of chili for the recipe?

Costs of Cans of Chili

10 oz for $1.50   **15 oz for $2.25**   **20 oz for $3.00**

ACTIVITY 5.2
MISSING VALUES IN CONTEXT

This activity builds on the comparing ratio tasks in Activity 5.1, using the same contexts but solving missing value proportion tasks. For example, you can pair Problem A from Activity 5.1 with Problem A below. Or you can simply begin here and explore these tasks (using the information in Activity 5.1). For any or all of these, they can be used to help students learn to use a representation or a strategy. For example, you can have students solve using tape diagrams. Or you can use these tasks to have students choose from among their strategies, asking them to use one of the strategies in a menu of options.

Problem A: Select your favorite food coloring recipe (see page 117). How many drops of yellow food coloring will you need for a recipe using 60 drops of blue food coloring?

Problem B: Select a mac and cheese recipe and determine the amount of milk and cheese needed for 24 oz of noodles.

Problem C: What is the most chili you can buy with $18?

Once students have solved the problem, ask:

- How do you know the recipes (or values) are equivalent?

- What connections do you see across problems?

- What connections do you see across strategies?

- Which strategy makes the most sense to you and why?

ACTIVITY 5.3
PROPORTIONAL PRICING

Finding equivalent ratios for more than one missing value provides a context that lends to using a Build Up/Break Down strategy or using $y = mx$. In this exploration, the situation is that the company wants to have each size option be the same value. Students select a strategy to figure out what to charge for each bag.

Problem: If the prices are proportional to the amount of dog food in the bag, what is the price of Bags 1, 2, and 4?

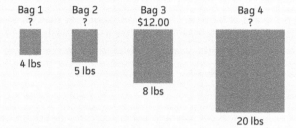

Ask students to conclude their work by explaining to the pet store how they can decide on a price for any sized bag.

Have students prepare an explanation on a vertical board (flip chart paper or white board) at various places around the room. Then, have students rotate to the various stations and discuss what they notice about the strategy used. As appropriate, name the strategies so that students can discuss and compare strategies.

ACTIVITY 5.4
PLANNING FOR PIZZA

Story situations help students to create visuals and to reason with numbers. This activity is designed to elicit more than one reasoning strategy and then compare those strategies. This activity extends the thinking in Activity 5.1 because students now must not only figure out whether the two options are equal, but then determine which one results in more (or less) pizza per person. The numbers in the ratios are small enough that several strategies are efficient. Tell a story like this one (adapted to your school setting):

The marching band is ordering pizza at band camp. The director suggests that for every 8 band members, they will order 3 medium pizzas. The assistant director suggests that they order 4 medium pizzas for every 10 band members. The directors decide to leave it to the students, asking each student to stand with the director whose plan they like the best.

Ask students which director's option they would pick and why.

Notice that this task has no right answer—it is not asking which option provides them the most pizza, though this could be a justification for picking one option. Also, notice that the ratios are written into the story in a different order. This is so that students attend to the units as they set up their ratios. Ask students to compare each option, using any strategy.

Here are two different student solutions:

Find a Unit Rate Strategy	Build Up/Break Down Strategy
(How much pizza for one person?)	(If the number of pizzas is the same, which option is better?)
D: $3 \div 8 = 0.375$ AD: $4 \div 10 = 0.4$	$\dfrac{3}{8} \times \dfrac{2}{2} = \dfrac{6}{16}$ $\dfrac{4}{10} = \dfrac{2}{5} \times \dfrac{3}{3} = \dfrac{6}{15}$

Students might respond that they like the director's option because they don't eat as much, or the assistant director's option because it is more pizza. Or, they may say, these two options are so similar it doesn't matter. The key to the explanations is that they are interpreting their strategy. For example, for the Build Up/Break Down strategy, the student might explain that for the same amount of pizza (6) the first option has more eaters (16), so less pizza for each.

To extend or adapt this context to solving missing value proportions, pose the following task:

> *Problem:* There are 40 band members and 20 of them want cheese pizza, 12 of them want pepperoni pizza, and 8 want sausage pizza. If they are going to order 15 pizzas, how many of each should they order?

Ask students to select a strategy to solve the problem (in small groups). As an option, ask groups to use at least two different strategies to solve the problem. Then, justify which strategy they would choose to use if solving a problem like this in the future.

Examples of reasoning strategies:

Break Down Strategy						
	people	40	20	8	4	12
	pizza	15	(7.5)	(3)	1.5	(4.5)

Use a Scale Factor Strategy

$$\div2\left(\frac{40}{20} = \frac{15}{7.5}\right)\div2 \qquad \div5\left(\frac{40}{8} = \frac{15}{3}\right)\div5 \qquad \frac{40}{12} = \frac{10}{3} = \frac{15}{4.5}$$

$\times1.5$ ... $\times1.5$

Find a Unit Rate Strategy

$$\frac{15 \text{ pizzas}}{40 \text{ people}} = \frac{3}{8} \text{ pizza per person} \rightarrow \frac{5}{20} \times \frac{3}{8}_2 = \frac{15}{2} = (7.5) \quad \frac{3}{12} \times \frac{3}{8}_2 = \frac{9}{2} = (4.5) \quad 8 \times \frac{3}{8} = (3)$$

ACTIVITY 5.5
B-W (B-DUBS) OR GO SOMEWHERE ELSE?

When there is an obvious scale factor to compare ratios or solve a missing value proportion, then other strategies are not needed. In this activity, students first label (or cut out and sort) the problems for which they will use a *between* (B) or *within* (W) ratio to solve, or if they will go to another option. After labeling or sorting, students then compare the ratios or solve for the missing value. Afterward, discuss problems for which many students labeled/sorted a problem into the same group (e.g., Why did you put $\frac{5}{2}$ and $\frac{14}{6}$ in the B-Dubs pile?). Then, discuss cards for which students made different decisions. To do this activity with missing value proportions, replace examples with a missing value. You can have students sort two ways:

1. Two Piles: Use a Scale Factor or Use Another Strategy

2. Three Piles: Use *Between Ratio*, Use *Within Ratio*, or Use Another Strategy

RESOURCE(S) FOR THIS ACTIVITY

COMPARING RATIO CARDS

$\frac{15}{20}$ and $\frac{3}{4}$	$\frac{5}{20}$ and $\frac{9}{36}$
$\frac{9}{15}$ and $\frac{8}{18}$	$\frac{7}{5}$ and $\frac{15}{10}$
$\frac{25}{20}$ and $\frac{5}{4}$	$\frac{8}{10}$ and $\frac{24}{32}$
$\frac{21}{7}$ and $\frac{15}{5}$	$\frac{3}{2}$ and $\frac{9}{5}$

FIND THE MISSING VALUE CARDS

$\frac{15}{20} = \frac{3}{a}$	$\frac{b}{20} = \frac{9}{36}$
$\frac{36}{c} = \frac{42}{7}$	$\frac{24}{2} = \frac{48}{d}$
$\frac{e}{18} = \frac{14}{21}$	$\frac{9}{15} = \frac{f}{18}$
$\frac{g}{5} = \frac{15}{10}$	$\frac{8}{h} = \frac{9}{27}$

These resources can be downloaded at **resources.corwin.com/FOF/rationalnumbersalgequations**.

ACTIVITY 5.6
PROMPTS FOR TEACHING COMPARING RATIOS AND MISSING VALUE PROPORTIONS

Use the following prompts as opportunities to develop understanding of reasoning strategies. These prompts can be used for class discussions and/or for collecting evidence of student understanding. These prompts are just a beginning; each prompt can be modified to feature different numbers or adapted in various ways (e.g., changing from comparing ratios to solving for a missing value proportion).

- How can you use *between* or *within* ratios to compare $\frac{6}{18}$ and $\frac{15}{45}$? $\frac{6}{16}$ and $\frac{15}{40}$?

- How can you use *between* or *within* ratios to find the missing value for $\frac{10}{15} = \frac{x}{45}$?

- Alyssa says that any time a ratio can be simplified (e.g., $\frac{15}{45}$ simplifies to $\frac{1}{3}$), this is a good first step for comparing (or finding a missing value). Do you agree or disagree? Explain.

- Explain why the cross products algorithm works. Use an example in your explanation.

- When would you use the $y = mx$ strategy?

- For which pairs of ratios is the Find a Unit Rate strategy an efficient option? For which pairs is it not an efficient option? Explain.

$\frac{34}{10}$ and $\frac{15}{4}$	$\frac{15}{9}$ and $\frac{5}{3}$	$\frac{5}{2}$ and $\frac{9}{4}$	$\frac{14}{5}$ and $\frac{25}{8}$

- Solve this proportion using two different strategies. Afterward, explain which method is more efficient: $\frac{12}{5} = \frac{42}{x}$

- How is the equation $y = \frac{3}{4}x$ useful in determining ratios equivalent to 3:4? How is it useful if you are given a value for y and need to find an equivalent ratio?

PRACTICE ACTIVITIES for Ratios and Proportions

As described in Part I (see page 20), fluency develops through quality practice that is *focused*, *varied*, *processed*, and *connected*. This table offers fluency look-fors as students are engaged in quality practice in using proportional reasoning strategies.

FLUENCY COMPONENT	WHAT TO LOOK FOR AS STUDENTS PRACTICE USING STRATEGIES TO COMPARE RATIOS AND SOLVE MISSING VALUE PROPORTIONS
Efficiency	• Do students choose a strategy that is a good fit for the problem? • Are students using their selected strategy efficiently (not getting bogged down in enacting the strategy)?
Flexibility	• Are students carrying out the strategies in flexible ways (e.g., for Use a Scale Factor strategy, focusing on numerators sometimes and denominators other times)? • Do students change their approach to or from a strategy as it proves inappropriate or overly complicated for the problem?
Accuracy	• Are students implementing the strategy accurately? (Are they using same-sized bars for creating visual comparisons?) • Are students finding accurate solutions? • Are students considering the reasonableness of their solutions?

ACTIVITY 5.7
WORKED EXAMPLES FOR RATIOS AND PROPORTIONS

As described in Part 1, correctly worked examples and partially solved worked examples help students make sense of a strategy, while incorrectly worked examples help students notice and avoid common errors. Common errors and challenges include:

- Using additive reasoning when the situation requires multiplicative reasoning. For example, when comparing $6 for 10 pens or $8 for 12 pens, thinking the ratios are the same because of the common difference (Canada et al., 2008; Dougherty et al., 2016).

- Understanding the whole in a part-to-part ratio. For example, if the ratio is 4 parts sugar to 1 part water, understanding that the whole is 5 parts (I, Martinez, & Dougherty, 2018).

- Not attending to covariation. For example, in looking at a ratio table, students may only look at the pattern from one column (or row) to the next without thinking about how two quantities vary together (Carlson, Jacobs, Coe, Larsen, & Hsu, 2002; Dougherty et al., 2016).

(Continued)

(Continued)

Questions to support student thinking for each type include:

CORRECTLY WORKED EXAMPLES	PARTIALLY WORKED EXAMPLES	INCORRECTLY WORKED EXAMPLES
What did _____ do? Why does it work? Is this a good method for this problem?	Why did _____ start the problem this way? What does _____ need to do to finish the problem?	What did _____ do? What mistake does _____ make? How can this mistake be fixed?

Worked examples are found throughout this module. A sampling of additional ideas is provided in the following table.

WORKED EXAMPLES		
TYPE OF EXAMPLE	**COMPARING RATIOS EXAMPLES**	**MISSING VALUE PROPORTIONS EXAMPLES**
Correctly Worked Example	Analesia is comparing these two recipes to see which option is more chocolatey: 2 cups milk 3 cups milk 3 tablespoons chocolate 5 tablespoons chocolate $\boxed{m}\ \boxed{m}\ \boxed{c}\ \boxed{c}\ \boxed{c}$ $\boxed{m}\boxed{m}\boxed{m}\boxed{c}\boxed{c}\boxed{c}\boxed{c}\boxed{c}$ The second option is more chocolatey	$\frac{18}{16} = \frac{27}{n}$ Ben solution: $$\frac{18}{16} = \frac{27}{n}$$ $$\frac{9}{8} \xrightarrow{\times 3} \frac{27}{n}$$ $$\xrightarrow{\times 3}$$ $$n = 24$$
Partially Worked Example	Jaena is working to figure out which is the better deal, 8 markers for $1.50 or 12 markers for $2.00: $$\frac{8 \xrightarrow{\times 3} 24}{1.5 \quad 4.50}$$ $$\xrightarrow{\times 3}$$	*Problem:* Kiwi are on sale, 5 for $2.00. What is the cost to buy 12 kiwi? Sam sets up an equation: $$y = \frac{5}{2}x$$
Incorrectly Worked Example	Patrick was comparing these prices, $6 for 10 pens or $8 for 12: Both prices are the same. For both you get 4 more pens than the cost.	*Problem:* In a classic cake recipe, the ratio of eggs to flour is 4:3. With $4\frac{1}{2}$ cups of flour, how many eggs are needed? $$\frac{4}{3} = \frac{4.5}{x}$$ $$4x = 13.5$$ $$x = 3.375$$

ACTIVITY 5.8

Name: "A String of Equal Ratios"   **Type:** Routine

About the Routine: This routine was shared in other *Figuring Out Fluency* books as a String of Halves. It is now extended to focus on generating equivalent ratios. Being able to flexibly use the between and within relationships to generate new equal ratios will help students to efficiently compare ratios and find missing values in proportions.

Materials: Prepare a series of fractions with either numerators or denominators that are intentionally related (see examples below).

Directions:

1. Post a set of four ratios with all of the numerators (or denominators) and just one of the denominators (or numerators) provided. See Set A below.

2. Provide individual think time for students to mentally find the missing values for each ratio.

3. If students are unable to find all of the missing values, pair students to discuss strategies.

4. Ask one student to share how they figured out the missing numbers. Ask other students to share their reasoning, if different. Once the values are filled in for A, ask students what multiplicative relationships they notice in the string.

5. Repeat for new strings.

A	$\dfrac{5}{}$	$\dfrac{10}{}$	$\dfrac{15}{6}$	$\dfrac{30}{}$	**C**	$\dfrac{10}{48}$	$\dfrac{}{12}$	$\dfrac{}{24}$	$\dfrac{}{36}$
B	$\dfrac{}{8}$	$\dfrac{9}{12}$	$\dfrac{}{16}$	$\dfrac{}{20}$	**D**	$\dfrac{10}{3.25}$	$\dfrac{20}{}$	$\dfrac{40}{}$	$\dfrac{50}{}$

ACTIVITY 5.9

Name: "Or You Could . . .?" **Type:** Routine

About the Routine: This routine helps students think about all their options for comparing ratios. It begins with the teacher saying something one way, and then students are charged to think of another way. If a strategy is being overused by students, it is a good one for the start of the sentence.

Materials: Prepare problems to pose.

Directions: 1. Pose a problem to students, using one of the following sentence frames.

> To compare _____ and _____ you could _____ or you could . . .
>   Ratio   Ratio   One Strategy

> To solve _____ you could _____ or you could . . .
>   Problem   One Way

2. Provide time for students to individually think of other options.

3. Pair students to talk about options.

4. Have partners pick one of their ideas and use it to compare the ratios.

5. As a class, discuss how *you could* solve the problem.

6. Summarize the discussion about how *they would* solve the problem (i.e., which methods are efficient, which ones make sense, etc.).

For example, the teacher says, "You can compare $\frac{20}{14}$ and $\frac{50}{35}$ by finding a common denominator, *or you could* . . .". In this case, students might suggest finding unit rates or cross products. For missing values, the teacher says, "To solve $\frac{15}{20} = \frac{a}{16}$, you could find the cross product, *or you could* . . .".

This routine can also be used with contexts. For example:

Which is the better deal: 12 apples for $4.00 or 10 apples for $3.00?

You could solve this by finding the cost for one apple, *or you could* . . .

ACTIVITY 5.10

Name: Proportion Fortune   **Type:** Game

About the Game: Students build missing value proportions in which there are whole-number scale factors. Thus, as they solve for the missing value, they are able to use various strategies—in particular, Use a Scale Factor.

Materials: 120-digit cards, 0–9 or three decks of playing cards (aces = 1, queens = 0, remove kings and jacks); *Optional: Proportion placemat*

Directions: 1. Deal 12 cards to each player. Cards can be hidden or face up; the group can decide.

2. Players each look at their cards and use as many cards as they want to create a missing value proportion <u>for which there is a whole-number answer</u> for the missing value (e.g., $\frac{7}{4} = \frac{21}{\Box}$ works, but $\frac{7}{4} = \frac{\Box}{2}$ does not).

3. Players place their proportions in front of them.

4. When players are ready, it is time to look for *Proportion Fortune*. Players see if their cards can form any of the missing values (including their own). If so, they place the card or cards on the table (e.g., if they have an ace and a 2 card, they set the two cards in front of them because 12 is the missing value for $\frac{7}{4} = \frac{21}{\Box}$).

5. If a player clears all 12 cards in one round, they win! If not, play continues to Round 2.

6. In Round 2 and beyond, players are dealt new cards to replace the cards they used in the last round (if a player used 8 cards, they receive 8 new cards).

7. Repeat Steps 2–6 until (1) someone wins (clears all cards in a single round) or (2) the deck is gone. In the latter case, the player who placed the most cards wins.

RESOURCE(S) FOR THIS ACTIVITY

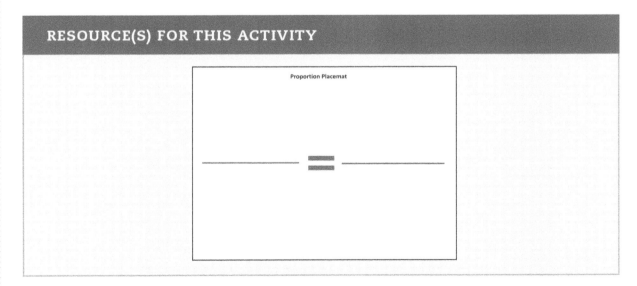

Proportion Placemat

online resources These resources can be downloaded at **resources.corwin.com/FOF/rationalnumbersalgequations**.

ACTIVITY 5.11

Name: Missing Value Stack or Attack   **Type:** Game

About the Game: Students roll to get possible missing values and strategically decide if they are going to stack on their own squares or attack by removing another player's chip from a square. This game can be adapted using more or fewer chips per player, changing the problems, or by changing player options (e.g., stacks must have 3 in them to be "safe" from attack).

Materials: *Missing Value Stack or Attack* game board per group, three 10-sided dice per group, 12 same-colored chips per player (each player in a different color)

Directions: 1. Roll a die to see who goes first.

2. On a player's turn, they roll the three dice and can use 1, 2, or all 3 numbers to form a missing value on the game board. For example, a roll of 0, 3, and 5 can be various values, including 3, 5, 30, 35, 50, or 350. Player chooses any option that is a missing value on the *Missing Value Stack or Attack* game board.

   Player Options:

   ● Take an unoccupied square.

   ● *Stack:* Place on a square the player occupies to make a two-counter stack. This protects the player so their opponent(s) cannot attack them.

   ● *Attack:* Place on a square that has one counter from another player (thus sending that counter off the game board back to that player).

3. Play continues until one player has placed all their chips on the game board—the winner!

RESOURCE(S) FOR THIS ACTIVITY

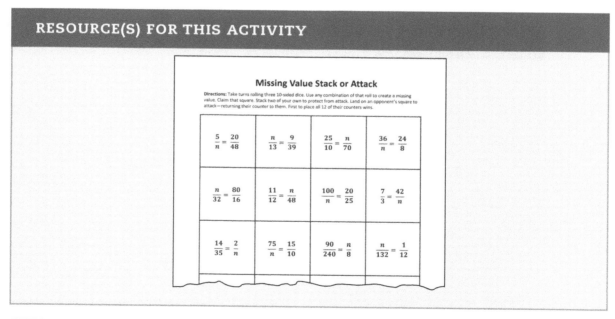

These resources can be downloaded at **resources.corwin.com/FOF/rationalnumbersalgequations**.

ACTIVITY 5.12

Name: The Collector   **Type:** Game

About the Game: As students look for a match between missing value proportion cards and the dice that they roll, they are using strategies for solving missing value proportions—in particular, Use a Scale Factor. This game can also be an independent activity wherein a student tries to collect as many cards as they can in 10 rolls (rolling 3 die each time).

Materials: Deck of digit cards (0–9) or playing cards (queens = 0, aces = 1; remove 10s, kings, and jacks) or three 10-sided dice; missing value proportion cards (or cut up a worksheet that has problems that lend to using proportional reasoning strategies)

Directions: 1. Students place the missing value cards in front of them, face up.

2. On a player's turn, they generate three numbers (e.g., draw three cards or roll three dice).

3. The player gets to collect any card for which they can make the solution with any of their three numbers. The player explains their reasoning.

4. When the player cannot find any more matches, their opponent has a chance to collect.

5. Play goes to the next player and the process repeats.

6. Winner is the one who collects the most cards.

For example, Keira draws a 1, 4, 5, and finds a card for which the missing value is 14, so she uses those numbers to collect that card. She can't find any others, so she ends her turn. But Natasha notices a card for which the missing value is 5, so she collects that card. It is Natasha's turn, and she draws three new cards.

RESOURCE(S) FOR THIS ACTIVITY

$\dfrac{15}{20} = \dfrac{3}{a}$	$\dfrac{b}{20} = \dfrac{9}{36}$	$\dfrac{25}{20} = \dfrac{k}{4}$	$\dfrac{8}{m} = \dfrac{24}{32}$
$\dfrac{36}{c} = \dfrac{42}{7}$	$\dfrac{24}{2} = \dfrac{48}{d}$	$\dfrac{5}{2} = \dfrac{n}{6}$	$\dfrac{9}{6} = \dfrac{p}{10}$
$\dfrac{e}{18} = \dfrac{14}{21}$	$\dfrac{9}{15} = \dfrac{f}{18}$	$\dfrac{12}{15} = \dfrac{q}{10}$	$\dfrac{r}{7} = \dfrac{15}{5}$
$\dfrac{g}{5} = \dfrac{15}{10}$	$\dfrac{8}{h} = \dfrac{9}{27}$	$\dfrac{3}{2} = \dfrac{s}{5}$	$\dfrac{t}{16} = \dfrac{8}{30}$

ACTIVITY 5.13

Name: Stack 'Em Ratios

Type: Game

About the Game: This task can be used over and over to give students opportunities to use reasoning to create equivalent ratios, as well as ones that are not equivalent. It can also be a partner game wherein a player tries to complete their stacks first.

Materials: *Stack 'Em* game board; playing cards (aces = 1, jacks = 11, queens = 12, kings = 13)

Directions: 1. Students draw three cards and use at least two of the cards to form a ratio.

2. Students decide where they want to place the ratio on their game board. Once the ratio is placed, it cannot be moved. Ratio placing rules:

 • Ratios in the same stack must be equivalent ratios, but not the same.

 • Ratios in other stacks must not be equal to any other stacks.

3. Each subsequent turn, students choose at least two of their three cards to make a ratio.

4. The goal is to complete all stacks before the deck runs out.

For example, Morgan first draws 1, 2, and 6; she decides to make the ratio $\frac{6}{12}$ and records it in the tallest stack. Next, she draws a 2, 3, and 5 and decides to use only the 2 and 3 to make a new ratio $\frac{2}{3}$. On her third draw, she gets 4, 8, and 11 and creates the ratio $\frac{4}{8}$.

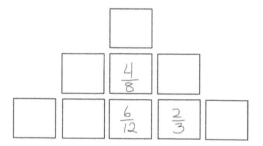

RESOURCE(S) FOR THIS ACTIVITY

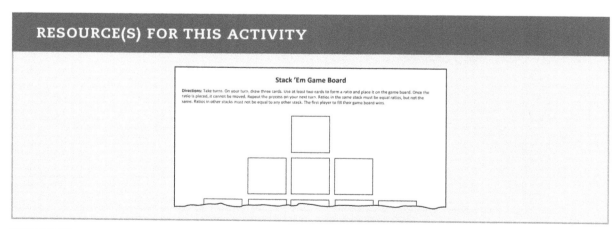

online resources ↖ These resources can be downloaded at **resources.corwin.com/FOF/rationalnumbersalgequations**.

Strategies for Solving Equations for an Unknown

In this module we highlight two significant strategies for reasoning with algebraic expressions and equations:

- Use Relational Reasoning

- Choose a Basic Transformation

The focus of this module is on developing an understanding of how each strategy works, practicing it, and determining when either is a good choice. Part 3 of this book offers additional engaging activities that focus on choosing among strategies.

STRATEGIES FOR SOLVING EQUATIONS FOR AN UNKNOWN

How might a student solve $x + 3 = 5$? One option is to examine the equation and think, "What number added to 3 equals 5?" It is 2. Another—and commonly taught—method is to "subtract 3 from both sides," resulting in $x = 2$. The first method describes Use Relational Reasoning and the second method describes one of four Basic Transformations that can be used to solve equations.

STRATEGY OVERVIEW:
Using Relational Reasoning

What Is Use Relational Reasoning?

Use Relational Reasoning involves looking at a problem holistically and thinking about what the variable must be. It looks and sounds like this:

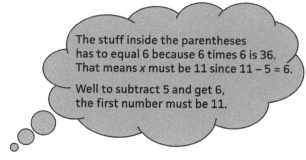

The stuff inside the parentheses has to equal 6 because 6 times 6 is 36. That means x must be 11 since $11 - 5 = 6$.

Well to subtract 5 and get 6, the first number must be 11.

$6(x - 5) = 36 \rightarrow$

$x - 5 = 6 \rightarrow$

$x = 11$

HOW DOES USE RELATIONAL REASONING WORK?

Use Relational Reasoning involves analyzing the structure of each side of the equation to identify relationships that can lead to knowing the value of the variable. This strategy utilizes inverse operations and understanding of the equal sign as a balance, as illustrated in the two examples below.

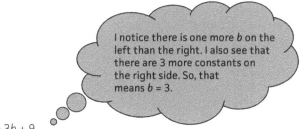

Example 1: $4b + 6 = 3b + 9$

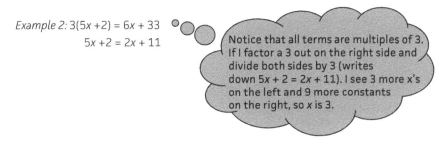

Example 2: $3(5x + 2) = 6x + 33$

$\quad\quad\quad\quad\quad 5x + 2 = 2x + 11$

Note that this strategy may be mental or it may be written. The defining characteristic is that relationships are used to simplify, rather than operating on one or both sides of the equation.

WHEN DO YOU CHOOSE USE RELATIONAL REASONING?

With one-step equations, this strategy is commonly efficient and builds on and supports students' number sense. With two-step equations, this strategy is useful when quantitative relationships are easily identified between terms in the equation. It is important to begin by asking if there are relationships that can readily simplify or solve the equation before moving to another strategy.

STRATEGY OVERVIEW:
Choosing a Basic Transformation

What Is Choosing a Basic Transformation? Transformations are essentially steps that preserve equivalence. Using transformations involves choosing which transformation to use to start solving the equation and, with each new step, revisiting what to do next with the eventual goal of solving for *x*. There are four basic transformations for solving equations (Star & Rittle-Johnson, 2008):

1. Combine like terms.
2. Add or subtract like terms on both sides of the equation.
3. Multiply or divide on both sides of the equation.
4. Use distributive property.

MODULE 1 Strategies for Addition

MODULE 2 Strategies for Subtraction

MODULE 3 Strategies for Multiplication

MODULE 4 Strategies for Division

MODULE 5 Strategies for Ratios and Proportions

MODULE 6 Strategies for Solving Equations for an Unknown

MODULE 7 Strategies for Solving Systems of Linear Equations

Students decide which transformation to select based on the numbers and operations in the equation. Each transformation is briefly described in the following table.

BASIC TRANSFORMATION	DESCRIPTION	EXAMPLES OF FIRST STEPS	WHEN TO CHOOSE
Combine Like Terms	Combining like terms on the same side of an equation.	$7x + 5 + 3x = 5x + 5$ $10x + 5 = 5x + 5$	When you notice that there are like terms on the same side of the equation.
Add or Subtract on Both Sides	This idea is grounded in "balancing" an equation – if you add or remove the same amount from two sides of an equation, the resulting expressions are still equal.	$6 - 3x = 15 - 4x$ $\underline{+4x \qquad\quad +4x}$ $6 + x = 15$	When an expression on one side cannot be simplified, then it may be necessary to add or subtract on both sides in order to combine like terms.
Multiply or Divide on Both Sides	This option involves multiplying on both sides (perhaps to eliminate fractions) or identifying a common factor and dividing to simplify the equation. Dividing or multiplying by a reciprocal have the same result, but may look different.	$4\left(\frac{1}{4}x + 3 = x\right)$ $x + 12 = 4x$ $3(x + 1.2) = 12$ $x + 1.2 = 4$ $\frac{3}{2} \cdot \frac{2}{3}(5x + 4) = {}^-14 \cdot \frac{3}{2}$ $5x + 4 = {}^-21$	When there is a common factor on both sides of the equation, dividing by that number (or multiplying by the reciprocal) results in an equation with smaller (and usually easier) numbers. It is also useful when fractions are involved.
Use Distributive Property	The distributive property $[a(b + c) = ab + ac]$ may be used in either direction (e.g., to eliminate the parentheses or to factor out a like term).	$5(x - 3) = 22.5$ $5x - 15 = 22.5$ $7(3x + 4) = 7x + 14$ $7(3x + 4) = 7(x + 2)$	Notice this is listed last. It is a good idea *after* you decide it is not easy to do the other transformations. Factoring is a good option when it leads to a common term on both sides that can then be eliminated.

TEACHING TAKEAWAY

Using the distributive property is not always the best first step, so do not say, "First eliminate parentheses." This works against flexibility and fluency.

Importantly, all of these options are just that—options. And, within each are options. For example, with $9e - 7 = 7e - 11$, you might decide to add to both sides, then you decide which side you want to have a variable. In this case, you might add ^-7e so that variable coefficient is positive: $2e - 7 = {}^-11$.

TEACHING ACTIVITIES for Solving Equations for an Unknown

A key to fluently knowing when to choose a strategy is being able to fully use and understand it. Too often, students are only taught a rote method for solving equations: First, . . . Then, . . . Yet each of the strategies (using relational understanding and any of the four transformations) is sometimes the most efficient. Thus, the activities in this section focus on making sense of these strategies and exploring when to use them, developing students' flexibility and efficiency with algebraic equations.

ACTIVITY 6.1
WHAT'S MY NUMBER?

This classic activity is well-liked by students because it sounds like a puzzle. Start with a one-step equation and describe it verbally without disclosing the actual equation. Examples include:

$2n = 14$ "I'm thinking of a number. I double it and get 14. What's my number?"

$n - 15 = 8$ "I'm thinking of a number. I subtract 15 and get 8. What's my number?"

Have students record their answers on white boards, or whisper to a partner. Then, have students record the equation that fits your number clue.

Move to two-step equations and repeat the process:

$3n + 1 = 16$ "I'm thinking of a number. I triple it, add 1, and get 16. What's my number?"

Then, reverse the activity. Pose an equation and ask students to give the clue. This can be done in partners, or independently.

Finally, give students some written problems and ask them to use reasoning to figure out what the number (n) is.

ACTIVITY 6.2
IF I KNOW THIS, THEN I KNOW THAT

This activity helps students notice structure and then use that structure to Use Relational Reasoning to solve an equation. Post equations that can be solved using reasoning (problems that are not too messy), and model the language of this activity:

PROBLEM	RELATED STATEMENT
$5 + 2x = 15$	If I know $5 + 2x$ equals 15, then I know that $2x$ must equal . . . [10]
	If I know $2x = 10$, then I know that x must equal . . . [5]

ACTIVITY 6.3
COVER AND UNCOVER

This is another activity to focus on relational reasoning. In this case, students place their finger over a term that has a variable.

For example:

$3a + 10 = 34 \rightarrow 3a + 10 = 34$

$$3a = 24$$

Then, ask students to share what they know about what they covered up. In this case, a student might say, "It has to equal 24." Then, they write what they uncovered—in this case, that $3a = 24$. Finalize by asking what a must be to make the equation true.

Source: pointing finger from Barks_japan/iStock.com

ACTIVITY 6.4
COMPARE AND DISCUSS
MULTIPLE STRATEGIES (CDMS)

Comparing strategies is a way to help students focus on why a strategy works and when it is a good fit for solving a problem (Star, Jeon, Comeford, Clark, Rittle-Johnson, & Durkin, 2021). The "CDMS" routine is described in Figure 6.1. First, ask students to make sense of what both students did. Second, ask students to look for similarities and differences between the two worked examples. The "CDMS" routine includes four possibilities for comparing (see Figure 14). The task in Figure 15 is an example of **"Which method is better?"** Next, have students prepare to discuss by applying their thinking to a new problem, in this example, asking, "If solving $5(x + 2) + 7$, which method would be better? Why?" As a class, students discuss connections they made and what they learned about when to use the methods (see prompts in Figure 14). Additional CDMS tasks are available at https://www.compareanddiscuss.com.

FIGURE 14 ● Phases of the "CDMS" Routine

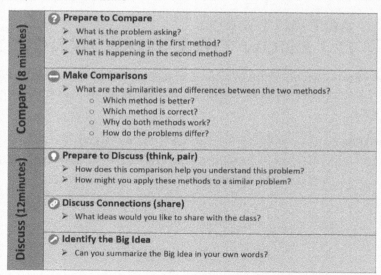

Source: Star, J., Rittle-Johnson, B., & Dirken, K. (2019). Compare and Discuss Multiple Strategies. Accessed at https://www.compareanddiscuss.com/. Used with Permission.

FIGURE 15 ● Sample CDMS Linear Equations Task

Gloria and Tim were asked to solve $5(x + 3) = 20$.

Gloria's "distribute first" way	Tim's "divide first" way

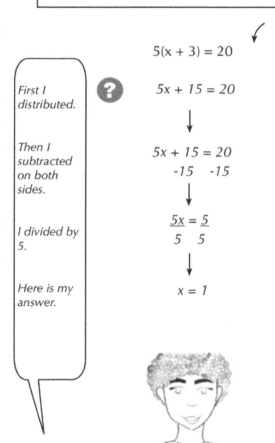

First I distributed.

Then I subtracted on both sides.

I divided by 5.

Here is my answer.

$5(x + 3) = 20$

$5x + 15 = 20$

$5x + 15 = 20$
$-15 \quad -15$

$\dfrac{5x}{5} = \dfrac{5}{5}$

$x = 1$

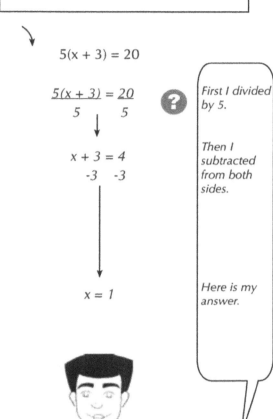

$5(x + 3) = 20$

$\dfrac{5(x + 3)}{5} = \dfrac{20}{5}$

$x + 3 = 4$
$-3 \quad -3$

$x = 1$

First I divided by 5.

Then I subtracted from both sides.

Here is my answer.

Source: Star, J., Rittle-Johnson, B., & Dirken, K. (2019). Compare and Discuss Multiple Strategies. Accessed at https://www.compareanddiscuss.com/. Used with Permission.

ACTIVITY 6.5
WHAT DO I NOTICE? WHAT DO I CHOOSE?

This activity focuses on choosing a basic transformation to begin. Pose an equation and ask students to silently notice structures about the equation. After a short time, have them turn and talk to their shoulder partner and share what they notice. Next, ask students to indicate which basic transformation they will choose (e.g., holding up two fingers to indicate the second basic transformation from a list). Select students to justify their choice. Have students continue making choices and finish the problem. In the end, students can compare their choices and what turned out to be more efficient.

For example, when presented with $4x + 8 = 8x - 4$, students notice x is on both sides, an addition expression on one side and a subtraction expression on the other, and all terms are multiples of 4. The teacher asks students to indicate which transformation they would use first. A few show a 2 (add or subtract to both sides), about half the students pick 3 (divide both sides), and several show a 4 (use distributive property). Students then implement their first step and finish the problem. After completing the problem, ask students to find someone in the room who solved it differently and have a "stand up conversation" comparing the two options. Here are a few more example equations. Any equations for which there are at least two good options work well for this activity.

$6(3x - 5) = 12(x + 10)$	$5x + 7x - 8 = 5x + 1$	$\frac{3}{4}x = 6$
$^-14 - 3x = {^-4}$	$\frac{x}{3} - 8 = 2$	$5(2x - 1) = 25$

ACTIVITY 6.6
MAKING GOOD CHOICES

Pose a problem along with a (fictional) student's transformation choice. Ask students to determine if they think it is a good choice or not and why. If not, ask what a better choice would be (and why). Treat the conversation as an efficiency discussion, making it clear that the purpose is to attend to choice, not for everyone to agree on an absolute answer.

EXAMPLES	TRANSFORMATION CHOICE	GOOD CHOICE? WHY OR WHY NOT?
$6x + 12 = 2(x + 7)$	Jasper distributed the 2 on the right side of the equation.	
$16y + 12 = 3y - 7$	Michael factored a 4 out of the left side of the equation.	
$\frac{3}{5}k + 4 = \frac{1}{10}k + 2$	Bailey decomposed $\frac{3}{5}k$ into $\frac{1}{10}k$ and $\frac{1}{2}k$.	

ACTIVITY 6.7
PROMPTS FOR TEACHING SOLVING EQUATIONS FOR AN UNKNOWN

These prompts can be used for class discussions and/or for collecting evidence of student understanding. After students work with the prompt(s), bring the class together to exchange ideas. During the discussion encourage students to justify their reasoning and analyze the reasoning of their peers.

- How might you Use Relational Reasoning in the equation $4q - 16 = 28$?

- Which transformation would you use to start solving:

  1. $3y + 17 = 7(y+1) + 2$

  2. $2b + 5b + 3 = {}^-1$

- Kennedy said that Use Relational Reasoning would *not* be efficient for solving these equations. Do you agree or disagree?

  1. $7a + 5 = 5a + 1$

  2. $10b - 3 = 2(b + 7)$

  3. $6(c + 8) = {}^-24$

- Andie looked at $5x - 5 = 25$ and without recording any steps said, "*x* equals 6." What reasoning do you think they used to solve this in their head?

- For each problem, share two basic transformations you could use to start solving them:

  1. $4(6y + 1) = 12y - 24$

  2. $6n + 20 = 2n + 4(1 + 3n)$

- Create an equation for which combining like terms would be a productive first step. Create another equation for which combining like terms would not be a productive first step. Justify your reasoning.

- Describe what process you go through to decide which transformation you will use to solve an equation.

PRACTICE ACTIVITIES for Solving Equations for an Unknown

Fluency is realized through quality practice that is focused, varied, processed, and connected. See Part 1, page 20, for more about quality practice. As students practice, you have the opportunity to assess. This chart offers ideas of what to look for.

FLUENCY COMPONENT	WHAT TO LOOK FOR AS STUDENTS REASON WITH SOLVING EQUATIONS FOR AN UNKNOWN
Efficiency	• Do students choose the appropriate strategy (Use Relational Reasoning or Choose a Basic Transformation) when it is a good fit for the problem? • Are students using basic transformations efficiently (not getting bogged down in selecting what to break apart or how to find the partial products)? • Are students aware of when Use Relational Reasoning might simplify an equation?
Flexibility	• Are students carrying out Choose a Basic Transformation in flexible ways? • Do students change their approach to or from either strategy as it proves inappropriate or overly complicated for the problem? • Are they seeing how to apply each strategy in "new" situations?
Accuracy	• Are students using the distributive property accurately (e.g., are they accurately decomposing, finding partial products, and adding them)? • Are students considering the reasonableness of their solutions? • Are students finding accurate solutions?

ACTIVITY 6.8

Name: "Two Truths and a Lie"　　　　　**Type:** Routine

About the Routine: As students continue to work with properties of operations and equality, they often need additional practice when applying them to new number types (e.g., rational numbers) or expressions (e.g., quantities with variables). This routine provides opportunities for students to examine and wrestle with common errors or missteps when solving equations for unknowns.

Materials: This routine does not require any materials.

Directions:　1. Present students with an equation to solve, pose three possible "first steps," and ask them which two are truths and which one is a lie.

　　　　　　　2. Have students discuss which is the lie.

　　　　　　　3. After students discuss with partners, bring the group together to share ideas. Have them share which "first step" they prefer and why.

For example, a teacher posts $\frac{x}{2} + 9 = 1$ and the three possible "first steps" shown below (mix up the order so the lie is not always presented last) for students to discuss. An excellent extension to this routine is for students to work to generate the examples. These student-generated sets can be used for repeating this routine on another day, or exchanged with other students/small groups as part of a full lesson.

EQUATION	TRUTH	TRUTH	LIE
$\frac{x}{2} + 9 = 1$	$2\left(\frac{x}{2} + 9 = 1\right)$	$\frac{x}{2} + 9 - 9 = 1 - 9$	$2\left(\frac{x}{2}\right) + 9 = 2(1)$
$^-8 - 5x = 12$	$^-8 - 5x + 5x = 12 + 5x$	$^-8 + 8 - 5x = 12 + 8$	$^-8 - 5x - 5x = 12 - 5x$
$12 + 6x = 2x - 14$	$\frac{12 + 6x}{2} = \frac{2x - 14}{2}$	$12 + 6x - 2x = 2x - 2x - 14$	$12 + 6x - 14 = 2x - 14 - 14$

ACTIVITY 6.9

Name: "Pick 2 Transformations"   **Type:** Routine

About the Routine: This routine helps students recognize that solving equations can be done in different ways, and notice features of problems that lend to different basic transformations. This routine can be used as an independent task or learning center, with the student solving it both ways and writing a sentence about how the solutions were the same and how they were different.

Materials: "Pick 2 Transformation" cards (optional)

Directions: 1. Place students in pairs, and letter off A and B.

2. Select a "Pick 2 Transformation" card (or use a problem you create) and have students solve the problem using the basic transformation option assigned to them.

$\frac{1}{2}(2x + 4) = 10$	
Option A	Option B
$(2)\frac{1}{2}(2x + 4) = (2)10$	$\frac{1}{2}(2x) + \frac{1}{2}(4) = 10$

3. Ask students to explain to their partner how they finished their problem.

4. Then, have partners discuss how the two problems were alike and different. Ask, "Which option is better, or are they both good options?"

5. Regroup as a whole class, and have students share their opinions about which option was better.

6. Conclude by asking students to summarize what features of the problem made the selected option(s) efficient.

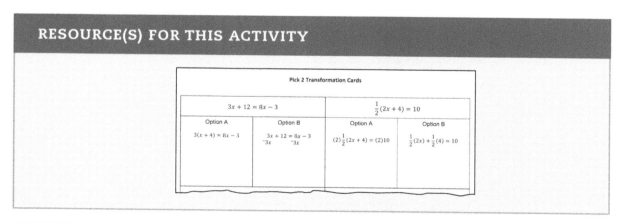

RESOURCE(S) FOR THIS ACTIVITY

online resources ⬂ This resource can be downloaded at **resources.corwin.com/FOF/rationalnumbersalgequations**.

ACTIVITY 6.10

Name: The Transformer   **Type:** Game

About the Game: This is a fun way to give students opportunities to choose and use different basic transformations to start solving equations.

Materials: *The Transformer* game board (one per player); *Solving for Unknowns* cards (or a worksheet cut up into cards—be sure the worksheet has problems with a variety of options for first steps), 10 counters per player

Directions: 1. Each player places their 10 counters on their game board. They must place at least 1 in each box, but can otherwise place as many as they want in a particular box.

2. At the same time, each player draws an equation card and determines the basic transformation (first step) they will use. In the space provided below the game board, they enact the step they chose and complete the problem.

3. Players then take turns showing the other players their first step and successful completion. If correct, they remove a chip from that box.

4. The first player to clear all their counters wins.

5. *Optional rule:* If a student can solve the problem using relational thinking, it is like a wild card and they can remove a counter from any box.

For example, Michael draws, $5 - 2(x + 1) = 1$. He decides to subtract 5 from both sides as his first step and solves the problem to get *x* equals 1. He removes one counter from the Add/Subtract on Both Sides of the Equation box.

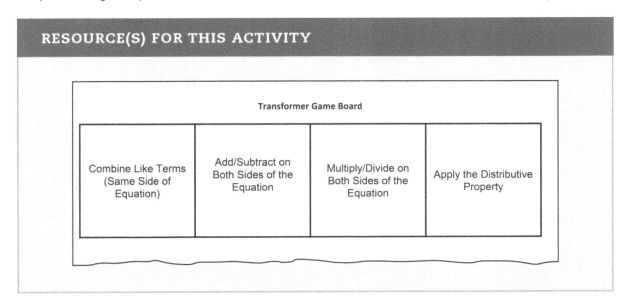

RESOURCE(S) FOR THIS ACTIVITY

Transformer Game Board

Combine Like Terms (Same Side of Equation)	Add/Subtract on Both Sides of the Equation	Multiply/Divide on Both Sides of the Equation	Apply the Distributive Property

[online resources] This resource can be downloaded at **resources.corwin.com/FOF/rationalnumbersalgequations**.

ACTIVITY 6.11

Name: Building Equations With Number Tiles

Type: Task

About the Task: This task encourages students to consider the structure of the expressions and equations in order to reason about the missing values.

Materials: One set of number tiles (0–9) per student, *Building Equations* recording sheet

1. The student uses the number tiles to strategically place one in each square to try to build an equation that works. Each tile can only be used one time.

2. After placing the tiles in the square the student will solve the equation to check to see if it works.

3. To challenge a student, ask them to create their own equation using the tiles (and variables) and then prepare a new card for other students to solve.

RESOURCE(S) FOR THIS ACTIVITY

BUILDING EQUATIONS WITH NUMBER TILES

Using number tiles with digits 0 through 9, create an equation so x = 1. You can use a digit only one time

$$\square x + \square x + \square\square = \square\square$$

Using number tiles with digits 0 through 9, create an equation so x = $\frac{1}{2}$. You can use a digit only one time.

$$\square x + \square x + \square\square = \square\square$$

Using number tiles with digits 0 through 9, create an equation so x = $\frac{1}{2}$. You can use a digit only one time.

$$\boxed{9}\, x + \boxed{7}\, x + \boxed{0}\boxed{8} = \boxed{1}\boxed{6}$$

Using number tiles with digits 0 through 9, create an equation so x = 1. You can use a digit only one time.

$$\boxed{7}\, x + \boxed{8}\, x + \boxed{2}\boxed{5} = \boxed{1}\boxed{0}$$

BUILDING EQUATIONS WITH NUMBER TILES

Using number tiles with digits 0 through 9, create an equation so x = 7. You can use a digit only one time.

$$\square(x + \square) = \square\square$$

Using number tiles with digits 0 through 9, create an equation so x = 5. You can use a digit only one time.

$$\square(\square x + \square) = \square\square$$

Using number tiles with digits 0 through 9, create an equation so x = 1. You can use a digit only one time.

$$\square(\square x + \square) = \square\square$$

BUILDING EQUATIONS WITH NUMBER TILES

Using number tiles with digits 0 through 9, create an equation so x = 3. You can use a digit only one time.

$$\boxed{3}(x + \boxed{2}) = \boxed{1}\boxed{5}$$

Using number tiles with digits 0 through 9, create an equation so x = 5. You can use a digit only one time.

$$\boxed{5}(\boxed{2}x + \boxed{6}) = \boxed{8}\boxed{0}$$

Using number tiles with digits 0 through 9, create an equation so x = 1. You can use a digit only one time.

$$\boxed{9}(\boxed{5}x + \boxed{4}) = \boxed{8}\boxed{1}$$

online resources — These resources can be downloaded at **resources.corwin.com/FOF/rationalnumbersalgequations**.

NOTES

MODULE 7

Strategies for Solving Systems of Linear Equations

In this module we highlight these significant strategies for solving systems of equations:

- Find the Intersection Point on a Graph
- Identify Values in a Table
- Use Substitution
- Use Elimination

The focus of this module is on developing an understanding of how these strategies work, practicing them, and determining when they are a good choice. Part 3 of this book offers additional engaging activities that focus on choosing among strategies.

STRATEGIES FOR Solving a System of Linear Equations

Systems of linear equations are two or more equations (or situations) with two or more variables. The typical task is to find a solution that is true in all the equations. Representations are central to reasoning with systems of equations. Representations include contexts, tables of values, graphs, and equations (Proulx, Beisiegel, Miranda, & Simmt, 2009). Significant strategies for solving systems are summarized in the table. Teaching these strategies is beyond the scope of this module. The focus of this module is on fluency—specifically, choosing an efficient strategy based on the features of the problems.

FIND THE INTERSECTION POINT ON A GRAPH		
DESCRIPTION	**EXAMPLE**	**WHEN IT IS USEFUL**
This strategy involves graphing both lines and finding the point of intersection.	$y = {}^-2x + 5$ $y = 4x - 1$ 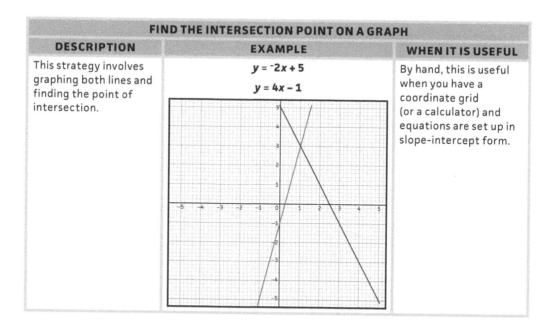	By hand, this is useful when you have a coordinate grid (or a calculator) and equations are set up in slope-intercept form.

146

IDENTIFY VALUES IN A TABLE

DESCRIPTION	EXAMPLE	WHEN IT IS USEFUL
Method 1: Select an x value, record it in the left column, substitute that value into both equations, and record in their respective columns. Continue until you find a match (i.e., $y1 = y2$).	<table><tr><td>x</td><td>$y_1 = 2x + 5$</td><td>$y_2 = -x + 2$</td></tr><tr><td>0</td><td>5</td><td>2</td></tr><tr><td>1</td><td>7</td><td>1</td></tr><tr><td>-1</td><td>3</td><td>3</td></tr></table> $(-1, 3)$	Either table method is a good choice when the equations are simple. The table enables students to better focus on the solution as coordinate pairs. It is also a good choice when values for x and y are whole numbers.
Method 2: Identify values for x and y that solve the first equation and record the x-values in the first column and the y-values in the second column. Substitute those values into the second equation and record the solution in the third column. Continue until Column 3 is a match to the constant in the second equation.	$x + y = 11$ $2x + 3y = 29$ $x + y = 11$ <table><tr><td>x</td><td>y</td><td>$2x + 3y = ?$</td></tr><tr><td>0</td><td>11</td><td>33</td></tr><tr><td>1</td><td>10</td><td>32</td></tr><tr><td>2</td><td>9</td><td>31</td></tr><tr><td>3</td><td>8</td><td>30</td></tr><tr><td>4</td><td>7</td><td>29</td></tr></table> $(4, 7)$	

USE SUBSTITUTION

DESCRIPTION	EXAMPLE	WHEN IT IS USEFUL
This strategy involves solving one equation for either x or y, then substituting that expression for the chosen variable into the second equation resulting in an equation with one variable, and solving for that variable.	$y = -2x - 9$ $6x - 5y = -19$ $6x - 5(-2x - 9) = -19$ $6x + 10x + 45 = -19$ $16x = -64$ $x = -4$ $y = -2(-4) - 9$ $y = -1$	This is a good choice when one equation is already in x= or y= form or can easily be transformed so that this is the case (i.e., either x or y does not have a coefficient).

(Continued)

MODULE 1 Strategies for Addition

MODULE 2 Strategies for Subtraction

MODULE 3 Strategies for Multiplication

MODULE 4 Strategies for Division

MODULE 5 Strategies for Ratios and Proportions

MODULE 6 Strategies for Solving Equations for an Unknown

MODULE 7 Strategies for Solving Systems of Linear Equations

(*Continued*)

USE ELIMINATION (ALSO CALLED LINEAR COMBINATION OR ADDITION METHOD)

DESCRIPTION	EXAMPLE	WHEN IT IS USEFUL
This strategy involves combining the two equations with the goal of eliminating one of the variables and solving for the one that remains. Sometimes you will have to manipulate one or both of the equations.	$x - 2y = -13$ $4x + 3y = 3$ $-4(x - 2y = -13)$ $-4x + 8y = 52$ $4x + 3y = 3$ $11y = 55$ $y = 5$ $4x + 3(5) = 3$ $x = -3$	This idea is useful when the coefficients of one of the variables are opposites of each other (or by multiplying one equation by a constant you can create a coefficient that is an opposite).

TEACHING ACTIVITIES for Solving Systems of Linear Equations

This section offers activities for helping students develop efficient ways to solve systems of linear equations. The goal is that students become adept at noticing features of the system equations and using those features to select an efficient option for solving the system.

ACTIVITY 7.1
VARIABLE-LESS PROBLEMS

A good way to begin reasoning with systems of equations is to begin with visual or contextual situations with two or more unknowns, leveraging students' conceptual understanding and relational thinking (Kindt et al., 2006). To begin, pose two balances with two objects (in this case, lollipops and cakes). Ask students what they notice across the two scales.

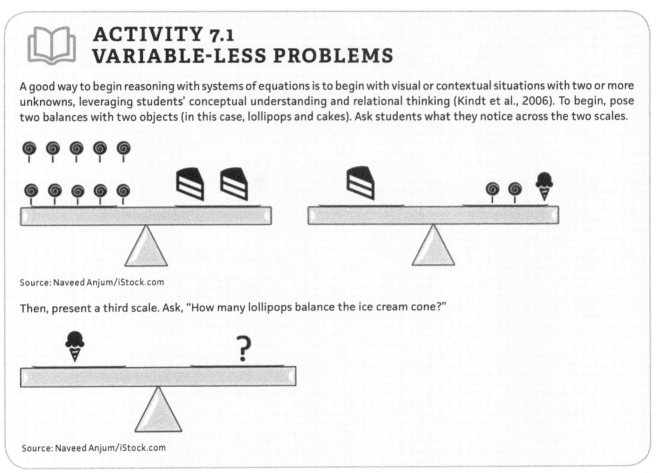

Source: Naveed Anjum/iStock.com

Then, present a third scale. Ask, "How many lollipops balance the ice cream cone?"

Source: Naveed Anjum/iStock.com

(Continued)

(Continued)

As students explain their reasoning, transition from the balance to the equal sign. Have students record their work using either the visuals, the variables, or both (L = lollipop; C = cake; I = ice cream cone). Both are shown here:

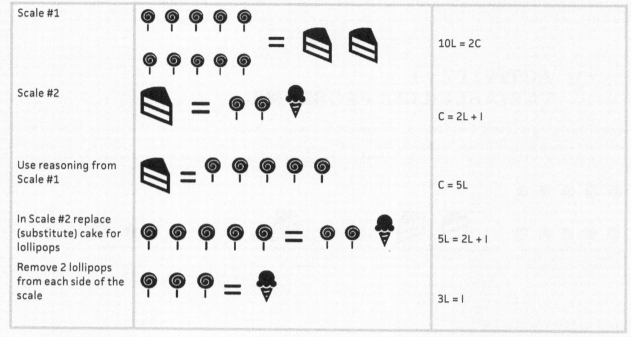

Scale #1		10L = 2C
Scale #2		C = 2L + I
Use reasoning from Scale #1		C = 5L
In Scale #2 replace (substitute) cake for lollipops		5L = 2L + I
Remove 2 lollipops from each side of the scale		3L = I

Source: Naveed Anjum/iStock.com

In this second example, the visuals begin to look even more like a system of equations. Again, ask students what they notice and then challenge them to use reasoning to find the cost of each item of clothing.

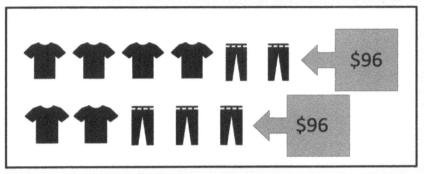

Source: Naveed Anjum/iStock.com

One approach students might use is to create a single equation and then eliminate common items on both sides:

This can also be translated into variables:

$$4T + 2P = 2T + 3P$$

$$2T = P$$

With this simplified relationship, substitution can be used to finish the problem (e.g., 2 T-shirts can be substituted into the first equation for each pair of pants, then 8 T-shirts cost $96, so one shirt costs $12 and a pair of pants is twice as much, so $24).

Another approach is to simply notice how the two rows are different and notice that 2T = P. Then, this relationship can be used to determine the cost of each:

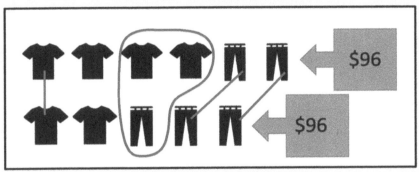

Source: Naveed Anjum/iStock.com

ACTIVITY 7.2
A VISIT TO THE DOG PARK

This activity presents a task that promotes a variety of approaches to solving it. Ask students to consider this scenario:

Andrew takes his dog to the dog park. To entertain himself he does some counting and then creates this puzzle for his mom to later solve at home: At the dog park, there were 19 dogs and people all together. I counted 62 legs. How many dogs were at the dog park?

Challenge students to solve this problem as many ways as they can—for example, using a vertical surface (e.g., chart paper; see examples below). After solutions are finished, identify two strategies and have students work in small groups to compare the two strategies (alternatively, they can pick 2). After students share findings from comparing, ask them to identify strategies they think were a good fit for this problem. As an alternative, print these worked examples and have students analyze each, explaining what the student did and why it works, and then discuss connections among the strategies.

RESOURCE(S) FOR THIS ACTIVITY

Student Solutions for Activity 7.2 Visit to the Dog Park

12 |||| I started by making groups of 4 until I got to 62 (15 ½). Then I broke them apart until I got 19 groups.

7

I started with 19 circles and put 2 legs in each circle. I kept adding 2 legs until I got to 62.

10×4=40   11×4=44   12×4=48
9×2=18   8×2=16   7×2=14
           60   62

---

online resources ⟶ This resource can be downloaded at **resources.corwin.com/FOF/rationalnumbersalgequations**.

Make connections between informal reasoning and the significant strategies for solving systems of linear equations. Present the system of equations in variable form. Ask students to revisit the other strategies and identify where they see D + P = 19 and 4D + 2P = 62 represented.

ACTIVITY 7.3
YOU BE THE JUDGE

Distribute or post a page that has a problem solved in several ways (see below). First, ask students to review each strategy and then judge it, defending why they think the strategy is a good way to solve that system or not. In the end ask, "Which strategy would you choose to solve this system? Why?" Second, provide students the *You Be the Judge* template that names or starts the strategies and have them complete the examples and then judge them. Third, just give students the problem and have them select three ways to solve it and then judge each one. For the second and third process, you can place students in trios and have each student solve it one way. Then, collectively, the students decide if the strategy was a good option for that problem or not.

RESOURCE(S) FOR THIS ACTIVITY

ACTIVITY 7.4
COMPARE AND DISCUSS
MULTIPLE STRATEGIES (CDMS)

Comparing strategies is a way to help students focus on why a strategy works and when it is a good fit for solving a system of linear equations (Star, Jeon, Comeford, Clark, Rittle-Johnson, & Durkin, 2021). Compare and Discuss Multiple Strategies (CDMS), described in Figure 16, is an instructional routine. First, ask students to make sense of what both students did. Second, ask students to look for similarities and differences between the two examples. The "CDMS" routine includes four possibilities for comparing (see Figure 16). The task in Figure 17 is an example of "**Which method is better?**" Next, have students prepare to discuss by applying their thinking beyond the example. In this case, you might ask, "Is there a situation where substitution would be better than elimination, or vice versa?" As a class, students discuss connections they made and what they learned about when to use the methods (see prompts in Figure 16). Additional CDMS tasks are available at https://www.compareanddiscuss.com.

FIGURE 16 ● Phases of the "CDMS" Instructional Routine

Compare (8 minutes)	**❓ Prepare to Compare** ➢ What is the problem asking? ➢ What is happening in the first method? ➢ What is happening in the second method? **➖ Make Comparisons** ➢ What are the similarities and differences between the two methods? ○ Which method is better? ○ Which method is correct? ○ Why do both methods work? ○ How do the problems differ?
Discuss (12 minutes)	**💡 Prepare to Discuss (think, pair)** ➢ How does this comparison help you understand this problem? ➢ How might you apply these methods to a similar problem? **🔗 Discuss Connections (share)** ➢ What ideas would you like to share with the class? **✎ Identify the Big Idea** ➢ Can you summarize the Big Idea in your own words?

Source: Star, J., Rittle-Johnson, B., & Dirken, K. (2019). Compare and Discuss Multiple Strategies. Accessed at https://www.compareanddiscuss.com. Used with permission.

FIGURE 17 ● Sample Systems of Linear Equations Task for the "CDMS" Instructional Routine

Tim and Emma were asked to solve the linear system
$$\begin{cases} 3x + 2y = 8 \\ x - 3y = 10 \end{cases}$$

Tim's "substitution" way	Emma's "elimination" way

Tim's "substitution" way

$$\begin{cases} 3x + 2y = 8 \\ x - 3y = 10 \end{cases}$$

↓

I solved the second equation for x.

$x = 3y + 10$

↓

I plugged this into the first equation.

$3(3y + 10) + 2y = 8$

↓

I then solved for y.

$9y + 30 + 2y = 8$
$11y + 30 = 8$
$11y = -22$
$y = -2$

I plugged y into the second equation to find x.

$x - 3(-2) = 10$
$x + 6 = 10$
$x = 4$

↓

The solution is (4, -2)

Emma's "elimination" way

$$\begin{cases} 3x + 2y = 8 \\ x - 3y = 10 \end{cases}$$

↓

I multiplied the bottom equation by -3.

$3x + 2y = 8$
$-3(x - 3y = 10)$

↓

I then used elimination and solved for y.

$3x + 2y = 8$
$\underline{-3x + 9y = -30}$
$11y = -22$
$y = -2$

↓

I plugged y into the second equation to find x.

$x - 3(-2) = 10$
$x + 6 = 10$
$x = 4$

↓

The solution is (4, -2)

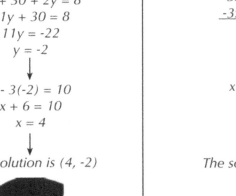

Source: Star, J., Rittle-Johnson, B., & Dirken, K. (2019). Compare and Discuss Multiple Strategies. Accessed at https://www.compareanddiscuss.com/. Used with Permission.

ACTIVITY 7.5
PROMPTS FOR TEACHING SOLVING SYSTEMS OF LINEAR EQUATIONS

These prompts can be used for class discussions and/or for collecting evidence of student understanding. After students explore a prompt, bring the class together to exchange ideas. During the discussion encourage students to justify their reasoning and analyze the reasoning of their peers. These prompts can be modified to feature different strategies or simpler/more complicated equations.

- Lyle said that Making a Graph would *not* be efficient to solve this system of equations: $2.5x + 4y = 25$ and $y = 5x + 12$. Do you agree or disagree? Explain.

- Solve this system using both methods for Identify Values in a Table:

$$y = 2x + 4$$

$$y = {}^-3x + 44$$

- Show two ways to Use Substitution to solve this system:

$$2x + 6 = 2y$$

$$x + 4y = 17$$

- Use Substitution and Use Elimination to solve this system. Then, explain which is better and why:

$$4x + 6y = 4$$

$$x - 2y = {}^-6$$

- Carlos, Peyton, and Anitta are solving $x + y = 4$ and $-3x - y = -8$. Carlos suggests they make a table of x and y values that equal 4 and test them in the second equation. Peyton suggests they rewrite the first equation in $y=$ form and Use Substitution. Anita doesn't like that idea because of the minus sign in front of the y, so she suggests they solve by multiplying the first equation by 3 and using elimination. With whom do you agree? Why?

- Tell which strategy you would use to solve each system and why:

$3x + 2y = 0$	$y = {}^-x + 1$
$y = \frac{1}{2}x - 1$	$y = 2x - 5$

- Create an equation for which substitution would be an efficient method. Create another equation for which substitution would not be a productive first step. Explain what features of the system make substitution a good or bad option.

PRACTICE ACTIVITIES for Solving Systems of Linear Equations

Quality practice is focused, varied, processed, and connected, See Part 1, page 20, for an overview about quality practice. More routines and games to practice choosing among strategies can be found in Part 3.

ACTIVITY 7.6

Name: "Strategize Your Strategy"   **Type:** Routine

About the Routine: This activity focuses on *choosing when* each strategy is the good option. This routine can be done quickly, with one problem, or can be a full lesson, using a set of 4 to 5 problems, looping through steps 1 – 5, then placing students in groups to compare and discuss.

Materials: Set of three to five systems of equation problems that lend to different strategies; supply coordinate grids or use graphing calculators

Directions:
1. Distribute or post the problems and ask, "For which of these problems would you want to use a Graph? Table? Substitution? Elimination?"

2. Give students time to select a strategy (not solve, just select).

3. Select one problem and have students hold up a number of fingers—(1) Graph, (2) Table, (3) Substitution, or (4) Elimination—to indicate a particular strategy.

4. Invite students to justify the strategy they picked.

5. After hearing different reasons for each option, have students solve using the method they now think is the best option.

6. Optional: If students have used different methods, compare the completed problems, and again ask students to discuss whether the selected options were efficient.

7. Conclude by asking, "What features of the equations influenced your choice?"

For example, for $y - x = 2$ and $y = -\frac{1}{4}x + 7$, students selected three different options, even after the strategies were justified. The teacher placed students in mixed-strategy groups to compare the strategies and report out which ones turned out to be good choices.

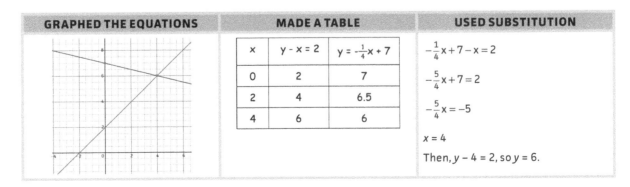

GRAPHED THE EQUATIONS	MADE A TABLE			USED SUBSTITUTION

	x	$y - x = 2$	$y = -\frac{1}{4}x + 7$	
	0	2	7	
	2	4	6.5	
	4	6	6	

USED SUBSTITUTION:

$-\frac{1}{4}x + 7 - x = 2$

$-\frac{5}{4}x + 7 = 2$

$-\frac{5}{4}x = -5$

$x = 4$

Then, $y - 4 = 2$, so $y = 6$.

ACTIVITY 7.7

Name: "Would You Rather...?"   **Type:** Routine

Version 1: Choose a Strategy

About the Routine: There are two versions of this routine with systems of linear equations—choosing different strategies (e.g., Use Tables or Use Graphs) and making choices within a strategy (e.g., For which variable will I substitute? Or Which variables will I eliminate?).

Materials: No materials are needed for this routine.

Directions:

Version 1: Focus on Choosing a Strategy

1. Post a "Would You Rather..." situation. Use numbers that will lend to different reasoning strategies.

2. Ask a "Would You Rather...?" question to prompt student to evaluate and then choose between two strategies.

3. Provide time for students to silently make a decision and then solve the problem with their choice.

4. Have students discuss both ways (either having students pair with someone who solved it the opposite way, or have someone share each way to the whole class).

5. Again ask, "Would you rather Make a Graph or Use Substitution to solve the system?" This time ask students to explain why.

6. Repeat with additional "Would you rather..." examples. Include examples wherein both named strategies are a good fit and when only one of them is a good fit.

For example, a teacher posts the following system of equations and asks, "Would you rather Make a Table or Use Substitution to solve the system?" Tables (and graphs) can be generated very efficiently using technology, such as a graphing calculator.

$$y = 2x - 5$$

$$y = {}^-x + 7$$

Make a Table		
x	● $2x-5$	● $^-x+7$
$^-2$	$^-9$	9
$^-1$	$^-7$	8
0	$^-5$	7
1	$^-3$	6
2	$^-1$	5
3	1	4
4	3	3

Use Substitution

$$2x - 5 = -x + 7$$
$$3x - 5 = 7$$
$$3x = 12$$
$$\boxed{x = 4}$$
$$y = 2(4) - 5$$
$$\boxed{y = 3}$$

ACTIVITY 7.8

Name: "Would You Rather . . .?"   **Type:** Routine

Version 2: Choose Within a Strategy

About the Routine: In this "Would You Rather," students make decisions within a strategy. For example, once they have decided to use substitution, there are still decisions to be made about which variable to eliminate and then what number(s) to multiply by.

Materials: No materials are needed for this routine.

Version 2: Focus on Choices Within a Strategy

Post a "Would You Rather . . ." situation. Use numbers that will lend to a particular reasoning strategy. Follow the same routine as described above but change what you would ask as the initial question.

- To focus on finding the point of intersection in a graph, ask about which method they will use to graph.

    Example:

    $y = 2x + 2$

    $y = x - 1$

    > "Would you rather graph using slope and y-intercept or using x-intercept and y-intercept?"

- To focus on identifying values in a table ask, "Would you rather select x values and substitute them into both equations until they result in the same y value (method 1) or find combinations of x and y that work for one equation and check to see if they work for the second (method 2)?

    Example:

    $y - x = 2$

    $3x - y = 14$

    > "Would you rather use method 1 or method 2?"

- To focus on Substitution ask, "Would you rather solve one equation for x and substitute into the other equation or solve one equation for y and substitute into the other equation?"

    Example:

    $5x - 7y = 58$

    $y + x = 2$

    > "Would you rather substitute for y or substitute for x?"

- If focused on Elimination ask, "Would you rather multiply first equation by ___, or the second equation by ___?

    Example:

    $-10x + 3y = 1$

    $-5x - 6y = 23$

    > "Would you rather multiply the first equation by 2 or multiply the second equation by -2?"

ACTIVITY 7.9

Name: *Choose and Go! Tic-Tac-Toe*　　　　　　　　**Type:** *Game*

About the Game: *Choose and Go! Tic-Tac-Toe* adds a fun twist to matching problems with a strategy to solve them. Students may want a particular space on the game board and therefore try to think of how they can use that strategy on the card they draw.

Materials: *Choose and Go! Tic-Tac-Toe* game board for players to share; Systems of Linear Equations cards

Directions:　1. Players place the stack of System of Linear Equations cards face down.

　　　　　2. Players take turns flipping over a card and deciding what strategy they would use to solve the problem and then follow that plan to find the correct solution.

　　　　　3. Players put a counter on a space that matches their thinking for the problem.

　　　　　4. The first player to get a *Tic-Tac-Toe* wins.

RESOURCE(S) FOR THIS ACTIVITY

Choose and Go! Tic-Tac-Toe

Directions: A player chooses a card and decides what method they would use to solve the system of equations. The player tells their partner their choice and solves the problem. The player puts a counter on a space that matches their thinking. Players take turns drawing cards. The first player to get a tic-tac-toe wins.

Use Substitution	Make a Graph	Use Elimination
Use Elimination	Make a Table	Use Substitution
Make a Graph	Use Substitution	Use Elimination

$y = 2x - 3$ $y = x - 1$	$3x + 2y = 0$ $y = \frac{1}{2}x - 1$
$4x - 2y = 8$ $2x + 2y = 4$	$x - 2y = 7$ $3x - 2y = 3$
$^-2x - y = ^-2$ $2x + 4y = 11$	$9x - 2y = 19$ $7x = 21$
$^-7x - y = 12$ $y = ^-8x = ^-14$	$y = 2x - 2$ $y = \frac{1}{3}x + 3$
$y = ^-x + 3$ $2x + 2y = 4$	$x + y = 3$ $x + 2y = 4$

 These resources can be downloaded at **resources.corwin.com/FOF/rationalnumbersalgequations**.

PART 3

PUTTING IT ALL TOGETHER

Developing Fluency

FLUENCY IS . . .

How might you finish a sentence that begins with "Fluency is . . ."? One way is "using procedures efficiently, flexibly, and accurately." Another option is "important." Or how about "an equity issue"? All of these are true statements. This section is the capstone of this book on fluency with rational numbers and algebraic equations. If students learn a strategy in isolation and never get to practice choosing when to use it, they will not become truly fluent. Part 3 focuses on learning to *choose* strategies. The table below summarizes the strategies developed in Modules 1–7.

OPERATION OR PROCEDURE	STRATEGIES
Addition	• Count On • Make Tens (and Make Hundreds, Make a Whole, Make a Zero, etc.) • Compensation • Partial Sums
Subtraction	• Count Back • Think Addition (Find the Difference) • Compensation • Partial Differences
Multiplication	• Break Apart by Addends (including Partial Products) • Break Apart by Factors (including Halve and Double) • Compensation
Division	• Think Multiplication (Use the Inverse Operation) • Partial Quotients
Ratios and Proportions	• Build Up/Break Down • Find a Unit Rate • Use a Scale Factor • Use $y = kx$ • Find Cross Products

Solving Equations for an Unknown	• Use Relational Reasoning
	• Choose a Basic Transformation:
	  • Combine like terms
	  • Add or subtract like terms on both sides of the equation
	  • Multiply or divide on both sides of the equation
	  • Use distributive property

Solving Systems of Equations	• Find the Intersection Point on a Graph • Identify Values in a Table • Use Substitution • Use Elimination

Once students know more than one strategy, they need opportunities to practice choosing strategies. In other words, you do not want to wait until they have learned four strategies and a standard algorithm before they begin choosing from among the strategies they know. And so, it is time to use a Part 3 activity. Then, add a new strategy to students' repertoire and return to activities that focus on choosing a strategy. This iterative process continues through the teaching of standard algorithms, as students continue to accumulate methods for adding and subtracting whole numbers. And, along the way, students also learn that sometimes there is more than one good way to solve a problem, and other times, one way really stands out from the others.

ALGORITHMS

Fluency includes knowing algorithms as well as strategies. An algorithm is a step-by-step process for solving a problem (as compared to a strategy, which is more flexible in how it is enacted). Computation algorithms vary from country to country. In the United States, most operations have one particular algorithm named as the "standard" method. For example, for adding or subtracting numbers, it is adding each place value, beginning with the smallest place value (farthest to the right) and working to the larger place values. Notations do not define an algorithm (Fuson & Beckman, 2012–2013). All three examples in the table, therefore, are versions of the standard algorithm for adding decimals. While the first one is more common, it can be the hardest for students to use.

TICK MARKS NOTATED ABOVE	TICK MARKS NOTATED BELOW	NO TICK MARKS, PARTIALS RECORDED
$$\begin{array}{r} {\scriptstyle 1\ \ 1} \\ 7.48 \\ + 1.76 \\ \hline 9.24 \end{array}$$	$$\begin{array}{r} 7.48 \\ + 1.76 \\ \hline {\scriptstyle 1\ 1} \\ 9.24 \end{array}$$	$$\begin{array}{r} 7.48 \\ + 1.76 \\ \hline .14 \\ 1.1 \\ 8. \\ \hline 9.24 \end{array}$$

Because standard algorithms are less intuitive and have numerous steps, it is even more important to focus on **reasonableness** (see Part 1). When the focus is on standard algorithms, students may see opportunities for reasoning strategies (great!). Use these moments to address efficiency. For example, ask, "How does dividing both sides compare to using the distributive property to solve $4(x + 3) = 16$?" Engaging the class in such a discussion places fluency as the focus (not just mastering an algorithm). **Estimation** is a means for encouraging reasonableness and an important "thinking tool" in developing algorithms.

CHOICE

Choosing strategies is at the heart of fluency. After a strategy is learned, it should always be an option for consideration. Too often, students feel like when they have moved on to a new strategy, they are supposed to use only the new one, as though it is more sophisticated or preferred by their teacher. But the strategies are additive—they form a collection from which students can select in order to solve the problem at hand.

Once students know how and why a strategy works, they need to figure out when it makes sense to use the strategy. That is when you need questions such as:

- When do you/might you use the _____ strategy for addition (or other operation)?
- When do you/might you *not* use _____ strategy/algorithm?
- Which strategies do you think of first when you see a problem?
- Which strategies do you choose only after other options don't work?
- When do you/might you use a standard algorithm?

This final question is particularly important to discuss with students. The answer is not "always." While standard algorithms always work, they are not always the best choice as described above. A standard algorithm is needed when:

1. Numbers in the problem do not lend themselves to a mental method.
2. Numbers in the problem do not lend themselves to a convenient written option (e.g., compensation).
3. You don't know an alternate method.
4. You want to check an answer, having used a different method.

Perhaps because standard algorithms are in state standards, a major part of our own learning, and applicable to all problems, there can be a hurry to get to them and significantly more time devoted to learning them than their reasoning alternatives. This is a mistake. A rush to the standard algorithm and memorizing procedures undermines students' confidence and may cause math anxiety, negatively impacting achievement (Boaler, 2014; Jameson, 2014; Ramirez, Shaw, & Maloney, 2018). Note that "fluently " does not mean "use the standard algorithm adeptly"; it means you use the standard algorithm adeptly *when it is the most efficient option.*

METACOGNITION

As students become more proficient with the strategies they have learned, and when to use them, they make decisions as to what they will do for a given problem. Taking time up front to make a good choice can save time in the enactment of a not-efficient strategy. We can help students with this reasoning by sharing a metacognitive process. This could be a bulletin board or a card taped to students' desks—a reminder that as we work, we make good choices about the methods we use. This is *flexibility* in action.

Metacognitive Process for Selecting a Strategy

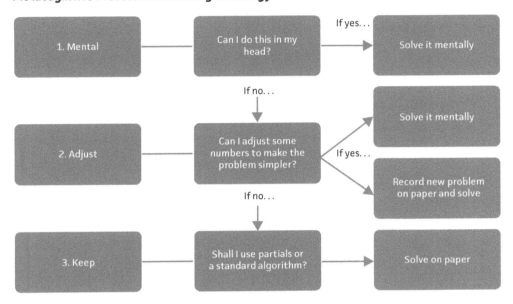

ASSESSING FLUENCY

Traditionally, fluency assessment has focused on speed and accuracy. While accuracy does matter, it is only one-third of what it means to be fluent. As you assess fluency, you want to intentionally look for each of the three fluency components and six fluency actions. Flexibility and efficiency can be observed as students engage in meaningful activities.

OBSERVATION TOOLS

Observation tools can help us focus on the "neglected" components of fluency and serve as a way to communicate with students and their parents about what real fluency looks like. Three examples are shared here.

See Chapter 7 (pp. 154–175) of the anchor book for more information about assessing fluency.

Fluency Component Checklist

Student/Student Group: _____   Date: _____

PROCEDURAL FLUENCY COMPONENTS	EVIDENT?			INSTRUCTIONAL NEXT STEPS
1. Efficiency	Yes	No	Not observed	
2. Flexibility	Yes	No	Not observed	
3. Accuracy	Yes	No	Not observed	

Comments:

Fluency Actions Checklist

Student/Student Group: _____   Date: _____

PROCEDURAL FLUENCY ACTIONS	EVIDENT?		
1. Selects appropriate strategy	Yes	No	Not observed
2. Solves in a reasonable amount of time	Yes	No	Not observed
3. Trades out or adapts a strategy	Yes	No	Not observed
4. Applies strategy to a new problem type	Yes	No	Not observed
5. Completes steps correctly	Yes	No	Not observed
6. Gets correct answer	Yes	No	Not observed

Comments:

 These resources can be downloaded at **resources.corwin.com/FOF/ rationalnumbersalgequations**.

GRADING ASSIGNMENTS AND ASSESSMENTS

All of your efforts to teach strategies and to teach students to choose efficient strategies must be continued through assessments. Too often, tests are graded for accuracy only. Instead, provide a fluency score using a rubric, such as this:

FOUR-POINT FLUENCY RUBRIC

BEGINNING 1	DEVELOPING 2	EMERGING 3	ACCOMPLISHED 4
Knows one algorithm or strategy but continues to get stuck or make errors.	Demonstrates efficiency and accuracy with at least one strategy/ algorithm but does not stop to think if there is a more efficient possibility.	Demonstrates efficiency and accuracy with several strategies, and sometimes selects an efficient strategy, though still figuring out when to use and not use a strategy.	Demonstrates efficiency and accuracy with several strategies and is adept at matching problems with efficient strategies (knowing when to use each and when not to).

 This resource can be downloaded at **resources.corwin.com/FOF/ rationalnumbersalgequations**.

With an eye on fluency and how to assess it, select fluency activities from Part 3, based on your students' needs and what type of activity you are seeking.

FLUENCY ACTIVITIES

The 12 activities in this section focus on all components of fluency, providing students with the opportunity to practice choosing an appropriate strategy or algorithm, enacting that method, and then reflecting on the efficiency of the strategy selected.

ACTIVITY F.1

Name: "Between and About"   **Type:** Routine

About the Routine: Estimation helps students determine reasonableness. Estimating can also provide insights into what strategy a student might select. There are a variety of ways to estimate; this routine offers practice in two of them.

Materials: This routine does not require any materials.

Directions:
1. Post a series of expressions to students, one at a time.

2. Have students determine the range for the answer as it is between ___ and ___. Record different ideas for the range and discuss as a class which ideas make the most sense.

3. After a "between" is agreed upon by the group, students then look to find an "about" number that is a reasonable estimate (using rounding, front-end, or compatibles, as they like). Students should not be asked to find the exact answer. It can be revealed after the between and about are identified.

PROBLEM POSED	BETWEEN	ABOUT
$7.32 + 8.48$	15 and 17 15.48 and 16.48 15.32 and 16.32	15, 16, 15.32
$13\frac{7}{20} - 2\frac{4}{5}$	10 and 12 $10\frac{1}{2}$ and 11	10, $10\frac{1}{2}$, 11
$-19 + 48$	0 and 40 10 and 40 10 and 30	28, 30
$\frac{4}{7} = \frac{?}{32}$	16 and 20	17, 18
$3x + 5 = 19$	3 and 5	4, 5

(Continued)

(Continued)

The routine works with any set of problems, including those that incorporate both fractions and decimals. Some to consider include:

FRACTION OPERATIONS	DECIMAL OPERATIONS	OPERATIONS WITH NEGATIVE NUMBERS
$3\frac{1}{5} + 5\frac{9}{10}$	$10.9 + 2.79$	$(^-2.9) + 10.3$
$34\frac{7}{16} + 14\frac{8}{15}$	$60.65 + 3.37$	$13\frac{3}{5} + 5\frac{1}{10}$
$13\frac{3}{5} - 5\frac{3}{8}$	$16.1 - 3.8$	$(^-33.7) - 14.545$
$24\frac{5}{6} - 5\frac{1}{4}$	$19.5 - 11.7$	$24\frac{5}{6} - \left(^-5\frac{3}{4}\right)$
$6\frac{1}{4} \times 4\frac{1}{3}$	1.6×5.4	$5.25 \times {}^-6.91$
$3\frac{1}{2} \times 4\frac{11}{12}$	3.8×4.9	$\left(^-2\frac{3}{4}\right) \times \left(^-5\frac{7}{8}\right)$
$12\frac{3}{4} \div 5$	$7.5 \div 3$	$(^-32.91) \div 7.18$
$22\frac{3}{4} \div 6\frac{1}{3}$	$22.6 \div 5.9$	$\left(^-36\frac{2}{5}\right) \div \left(^-5\frac{1}{3}\right)$
OPERATIONS WITH NEGATIVE MIXED REPRESENTATIONS	**MISSING VALUE PROPORTIONS**	**SOLVING EQUATIONS FOR AN UNKNOWN**
$3\frac{3}{5} + (^-7.9)$	$\frac{x}{15} = \frac{5}{6}$	$8 + 5x = 12$
$(^-2.19) + 10\frac{1}{6}$	$\frac{16}{7} = \frac{6}{x}$	$15 = {}^-3x + 7$
$33\frac{9}{19} - (^-14.545)$	$\frac{8}{x} = \frac{13}{27}$	$5x - 6 = 18$
$^-25.671 - 11\frac{2}{7}$	$\frac{2}{11} = \frac{9}{x}$	$^-48 = {}^-6 + (^-9x)$
$^-13\frac{3}{5} - (^-6.9)$	$\frac{3}{5} = \frac{8}{x}$	$^-6x - 6 = 19$
$3 \times (^-4.6)$	$\frac{10}{x} = \frac{13}{37}$	$2(x + 3) = 19$
$(^-12.2) \times \left(^-3\frac{7}{8}\right)$	$\frac{18}{5} = \frac{15}{x}$	$\frac{1}{2}x + 10 = 21$
$\left(^-15\frac{7}{10}\right) \div 5.35$	$\frac{x}{24} = \frac{1}{5}$	$7 + \frac{2}{3}x = 16$

ACTIVITY F.2

Name: "That One"   **Type:** Routine

About the Routine: This routine helps students consider when to use an algorithm (and when not to use it). An adaptation is to pick something other than the standard algorithm as the focus. For example, for systems of equations, the focus can be on which ones that will use substitution.

Materials: This routine does not require any materials.

Directions:
1. Pose a set of three to four problems to students.

2. Have students talk to a partner about which problems are good candidates for solving with an algorithm (or a selected strategy) and which are not.

3. Bring the group back together and point at each problem. When it is one where the pair think it is best solved with a standard algorithm (designated strategy), they call out, "That one." Continue through the list. When done, students who didn't pick one call out, "None."

4. Identify a problem for which there was not consensus and have students explain their decisions.

5. Summarize by asking students to reflect on whether they would keep or change their thinking on the problem(s) discussed.

"That One!" examples across content:

Adding Fractions	Subtracting Decimals	Adding Negative Numbers	Subtracting Negative Numbers
1. $2\frac{3}{4}+4\frac{1}{2}$ 2. $4\frac{3}{8}+5\frac{5}{8}$ 3. $6\frac{2}{3}+2\frac{3}{4}$	1. $47.2-37.6$ 2. $51.9-30.4$ 3. $85.6-44.8$	1. $^{-}45+{}^{-}98$ 2. $^{-}83+154$ 3. $36+{}^{-}96$ 4. $^{-}734+{}^{-}123$	1. $^{-}35-19$ 2. $23-{}^{-}47$ 3. $^{-}36-{}^{-}135$
Multiplying Fractions	Dividing Fractions	Dividing Decimals	Find Missing Value
1. $2\frac{1}{2}\times12$ 2. $2\frac{1}{4}\times4\frac{1}{2}$ 3. $1\frac{3}{8}\times4\frac{1}{4}$	1. $2\frac{1}{2}\div2$ 2. $\frac{6}{9}\div\frac{2}{9}$ 3. $2\frac{3}{8}\div\frac{1}{4}$ 4. $3\frac{1}{3}\div\frac{2}{9}$	1. $45.9\div0.9$ 2. $62.5\div0.25$ 3. $25.6\div0.8$ 4. $8.4\div6$	1. $\frac{32}{15}=\frac{58}{x}$ 2. $\frac{14}{21}=\frac{8}{x}$ 3. $\frac{3.50}{5}=\frac{2.80}{x}$

(Continued)

(*Continued*)

Adaptations for Algebraic Equations

Solving Equations for Unknowns: Identify one of the Basic Transformations. For example, for which will you divide both sides of the equation as your first step?

1. $4(x + 5) = 12$

2. $4(x + 5) - 3(x + 5) = 10$

3. $4(x + 5) = 2(x + 5) - 4$

Solving Systems of Linear Equations: Identify a strategy. For example, for which will you Use Elimination?

$y = x + 7$ $y = 2x + 3$	$4x + 6y = 4$ $x - 2y = {}^-6$	$2x + 3y = 12$ $5x - 3y = 9$

TEACHING TAKEAWAY

You can use related problems so that students can see relationships among the problem set, or use distinct problems where the focus is on each separate situation.

ACTIVITY F.3

Name: *A List of Ten*　　　　　　　　　　　　　　　　　　**Type:** *Game*

About the Game: In terms of procedural fluency, knowing when to use an algorithm is just as important as knowing how to use an algorithm. Yet students don't have frequent opportunities to consider when to use an algorithm. This modified version of *A List of Ten* is a game for considering when an algorithm is useful and when it isn't. Here it is shown with proportions but can work with any algorithm or procedure.

Materials: A deck expression or proportion cards for whichever operation or procedure you are working on; *A List of Ten* recording sheet

Directions:　
1. The expression cards are shuffled and placed face down.

2. Players take turns selecting a card and determining if the expression is best solved with or without a standard algorithm. Note that if a player can tell their opponent why an expression is better solved *without an algorithm* they can steal the card from their opponent.

3. The player records the equation in the appropriate column.

4. The first player to get *A List of Ten* wins.

5. After the game, both players solve each problem on their game board.

To adapt the game and game board for solving equations for unknowns or solving systems, trade out "standard algorithm" for a specific strategy (e.g., Use Distributive Property or Use Elimination).

For example, a student turns over this proportion card:

$$\frac{20}{x} = \frac{36}{27}$$

The student says "standard" (or "use cross products"). Their partner counters with "use equivalent fractions because both are equal to $\frac{4}{3}$." They agree this is more efficient, and the partner steals the card and places it on their *List of Ten* game board.

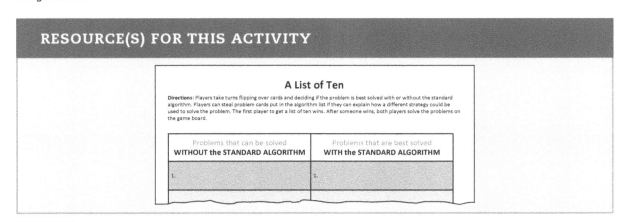

ACTIVITY F.4

Name: All Lined Up

Type: Game

About the Game: *All Lined Up* is a game of strategy and luck that gives students an opportunity to practice any operation with any number type. It appears in Module 2 with a focus on Think Addition. Here, encourage students to use efficient strategies. After the game, ask students to identify problems they created that were best solved with an algorithm or those that were not.

Materials: *All Lined Up* game board, playing cards (queens = 0, aces = 1; remove 10s, kings, and jacks)

Directions:

1. Players take turns making a number. *(The number of cards to take depends on the types of numbers you direct them to make. In the example, students would pull five cards to ensure they could make 2 two-digit integers discarding one of their choices.)*

2. A player records the sum in one of their six boxes. The game can be played with any operation but use the same operation for the entire game.

3. On subsequent turns, the student must record the sum in a box so that the sums are in order from least to greatest.

4. If a player can't place their sum, the player loses their turn.

5. The first player to fill all six boxes in order from least to greatest wins.

For example, a student pulled ⁻2, 5, 8, ⁻9, and 6. They made the problem ⁻92 + 85 and put ⁻17 on their board, as shown. On their next turn, they made ⁻16 + 19 and recorded the sum 3, as shown. On their third turn, they created ⁻61 + 48. They would lose their turn because there is no space for the ⁻13 between ⁻17 and 3 on their board.

All Lined Up

Directions: Make two numbers. Find the sum or difference of the numbers. Place the sum or difference in one of the boxes so that the numbers in the boxes are in order from least to greatest.

		−17	3		

To use fraction equations, students can use a set of fraction cards (e.g., with halves, fourths, and eighths) or use two cards to make a fraction (or three cards to make a mixed number). In this game, the player's fourth turn created a sum of $1\frac{3}{4}$. The player lost their turn because there is no space to place it on the game board.

All Lined Up

Directions: Make two numbers. Find the sum or difference of the numbers. Place the sum or difference in one of the boxes so that the numbers in the boxes are in order from least to greatest.

RESOURCE(S) FOR THIS ACTIVITY

All Lined Up

Directions: Make two numbers. Find the sum or difference of the numbers. Place the sum or difference in one of the boxes so that the numbers in the boxes are in order from least to greatest.

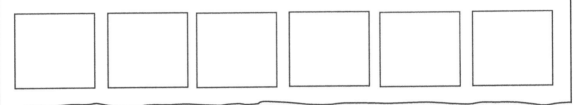

online resources | These resources can be downloaded at **resources.corwin.com/FOF/rationalnumbersalgequations**.

ACTIVITY F.5

Name: "Strategize First Steps"   **Type:** Routine

About the Routine: This routine involves sharing how to *start* a problem. It is at that first step that students are selecting a strategy. In its quickest version, that is the only step that is ever done. Simply ask, "Which step first and why?" A second option is to begin the same, but after students have shared ideas for first steps, they choose which first step they like and finish the problem.

Materials: List of three or four problems on the same topic but that lend to different strategies

Directions:
1. Show the first problem and ask students to mentally determine their first step (only) and signal when they're ready (since it is only the first step, they only need a few seconds).

2. Record first-step ideas by creating a list on the board.

3. Discuss which first steps seem reasonable (or not).

4. Repeat with two to four more problems, referring to the list created from the first problem, and adding to the list if/when new strategies are shared.

5. Conclude the series with a discussion: When will you use _____ strategy?

Example Problem Sets

FRACTION OPERATIONS	DECIMAL OPERATIONS	OPERATIONS WITH NEGATIVE NUMBERS
1. $2\frac{4}{5} + 3\frac{3}{10} =$	1. $6.9 + 4.4 =$	1. $12.2 + {}^-7.6 =$
2. $4 - 2\frac{1}{3} =$	2. $28.6 - 20.57 =$	2. ${}^-44.9 + {}^-7.4 =$
3. $4\frac{6}{8} - 1\frac{1}{5} =$	3. $32.91 - 7.18 =$	3. ${}^-7 - ({}^-3.7) =$
4. $6\frac{1}{8} \times 1\frac{1}{5} =$	4. $2.6 \times 3.5 =$	4. ${}^-5\frac{3}{8} + 1\frac{1}{4} =$
5. $12 \div \frac{2}{3} =$	5. $37.2 \div 0.6 =$	5. ${}^-10\frac{5}{6} - 2\frac{3}{5} =$
MISSING VALUE PROPORTIONS	SOLVING EQUATIONS FOR AN UNKNOWN	SOLVING SYSTEMS OF EQUATIONS
1. $\frac{8}{32} = \frac{x}{44}$	1. $2(x + 3) = 18$	1. $x + 2y = 7$ $x + y = 5$
2. $\frac{6}{x} = \frac{12}{20}$	2. $3(x - 2) = 4 + x$	2. $2x + 3y = 8$ $3x + 6y = 15$
3. $\frac{x}{25} = \frac{20}{100}$	3. $\frac{1}{2}x + 5 = 11$	3. $2x + 6y = 16$ $6x + y = 31$
4. $\frac{8}{x} = \frac{12}{24}$	4. $2(3x + 7) = 2x + 30$	
5. $\frac{25}{75} = \frac{6}{x}$	5. $4(x - 2) + 6(x - 2) = 10$	

For example, you post Problem 3 from the Missing Value Proportions set, $\frac{x}{25} = \frac{20}{100}$. The first steps you might hear for the first problem include:

"Look to see if you can multiply 20 by something to get 100."

"Think 25 times 4 equals 100."

"Simplify $\frac{20}{100}$ to $\frac{1}{5}$."

"Multiply 25 times 20 and 100 times x."

You can layer in strategy names at this point: for example, labeling the first and second ideas as "Scale Factor." Then, students will begin to use the strategy names as well.

ACTIVITY F.6

Name: "M-A-K-E a Decision"   **Type:** Routine

About the Routine: "<u>M</u>ental-<u>A</u>djust-<u>K</u>eep-<u>E</u>xpressions" is a routine that, like other routines, can function for assessment purposes. Project an illustration of the metacognitive process, like the one in the Part 3 overview (page 165). If a problem can be solved mentally, there is no need to use a written method such as a standard algorithm. Students tend to dive in without stopping to think if they can solve a problem mentally. There are two ways to use the tasks in this routine. One is to show one problem at a time, each time asking, "Which way will you solve it?" Or you can show the full set and ask, "Which ones might you solve mentally? Adjust and solve? Keep as is and solve?" The former is used below. To support student decision-making, keep a menu of strategy and algorithm options posted in a visible location. The first page of each module offers such a list.

Materials: Prepare a set of three to six expressions.

Directions:

1. Explain that you are going to display a problem. Students are not to solve it but simply MAKE a decision: Mental, Adjust and solve, or Keep and solve on paper?

2. Display the first problem, and give students about 10 seconds to decide.

3. Use a cue to have students share their choice (1 finger = mental, 2 fingers = adjust, 3 fingers = keep and solve on paper).

4. Ask a student who picked each decision to share why (and how).

5. Repeat Step 3, giving students a chance to change their minds.

6. Repeat for the next problem.

7. At the end of the set ask, "What do you 'see' in a problem that leads you to doing it mentally? Adjusting? Keeping and using paper?"

Possible problem sets to use with this routine include:

FRACTION OPERATIONS		DECIMAL OPERATIONS	
$\frac{4}{5}+7\frac{9}{10}$	$2\frac{2}{5}+3\frac{3}{4}$	29.9 + 6.72	1.35 + 4.65
$6\frac{1}{3}+8\frac{1}{3}$	$12\frac{1}{2}+8\frac{2}{10}$	25.16 + 9.013	36.9 + 4.01
$10-2\frac{7}{8}$	$6\frac{11}{12}-5\frac{7}{8}$	6.25 – 5.68	9.997 – 7.955
$5\frac{1}{7}-1\frac{1}{6}$	$2\frac{1}{3}-\frac{2}{3}$	10.57 – 6.17	52.17 – 18.84
$3\frac{1}{2}\times4$	$3\frac{2}{5}\times1\frac{2}{8}$	6.25 × 5	9.034 × 7.955
$5\times2\frac{1}{5}$	$7\frac{2}{5}-3\frac{3}{5}$	1.1 × 8.7	43.75 × 2.97

MISSING VALUE PROPORTIONS		ALGEBRAIC EQUATIONS	
$\frac{11}{88}=\frac{8}{x}$	$\frac{10}{25}=\frac{20}{x}$	$3(x + 5) = 18$	$\frac{1}{5}x+15=30$
$\frac{x}{12}=\frac{9}{36}$	$\frac{x}{10}=\frac{16}{60}$	$9x - 12 = 25$	$4x - 8 = 10$
$\frac{2}{5}=\frac{x}{12}$	$\frac{5}{8}=\frac{x}{25}$	$25 = 5(x - 3)$	$10 = 7(2x + 4)$
$\frac{8}{x}=\frac{18}{6}$	$\frac{12}{x}=\frac{20}{5}$	$5(x + 7) + 2(x + 7) = 49$	$3(x + 7) + 3(x - 2) = 28$
$\frac{25}{75}=\frac{6}{x}$	$\frac{x}{5}=\frac{6}{15}$	$3(x + 7) = 3x + 21$	$6(x + 4) = 4x + 20$
$\frac{x}{14}=\frac{1}{2}$	$\frac{3}{14}=\frac{5}{x}$	$5x + 6 + 2x = 2 + 7 + 4x$	$5x - 19 + 2x = 5x + 7$

ACTIVITY F.7

Name: "Share–Share–Compare"   **Type:** Routine

About the Routine: This routine can also be a longer classroom activity, depending on how many problems students are asked to solve. Each person first solves problems independently, then has the chance to have a one-on-one with a peer to compare their thinking on the same problem.

Materials: Prepare a list of three to five problems that lend to being solved different ways.

Directions:
1. Students work independently to solve the full set.

2. Students write if they solve it mentally by naming the strategy they used; if they solved it by writing, they do not need to name a strategy.

3. Once complete, everyone stands up with their page of worked problems.

4. Students find a partner who is *not* at their table. When they find a partner, they high-five each other and begin "Share–Share–Compare" for the first problem:

   - Share: Partner 1 *shares* their method.

   - Share: Partner 2 *shares* their method.

   - Compare: Partners discuss how their methods *compared*:

     · If their methods are different, they compare the two, discussing which one worked the best or if both worked well.

     · If their methods are the same, they think of an alternative method and again discuss which method(s) worked well.

After the exchange, the partners thank each other, raise their hands to indicate they are in search of a new partner, find another partner, and repeat the process of share–share–compare for Problem #2 (or any problem they haven't yet discussed).

Possible problem sets for this routine include:

DECIMAL OPERATIONS	FRACTION OPERATIONS	OPERATIONS WITH NEGATIVE NUMBERS	COMPARING RATIOS
$8.1 + 7.4$	$6\frac{3}{4} + 6\frac{1}{2}$	$12.1 + {}^{-}8.6$	$\frac{15}{40}$ and $\frac{5}{4}$
$34.5 - 7.65$	$8\frac{1}{2} - 7\frac{1}{4}$	$^{-}4.9 + {}^{-}17.4$	$\frac{18}{6}$ and $\frac{21}{7}$
$10.8 - 0.74$	$9\frac{1}{3} - 2\frac{1}{12}$	$^{-}9 - (^{-}2.8)$	$\frac{27}{15}$ and $\frac{9}{5}$
5.25×4	$6 \times 3\frac{1}{6}$	$6\frac{3}{10} \times (^{-}2)$	$\frac{2}{13}$ and $\frac{8}{52}$
$17.6 \div 4$	$12\frac{3}{4} \div \frac{1}{2}$	$^{-}16 \div \frac{1}{4}$	$\frac{18}{24}$ and $\frac{9}{18}$

SOLVING MISSING VALUE PROPORTIONS	SOLVING EQUATIONS FOR UNKNOWNS	SOLVING SYSTEMS OF LINEAR EQUATIONS
$\frac{15}{30} = \frac{x}{45}$	$\frac{1}{3}x + 12 = 23$	$2x + y = 12$ $2x = 10$
$\frac{12}{15} = \frac{48}{x}$	$6x - 8 = 10$	$3x + y = 15$ $x + 2y = 10$
$\frac{30}{x} = \frac{6}{24}$	$30 = 6(2x + 4)$	$x = 1 - 4y$ $2x + 4y = 6$
$\frac{3.5}{5} = \frac{14}{x}$	$3(x + 5) + 4(x + 5) = 56$	$\square + 4\square = 25$ $3\square - 6\square = {}^{-}33$

ACTIVITY F.8

Name: Strategy Spin   **Type:** Game

About the Game: This activity can be played in many ways with many different problem types. Spinners can focus on metacognition (mental, adjust, keep) or strategies for a particular operation or procedure.

Materials: *How Will I Solve It?* spinner or *Strategy Spin* spinner (one per group); paperclips; card sets with problems that lend to different strategies (a sampling of card sets are available online; see examples below)

Directions: 1. Players take turns spinning the spinner.

2. The player looks through the set of problems to find a problem that fits what they spun.

   For example, with the *How Will I Solve It?* spinner, if the paper clip stops at "mental," they look for a problem they can solve in their head. Or, with the *Multiplication* spinner, if the paper clip lands on "compensation," they look for a problem they can solve using compensation.

3. If they are successful in finding a problem and solving it correctly, they score 10 points (or keep the card). Other players can check the answers, or you can use a calculator.

4. If a player cannot find a match, they forfeit their turn.

5. Repeat until every player has had five turns. High score wins.

RESOURCE(S) FOR THIS ACTIVITY

How Will I Solve It?

Directions: Spin the spinner. Find a problem card that matches the approach you spin. Keep the problem card if you solve it correctly.

KEEP:
Don't change and use written method.

MENTAL:
Solve in my head.

ADJUST:
Change one or both numbers to make a simpler problem.

Missing Value Proportions: How Will I Solve It?

Directions: Spin the spinner. Find a problem card that matches the approach you spin. Keep the problem card if you solve it correctly.

Build Up/Break Down

Find a Unit Rate

Use a Scale Factor

Find Cross Products

Use $y = kx$

online resources — Sample spinners and card sets can be downloaded at **resources.corwin.com/FOF/ rationalnumbersalgequations**.

ACTIVITY F.9

Name: Just Right   **Type:** Game

About the Game: The game board can be adapted to incorporate the strategies students have learned. So, earlier in the year, it may have three options, and later in the year, it may have five options. Students may be tempted to use inefficient strategies in order to get four in a row. To counter this, require students to record the equations and the strategy they used.

Materials: *Just Right* game board, card sets with problems that lend to different strategies (see cards with Activity F.8), two-sided counters

Directions: 1. Players take turns flipping cards.

2. Player selects a "just right" strategy and solves it thinking aloud or on paper.

3. Opponents confirm accuracy with calculators (for decimals).

4. Having correctly solved the problem, the player places a marker on the strategy they used on the *Just Right* game board.

5. The first player to place four markers in a row on the game board wins.

For example, Sydney draws 6.8 + 2.8. She says, "My 'just right' strategy is Compensation. 7 + 3 equals 10, but that is four tenths too much, so I subtract four tenths and it equals 9.6." Sydney covers her choice of a Compensation square.

RESOURCE(S) FOR THIS ACTIVITY

 These resources can be downloaded at **resources.corwin.com/FOF/rationalnumbersalgequations**.

ACTIVITY F.10

Name: Strategories   **Type:** Game

About the Game: This game is an excellent opportunity for practice or assessment once a variety of strategies are learned. Students generate three to six examples of problems that lend to using a certain strategy, such as $\frac{3}{7} = \frac{9}{x}$, $\frac{4}{9} = \frac{x}{81}$, or $\frac{13}{4} = \frac{x}{8}$ could be used for Use a Scale Factor. For integer addition, students might use $^-91 + 44$, $^-65 + 116$, or $71 + {}^-64$ for Make a Zero. The instructions below are described for a small group. They can be modified for students to use independently. An alternative to this game is just to focus on one strategy (e.g., Make a Zero).

Materials: *Strategories* game card, one per student

Directions: 1. Each player works independently to generate a problem for which they would use that strategy (alternatively, students can work with a partner to discuss problems that would fit in each strategory).

2. After players have completed their *Strategories* game card (i.e., have one example expression in each strategory), place students in groups of three.

3. On a player's turn, they ask one of the other group members to share the problem on their *Strategories* card for _____ strategy. If the player explains the problem using that strategy, they score 5 points. If not, the third player gets a chance to "steal" by explaining the problem using that strategy. If the third player cannot, the author of the problem must explain using that strategy. If they cannot, they lose 10 points.

4. Play continues until all strategies have been solved, or three rounds. High score wins!

5. To discuss after play, ask, "What do you notice about the problems in _____ strategory?" and "When is this strategy useful?"

RESOURCE(S) FOR THIS ACTIVITY

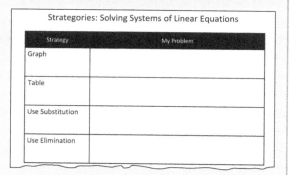

Strategories: Addition	
Strategy	My Problem
Count On	
Make a Zero	
Use Compensation	
Partial Sums	

Strategories: Solving Systems of Linear Equations	
Strategy	My Problem
Graph	
Table	
Use Substitution	
Use Elimination	

online resources These resources can be downloaded at **resources.corwin.com/FOF/rationalnumbersalgequations**.

ACTIVITY F.11

Name: Strategy Problem Sort   **Type:** Task

About the Task: Just because a problem can be solved with a given strategy does not mean the strategy is a good fit for the problem. It is a good fit when it is the most appropriate option from a student's set of known strategies (See Part 1 discussion of appropriate strategies). You can extend the activity by having students go through the "Does Not Fit the Strategy" category and identify which strategy would work well for that problem.

Materials: *Strategy Sort* placemat, card sets with problems that lend to different strategies (see cards with Activity F.8 and example set below)

Directions: 1. Students flip over a problem card.

2. Students determine if the problem fits the strategy or doesn't fit the strategy.

3. Students then solve the problem.

To create assessment artifacts, you can take a picture of a student's completed sort. Or you can ask students to provide written responses to entries like the following:

I placed _____ in the "Fits the Strategy" side because . . .

I placed _____ in the "Does Not Fit the Strategy" side; it did not fit because . . .

Possible expressions for integer subtraction could include:

39 – ⁻47	⁻616 – 828	⁻298 – 4	399 – ⁻859
⁻601 – 99	314 – ⁻44	99 – ⁻313	⁻739 – ⁻417
⁻119 – ⁻45	⁻554 – ⁻497	⁻73 – ⁻92	⁻54 – 564
51 – 529	775 – 695	19 – 242	903 – ⁻878
⁻452 – ⁻463	⁻774 – ⁻159	⁻192 – ⁻78	⁻932 – 99

RESOURCE(S) FOR THIS ACTIVITY

Strategy Sort Placemat

Strategy: _____

Fits the Strategy	Does Not Fit the Strategy

online resources These resources can be downloaded at **resources.corwin.com/FOF/rationalnumbersalgequations**.

ACTIVITY F.12

Name: A-Maze-ing Race   **Type:** Game

About the Game: This game is not about speed! Putting time pressure on students works against fluency, as the stress can block good reasoning. The purpose of this game is to practice selecting and using strategies that are a good fit for the numbers in the problem. It can be adapted for any operation problem sets. You can also use it as an independent work activity in which students highlight their path, record the problems, find the solutions, and show their strategy.

Materials: *A-Maze-ing Race* game board, one per pair; two-sided counters, calculator

Directions: 1. Players both put their marker on Start.

2. Players take turns selecting an unoccupied square that shares a border with their current position.

3. Players talk aloud to say the answer and explain how they solved the equation.

4. Opponents confirm accuracy with calculators. If correct, the player moves to the new square.

5. Note that the dark lines cannot be crossed.

6. The winner is the first to reach the finish.

RESOURCE(S) FOR THIS ACTIVITY

A-MAZE-ing Race	A-MAZE-ing Race	A-MAZE-ing Race	A-MAZE-ing Race

online resources These resources can be downloaded at **resources.corwin.com/FOF/rationalnumbersalgequations**.

Appendix
Tables of Activities

Figuring out fluency is a journey. Each and every child must have access and ample opportunities to develop their understanding and to use reasoning strategies. It is critical to remember these points:

- Fluency needs to be a daily part of mathematics instruction.

- There are no shortcuts or quick fixes to developing fluency.

- Fluency requires instruction *and* ongoing reinforcement.

- Different students require different types and quantities of experiences to develop fluency.

- While strategy choice is about the individual student, every student must learn and practice significant strategies so that they *can* choose to use them.

- Fluency practice must *not* be stressful. Stress complicates thinking.

- Fluency is more than accuracy; you must assess the other components.

This book is packed with activities for instruction, practice, and assessment to support your fluency efforts. The following pages provide activity lists by module and by type of activity. These tables can help you achieve the following:

- Jump between strategies, as you may not teach them sequentially.

- Locate ideas for teaching a strategy.

- Identify a specific type of activity to incorporate into your fluency instruction.

- Take notes about modifying an activity (e.g., for another strategy) or revisiting an activity later in the year or future years.

- Identify an activity that is particularly useful for assessment.

NO.	TYPE	NAME	NOTES
		MODULE B: GOOD BEGINNINGS FOR REASONING STRATEGIES (ONLINE ONLY): This module and related activities can be downloaded at resources.corwin.com/FOF/rationalnumbersalgequations.	
B.1	G	*Five Ways, Most Ways*	
B.2	G	*Lose It*	
B.3	R	"Common or Unique?"	
B.4	G	*Cover the Line*	
B.5	G	*Combinations of 0*	
B.6	G	*Farthest From*	
B.7	R	"The Stand"	
B.8	G	*Multiple Cover Up*	
B.9	G	*Six Charts*	
B.10	R	"Another Way to Say It"	
B.11	G	*PoNeg Products Three by Threes*	
B.12	R	"The Truth"	
B.13	R	"The One and Done"	
B.14	R	"The Missing"	
B.15	R	"If I Know This . . ."	

R (Routine) • G (Game)

MODULE 1: STRATEGIES FOR ADDITION				
NO.	PAGE	TYPE	NAME	NOTES
1.1	28	W	Number Line Comparisons With Worked Examples	
1.2	29	T	Connecting Bonds and Number Lines	
1.3	30	G	*Make It Close*	
1.4	32	IT	Greatest Sum/Smallest Sum	
1.5	34	T	Same Different	
1.6	34	T	Expression Match	
1.7	35	R	"Say It as Make a Zero"	
1.8	36	G	*Make Zero a Hero*	
1.9	38	T	One or Both and I Prefer	
1.10	39	T	Four Compensation	
1.11	40	R	"Or You Could . . ."	
1.12	41	G	*Estimation Cover*	
1.13	44	T	Place Value Discs for Partial Sums	
1.14	45	T	Missing Partials, Missing Problem	
1.15	46	R	"Complex Number Strings"	
1.16	47	G	*Take 5* Target	

T (Teaching) • W (Worked Examples) • R (Routine) • G (Game) • IT (Independent Task/Center)

MODULE 2: REASONING STRATEGIES FOR SUBTRACTION				
NO.	PAGE	TYPE	NAME	NOTES
2.1	50	T	It Always Works?	
2.2	51	T	Truth and Lies	
2.3	52	G	*Pick Your Jumps*	
2.4	53	IT	What's the Difference?	
2.5	56	T	Teaching Prompts for Think Addition	
2.6	56	T	The Match	
2.7	58	W	Worked Examples	
2.8	59	G	*All Lined Up*	
2.9	62	T	Compensation Lane	
2.10	63	T	Constant Difference Proofs	
2.11	64	R	"Why Not?"	
2.12	65	G	*The Absolute Difference*	
2.13	67	W	Yeah…But…	
2.14	68	T	The Missing Problem	
2.15	69	R	"Over/Under"	
2.16	70	G	*For Keeps*	

T (Teaching) • W (Worked Examples) • R (Routine) • G (Game) • IT (Independent Task/Center)

MODULE 3: REASONING STRATEGIES FOR MULTIPLICATION				
NO.	PAGE	TYPE	NAME	NOTES
3.1	74	T	Models and Partials	
3.2	76	T	Negative Arrays	
3.3	77	R	"The Breaks"	
3.4	78	G	*Lucky Highs or Lows*	
3.5	79	IT	Backward Breaks	
3.6	82	T	Equal Group Arguments	
3.7	82	T	Halve and Double Proofs With Cuisenaire Rods	
3.8	83	T	Addends or Factors?	
3.9	84	R	"About or Between"	
3.10	85	R	"A String of Halves"	
3.11	87	T	Seeing Is Believing	
3.12	88	T	True or False Statements	
3.13	89	R	"A Little More, A Little Less"	
3.14	90	G	*Give Some to Get Some*	
3.15	91	IT	Creating Compensations	

T (Teaching) • W (Worked Examples) • R (Routine) • G (Game) • IT (Independent Task/Center)

MODULE 4: REASONING STRATEGIES FOR DIVISION				
NO.	PAGE	TYPE	NAME	NOTES
4.1	94	T	Is It the Inverse?	
4.2	95	T	Decomposing Dividends	
4.3	96	T	Teaching Prompts	
4.4	97	G	*Paper Clip Connections*	
4.5	98	G	*Missing Numbers—Triangle Cards*	
4.6	101	T	Are They the Same?	
4.7	102	T	Areas and Lists	
4.8	103	W	Worked Examples for Partial Quotients	
4.9	104	R	"Breaking Dividends"	
4.10	105	R	"Could It Be?"	
4.11	106	G	*Quotient Connect*	

T (Teaching) • W (Worked Examples) • R (Routine) • G (Game)

MODULE 5: REASONING STRATEGIES FOR COMPARING RATIOS AND PROPORTIONS				
NO.	PAGE	TYPE	NAME	NOTES
5.1	117	T	Comparing Ratios in Context	
5.2	118	T	Missing Values in Context	
5.3	119	T	Proportional Pricing	
5.4	120	T	Planning for Pizza	
5.5	121	T	B-W (B-Dubs) or Go Somewhere Else?	
5.6	122	T	Teaching Prompts	
5.7	123	W	Worked Examples for Ratios and Proportions	
5.8	125	R	"A String of Equal Ratios"	
5.9	126	R	"Or You Could ..."	
5.10	127	G	*Proportion Fortune*	
5.11	128	G	*Missing Value Stack or Attack*	
5.12	129	G	*The Collector*	
5.13	130	G	Stack 'Em Ratios	

T (Teaching) • W (Worked Examples) • R (Routine) • G (Game)

MODULE 6: STRATEGIES FOR SOLVING EQUATIONS FOR AN UNKNOWN				
NO.	PAGE	TYPE	NAME	NOTES
6.1	135	T	What's My Number?	
6.2	135	T	If I Know This, Then I Know That	
6.3	136	T	Cover and Uncover	
6.4	136	W	Compare and Discuss Multiple Strategies	
6.5	138	T	What Do I Notice? What Do I Choose?	
6.6	138	T	Making Good Choices	
6.7	139	T	Teaching Prompts	
6.8	141	R	"Two Truths and a Lie"	
6.9	142	R	"Pick 2 Transformations"	
6.10	143	G	*The Transformer*	
6.11	144	IT	Building Equations With Number Tiles	

T (Teaching) • W (Worked Examples) • R (Routine) • G (Game) • IT (Independent Task/Center)

MODULE 7: STRATEGIES FOR SYSTEMS OF LINEAR EQUATIONS				
NO.	PAGE	TYPE	NAME	NOTES
7.1	149	T	Variable-less Problems	
7.2	152	T	A Visit to the Dog Park	
7.3	153	T	You Be the Judge	
7.4	154	W	Compare and Discuss Multiple Strategies	
7.5	156	T	Prompts for Teaching Solving Systems of Equations	
7.6	157	R	"Strategize Your Strategy"	
7.7	158	R	"Would You Rather…"	
7.8	159	G	*Choose and Go! Tic-Tac-Toe*	

T (Teaching) • W (Worked Examples) • R (Routine) • G (Game)

PART 3: PUTTING IT ALL TOGETHER: DEVELOPING FLUENCY				
NO.	PAGE	TYPE	NAME	NOTES
F.1	167	R	"Between and About"	
F.2	169	R	"That One"	
F.3	171	G	*A List of Ten*	
F.4	172	G	*All Lined Up*	
F.5	174	R	"Strategize First Steps"	
F.6	176	R	"M-A-K-E a Decision"	
F.7	178	R	"Share–Share–Compare"	
F.8	180	G	*Strategy Spin*	
F.9	181	G	*Just Right*	
F.10	182	G	*Strategories*	
F.11	183	IT	Strategy Problem Sort	
F.12	184	G or IT	*A-MAZE-ing Race*	

R (Routine) • G (Game) • IT (Independent Task/Center)

References

Bailey, D. H., Hoard, M. K., Nugent, L., & Geary, D. C. (2012). Competence with fractions predicts gains in mathematics achievement. *Journal of Experimental Child Psychology*, 113(3), 447–455. https://doi.org/10.1016/j.jecp.2012.06.004

Baroody, A. J., & Dowker, A. (Eds.). (2003). *Studies in mathematical thinking and learning. The development of arithmetic concepts and skills: Constructing adaptive expertise.* Lawrence Erlbaum Associates.

Baroody, A. J., Purpura, D. J., Eiland, M. D., Reid, E. E., & Paliwal, V. (2016). Does fostering reasoning strategies for relatively difficult combinations promote transfer by K–3 students? *Journal of Educational Psychology*, 108(4), 576–591.

Bay-Williams, J., & Kling, G. (2019). *Math fact fluency: 60+ games and assessment tools to support learning and retention.* Association for Supervision and Curriculum Development.

Bay-Williams, J. M., & SanGiovanni, J. (2019). *Figuring out fluency in mathematics teaching and learning, K–8.* Corwin.

Bishop, J. P., Lamb, L. L., Philipp, R. A., Whitacre, I., Schappelle, M. P., & Lewis, M. L. (2014). Obstacles and affordances for integer reasoning: An analysis of children's thinking and the history of mathematics. *Journal for Research in Mathematics Education*, 45(1), 19–61.

Boaler, J. (2014). Research suggests that timed tests cause math anxiety. *Teaching Children Mathematics*, 20(8), 469–474.

Braithwaite, D. W, Tian, J., & Siegler, R. S. (2018). Do children understand fraction addition? *Developmental Science*, 21(4), e12601. https://doi.org/10.1111/desc.12601

Brendefur, J., Strother, S., Thiede, K., & Appleton, S. (2015). Developing multiplication fact fluency. *Advances in Social Sciences Research Journal*, 2(8), 142–154.

Byrd, C. E., McNeil, N. M., Chesney, D. L., & Matthews, P. G. (2015). A specific misconception of the equal sign acts as a barrier to children's learning of early algebra. *Learning and Individual Differences*, 38, 61–67. https://doi.org/10.1016/j.lindif.2015.01.001

Canada, D., Gilbert, M., & Adolphson, K. (2008). Conceptions and misconceptions of elementary preservice teachers in proportional reasoning. In O. Figueras, J. L. Cortina, S. Alatorre, T. Rojano, & A. Sepúlveda (Eds.), *Proceedings of the joint meeting of Psychology of Mathematics Education 32nd meeting and of the North American Chapter of the International Group for the Psychology of Mathematics Education 30th meeting* (Vol. 2, pp. 249–256). Morelia, Mexico: Universidad Michoacana de San Nicolás de Hidalgo.

Carlson, M., Jacobs, S., Coe, E., Larsen, S., & Hsu, E. (2002). Applying covariational reasoning while modeling dynamic events: A framework and a study. *Journal for Research in Mathematics Education*, 33, 352–378. doi:10.2307/4149958

Cramer, K. A., Post, T. R., & delMas, R. C. (2002). Initial fraction learning by fourth- and fifth-grade students: A comparison of the effects of using commercial curricula with the effects of using the Rational Number Project Curriculum. *Journal for Research in Mathematics Education*, 33(2), 111–144. https://doi.org/10.2307/749646

Cramer, K. A., & Whitney, S. (2010). Learning rational number concepts and skills in elementary school classrooms. In D. V. Lambdin & F. K. Lester Jr. (Eds.), *Teaching and learning mathematics: Translating research for elementary school teachers* (pp. 15–22). National Council of Teachers of Mathematics.

Dougherty, B., Bryant, D. P., Bryant, B. R., & Shin, M. (2016). Helping students with difficulties understand ratios and proportions. *Teaching Exceptional Children*, 49(2), 96–105.

Durkin, K., Star, J. R., & Rittle-Johnson, B. (2017). Using comparison of multiple strategies in the mathematics classroom: Lessons learned and next steps. *ZDM Mathematics Education, 49*, 585–597.

Empson, S. B., & Levi, L. (2011). *Extending children's mathematics: Fractions & decimals.* Heinemann.

"Explicit." (2021). *Merriam-Webster.com.* https://www.merriam-webster.com/dictionary/explicit

Falkner, K. P., Levi, L., & Carpenter, T. P. (1999). Children's understanding of equality: A foundation for algebra. *Teaching Children Mathematics, 6*(4), 232–236.

Fuson, K. C., & Beckmann, S. (2012–2013, Fall/Winter). Standard algorithms in the Common Core State Standards. *Leadership in Mathematics Education Network Communicate Support Motivate*, pp. 14–30.

Hurst, M. A., & Cordes, S. (2018). Children's understanding of fraction and decimal symbols and the notation-specific relation to pre-algebra ability. *Journal of Experimental Child Psychology, 168*, 32–48. https://doi.org/10.1016/j.jecp.2017.12.003

I, J. Y., Martinez, R., & Dougherty, B. (2018). Misconceptions on part–part–whole proportional relationships using proportional division problems. *Investigations in Mathematics Learning.* doi:10.1080/19477503.2018.1548222

Jameson, M. M. (2014). Contextual factors related to math anxiety in second-grade children. *Journal of Experimental Education, 82*, 518–536.

Kilpatrick, J., Swafford, J., & Findell, B. (Eds.). (2001). *Adding it up: Helping children learn mathematics.* Mathematics Learning Study Committee, Center for Education, Division of Behavioral and Social Sciences and Education. National Academy Press.

Kindt, M., Abels, M., Dekker, T., Meyer, M. R., Pligge M. A., & Burrill, G. (2006). Comparing quantities. In Wisconsin Center for Education Research & Freudenthal Institute (Eds.), *Mathematics in context.*

Knuth, E. J., Alibali, M. W., Hattikudur, S., McNeil, N. M., & Stephens, A. C. (2008). The importance of equal sign understanding in the middle grades. *Mathematics Teaching in the Middle School, 13*(9), 514–519.

Lamb, L. L., Bishop, J. P., Philipp, R. A., Whitacre, I., & Schappelle, B. P. (2018). A cross-sectional investigation of students' reasoning about integer addition and subtraction: Ways of reasoning, problem types, and flexibility. *Journal for Research in Mathematics Education, 49*(5), 575–613.

Lamon, S. (2020). *Teaching fractions and ratios for understanding: Essential content knowledge and instructional strategies* (4th ed.). Taylor & Francis Group.

Laskowski, E. R. (2021, September). How much should the average adult exercise every day? Accessed at Mayoclinic.org (https://www.mayoclinic.org/healthy-lifestyle/fitness/expert-answers/exercise/faq-20057916).

Lobato, J., Ellis, A. B., Charles, R. I., & Zbiek, R. M. (2010). *Developing essential understanding of ratios, proportions, and proportional reasoning: Grades 6–8.* National Council of Teachers of Mathematics.

Lortie-Forgues, H., Tian, J., & Siegler, R. S. (2015). Why is learning fraction and decimal arithmetic so difficult? *Developmental Review, 38*, 201–221. https://doi.org/10.1016/j.dr.2015.07.008

Martinie, S. L. (2014). Decimal fractions: An important point. *Mathematics Teaching in the Middle School, 19*(7), 420–429. https://doi.org/10.5951/mathteacmiddscho.19.7.0420

McMillan, B. G., & Sagun, T. (2020). Extending choral counting. *Mathematics Teacher: Learning & Teaching PreK–12, 113*(8), 618–627. https://doi.org/10.5951/MTLT.2019.0361

Monson, D., Cramer, K., & Ahrendt, S. (2020). Using models to build fraction understanding. *Mathematics Teacher: Learning & Teaching PreK–12, 113*(2), 117–123. https://doi.org/10.5951/MTLT.2019.0105

National Center for Education Statistics (NCES). (n.d.). *NAEP report card: 2019 NAEP mathematics assessment.* https://www.nationsreportcard.gov/mathematics/nation/achievement/?grade=8

National Council of Teachers of Mathematics (NCTM). (2014). *Principles to actions: Ensuring mathematical success for all.* NCTM.

Newton, K. J., Willard, C., & Teufel, C. (2014). An examination of the ways that students with learning disabilities solve fraction computation problems. *Elementary School Journal, 39,* 258–275.

OECD. (2010). *Mathematics teaching and learning strategies in PISA.* http://www.oecd.org/education/school/programmeforinternationalstudentassessmentpisa/mathematicsteachingandlearningstrategiesinpisa.htm

OECD. (2016). Is memorisation a good strategy for learning mathematics? *PISA in Focus, 61.* OECD Publishing. https://doi.org/10.1787/5jm29kw38mlq-en

Parrish, S., & Dominick, A. (2016). *Number talks: Fractions, decimals and percentages.* Math Solutions.

Petit, M. M., Laird, R. E., Wyneken, M. F., Huntoon, F. R., Abele-Austin, M. D., & Sequeira, J. D. (2020). *A focus on rations and proportions: Bringing mathematics education research to the classroom.* Routledge.

Proulx, J., Beisiegel, M., Miranda, H., & Simmt, E. (2009). Rethinking the teaching of systems of equations. *Mathematics Teacher, 102*(7), 526–533.

Ramful, A. (2015). Reversible reasoning and the working backwards problem solving strategy. *The Australian Mathematics Teacher, 71*(4), 28–32.

Ramirez, G., Shaw, S. T., & Maloney, E. A. (2018). Math anxiety: Past research, promising interventions, and a new interpretation framework. *Educational Psychologist, 53*(3), 145–164. https://doi.org/10.1080/00461520.2018.1447384

Rittle-Johnson, B., & Star, J. (2007). Does comparing solution methods facilitate conceptual and procedural knowledge? An experimental study on learning to solve equations. *Journal of Educational Psychology, 99*(3), 561–574.

Rittle-Johnson, B., Star, J., & Durkin, K. (2012). Developing procedural flexibility: Are novices prepared to learn from comparing procedures? *British Journal of Educational Psychology, 82,* 436–455. doi:10.1111/j.2044-8279.2011.02037.x

SanGiovanni, J. J. (2019). *Daily routines to jump-start math class: Elementary school.* Corwin.

SanGiovanni, J. J., Katt, S., & Dykema, K. J. (2020). *Productive math struggle: A 6-point action plan for fostering perseverance.* Corwin.

SanGiovanni, J. J., & Milou, E. (2018). *Daily routines to jump-start math class: Middle school.* Corwin.

Siegler, R. S., Carpenter, T., Fennell, F., Geary, D., Lewis, J., Okamoto, Y., Thompson, L., & Wray, J. (2010). *Developing effective fractions instruction for kindergarten through 8th grade: A practice guide* (NCEE 2010–4039). https://ies.ed.gov/ncee/wwc/practiceguides

Siegler, R. S., Duncan, G. J., Davis-Kean, P. E., Duckworth, K., Claessens, A., Engel, M., . . . Chen, M. (2012). Early predictors of high school mathematics achievement. *Psychological Science, 23,* 691–697. https://doi.org/10.1177/0956797612440101

Star, J. R. (2005). Reconceptualizing conceptual knowledge. *Journal for Research in Mathematics Education, 36*(5), 404–411. https://doi.org/10.2307/30034943

Star, J. R., Jeon, S., Comeford, R., Clark, P., Rittle-Johnson, B., & Durkin, K. (2021). Compare and discuss multiple strategies. *Mathematics Teacher: Learning and Teaching PK–12, 114*(11), 853–859. doi: 10.5951/MTLT.2021.0051

Star, J., Rittle-Johnson, B., Durkin, K., Shero, M., & Sommer, J. (2020). Teaching for improved procedural flexibility in mathematics. In M. Gresalfi and I. S. Horn (Eds.), *The Interdisciplinarity of the Learning Sciences,* 14th International Conference of the Learning Sciences (ICLS) 2020, Vol. 4 (pp. 2285–2288). International Society of the Learning Sciences.

Torbeyns, J., Schneider, M., Ziqiang, X., & Siegler, R. (2015). Bridging the gap: Fraction understanding is central to mathematics achievement in students from three different continents. *Learning and Instruction, 37,* 5–13. https://doi.org/10.1016/j.learninstruc.2014.03.002

Van de Walle, J. A., Karp, K. S., & Bay-Williams, J. M. (2019). *Elementary and middle school mathematics: Teaching developmentally* (10th ed.). Pearson.

Van de Walle, J. A., Karp, K. S., & Bay-Williams, J. M. (2023). *Elementary and middle school mathematics: Teaching developmentally* (11th ed.). Pearson.

Index

CORWIN Mathematics

Supporting TEACHERS | Empowering STUDENTS

NOW AVAILABLE:
Supplement to modify the practices for different settings

PETER LILJEDAHL

14 optimal practices for thinking that create an ideal setting for deep mathematics learning to occur

Grades K–12

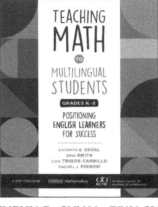

KATHRYN B. CHVAL, ERIN SMITH, LINA TRIGOS-CARRILLO, RACHEL J. PINNOW

Strengths-based approaches to support multilingual students' development in mathematics

Grades K–8

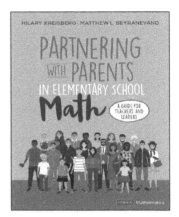

HILARY KREISBERG, MATTHEW L. BEYRANEVAND

Guidance on building productive relationships with families about math education

Grades K–5

BETH MCCORD KOBETT, FRANCIS (SKIP) FENNELL, KAREN S. KARP, DELISE ANDREWS, LATRENDA KNIGHTEN, JEFF SHIH, DESIREE HARRISON, BARBARA ANN SWARTZ, SORSHA-MARIA T. MULROE

Detailed plans for helping elementary students experience deep mathematical learning

Grades K–1, 2–3, 4–5

BETH MCCORD KOBETT, KAREN S. KARP

Your game plan for unlocking mathematics by focusing on students' strengths

Grades K–6

JOHN J. SANGIOVANNI, SUSIE KATT, KEVIN J. DYKEMA

A guide for empowering students to embrace productive struggle to build essential skills for learning and living—both inside and outside the classroom

Grades K–12

To order, visit corwin.com/math

**JENNIFER M. BAY-WILLIAMS,
JOHN J. SANGIOVANNI, ROSALBA SERRANO,
SHERRI MARTINIE, JENNIFER SUH**

Because fluency is so much more
than basic facts and algorithms

Grades K–8

**KAREN S. KARP,
BARBARA J. DOUGHERTY,
SARAH B. BUSH**

A schoolwide solution for students'
mathematics success

Elementary, Middle School, High School

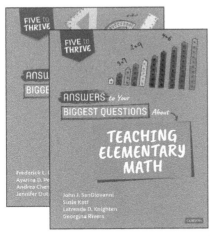

**JOHN J. SANGIOVANNI, SUSIE KATT,
LATRENDA D. KNIGHTEN, GEORGINA RIVERA,
FREDERICK L. DILLON, AYANNA D. PERRY,
ANDREA CHENG, JENNIFER OUTZS**

Actionable answers to your most pressing questions
about teaching elementary and secondary math

Elementary, Secondary

**SARA DELANO MOORE,
KIMBERLY RIMBEY**

A journey toward making
manipulatives meaningful

Grades K–3, 4–8

CORWIN

A SAGE Publishing Company

Helping educators make the greatest impact

CORWIN HAS ONE MISSION: to enhance education through intentional professional learning.

We build long-term relationships with our authors, educators, clients, and associations who partner with us to develop and continuously improve the best evidence-based practices that establish and support lifelong learning.